BORDERLAND

BORDERLAND

Essays from the US-Canadian Divide

BRUCE FISHER

excelsior editions
State University of New York Press
Albany, New York

Published by State University of New York Press, Albany

Printed in the United States of America

Excelsior Editions is an imprint of State University of New York Press

For information, contact State University of New York Press, Albany, NY
www.sunypress.edu

Production by Ryan Morris
Marketing by Fran Keneston

Library of Congress Cataloging-in-Publication Data

Fisher, Bruce, 1953–
Borderland : essays from the US-Canadian Divide / Bruce Fisher.
p. cm. — (Excelsior editions)
ISBN 978-1-4384-4223-5 (hardcover : alk. paper)
1. Buffalo (N.Y.)—History. 2. Buffalo (N.Y.)—Social life and customs. 3. Buffalo (N.Y.)—Biography. I. Title.

F129.B845F57 2012
974.7'97—dc23 2011025883

10 9 8 7 6 5 4 3 2 1

Contents

Preface

There is a very potent and enduring myth that has oppressed my generation, which is that only the big places are real. I embraced this concept early. When I left home at seventeen, I moved to the city. Then I left a small city for one of America's great cities, and there embraced the established tradition of big-city life, and got myself a place in it as a big-city journalist. After ten years of that, I went even bigger—to Washington, the capital of Earth. Yes, of course, New York and Los Angeles and London and Beijing are bigger than Washington. Even Atlanta is bigger than Washington. Istanbul, too. Kuala Lumpur and São Paolo?

Who knows. There is, however, no more powerful place than Washington. It is all big there. There are big fights over big ideas; people and institutions with big money do not matter as much as those with political power. There are lots of people with money, fame, beauty, and other such trinkets. It is the sheer immensity of the power in Washington, especially the power of the president and of Congress, that so awed me.

But then one day, after I'd worked on another big political triumph in Washington, and had been recognized as a player with a big future, a curious species of cowardice, or sanity, crept into my bones and settled there, and with it a recognition that the further development of my own life could well occur in such a context, a context ever shaped by someone else's power, but that it needn't be so.

It wasn't. I left it, returned to my small native region, married, helped create natives, and withal dived into life. Having come to adulthood elsewhere, though, meant that I was actually a stranger to the place in which I'd spent my childhood. My experience of the big world did not prepare me for this. There was such a sharp discontinuity in my understanding of this place—in such radical contrast to lifelong residents' understandings and expectations—that conflict over just about every issue ensued.

A native myself, from nine generations of presence here, I was nevertheless a newcomer, and was certainly seen as a newcomer.

So I really had no choice. I had to think about this conflict as well as to engage in it, and I did engage, first as a citizen, then as a leader in local government, now as a columnist and educator. There is much to report on: arts and historic preservation here, much more to be said about Canada, about Upstate New York's demographic collapse, about racial conflict, public finance, the economic dead-end that is legalized casino gambling, and about the policy directions my old home should take no matter who is in office. Those topics, which I write about regularly for the independent weekly *Artvoice*, are for a very different kind of book

This collection is something else entirely. This book is a short sequence of studies of peculiar and quite specific parts of the psychological, geological, historic, and personal landscape of this place. It is an idiosyncratic collection, too; there's not enough explanation of how some issues, terms, and even languages relate to the rest of it, but that's how it'll stay for now. Perhaps it is a risky book, because people in public life should not be so forthright about deeply held ideas as I am in these essays. But as my critics are already convinced of my numerous and deep flaws, it seems to me no new risk to put more of them on display.

Acknowledgments

"Choosing Icons," "Choosing Identity" ("The slave Daniel" in this volume), "The idea of the city," and "Obama's election" were first published in *Artvoice*. "Tree of Life" and "Flat at dawn and twilight" ("Sculls" in this volume) were first published in The King's English.com. "The ambiguities" was first published in Ducts.com. "Flags" was broadcast by WBFO-FM. "Ties" was first published by Narrativemagazine.com.

OLD NOTIONS

Democracy, equality, commonality

The happiest day in Buffalo is the day before the football team's home opener, for on that day, we stop moaning about our lost children. They're not lost, actually. Some of them have just moved, temporarily, to where it's warmer and drier. Gradually, some of the clever ones filter back to practice medicine or to inherit the family business, and to enjoy the water, the woods, the closeness of the unique interior life here, and Canada. These re-migrants avoid the general political discourse of Upstate New York, which has for decades consisted of a litany of blame. Loud people blame taxes for the region's failure to become a fast-expanding Sunbelt suburb. They caterwaul about the wages of cops, firemen, social workers, and highway-repair crews. Quiet people do not go unaffected by this rant, for even they believe that the region has utterly lost its population of clever young people, never to regain it. Even they have come to believe that despair is a rational response, and that deliverance will arrive if only democracy departs. This is sad.

This used to be such a dirty, fun, mobbed-up, and raucous town, like Carl Sandburg's Chicago—broad-shouldered, boozy. The Erie Canal ended (or started) here, and the lake boats brought all of the trade of America's interior to this port. You know what that means: sailors. And where there are sailors, there are saloons, girls for rent, dullard shopkeepers, loan sharks and cardsharps, immigrants, boat owners, speculators, puff-chested bankers, unions, and the free flow of money that nobody can quite keep track of. A port next to a border is even more trouble, because borders are all about smuggling, and that's where the real fun is to be had.

Buffalo's nostalgia would be more entertaining, certainly, if it were a true and genuine longing for its lost array of opportunities for vice and venery. We should encourage nostalgia for old Chippewa Street, for example: for one hundred years, Chippewa Street was a row of saloons in which sailors drank up their pay, and paid to watch women who danced without the interference of excessive clothing. Whatever funds remained available to these gypsy workers tended to get invested in the local economy—not in housing or in grain futures or in iron ore contracts, but in the short-term companionship arrangements that sent sailors back to their grain boats and ore boats, back to the Soo and to Duluth and to Milwaukee broke, and itchy.

Instead, Buffalo is nostalgic for steel plants and for the class warfare of the industrial age that so shaped the landscape and created enduring identities. Back when there was heavy metal industry, so the gripe goes, we had top-hatted tycoons who flaunted their wealth, and tough unions who wrestled it away from the bastards. Back then, folks knew their place—where to live, where to walk, eat, worship, flirt, dance, die. Back then, everybody worked, and everybody came home from college or from the service to do what everyone had always done.

But then came the great out-migration of capital from the whole Great Lakes region, and specific departures: after the Second World War, the mobsters and the violent unions scared the aerospace pioneers (Buffalo engineers invented the jet engine) into the warm arms of California. Others left, too, but cars stayed, chemicals stayed, colleges and banks stayed, and a huge university actually grew tenfold, but the big, visible blast furnaces and coke ovens and ingot works and rolling mills emptied, and no matter that it stayed a sweet place with nice water, good Canadian beer, old trees, pretty buildings, ducks to hunt, music to hear and books to borrow, the town set to whining, and hasn't stopped.

But then every town has its signature gripe. In Montreal, it's Toronto, still and always Toronto. In Toronto, it's America in general, and especially America's utter indifference to Canada, but in self-aware and thriving and now-sophisticated Toronto, which is barely one hundred miles from Buffalo and no longer the boring place where one's elderly Loyalist aunts dwelt amid lace antimacassars and sturdy oak pews, they still say to themselves "at least we're better than Buffalo." The gripe in Chicago is New York, except when it's Chicago's own embarrassment over its own ineradicable political corruption, but in Chicago, in that belligerent Chicago way, the embarrassment of living in a political cartoon gives way to a cocky, up-tempo arch of the brow as the chat turns to predicting which of the mayor's guys is going to squeal first.

Buffalo used to have scoundrels, for Buffalo used to be such a dirty, corrupt town, with the canal the source and conduit of its wealth and its dirt. The Erie Canal started or ended right at the foot of Main Street. New York State's schools teach all the kids about that day in October 1825 when Governor DeWitt Clinton scooped up a jug of Lake Erie water from Buffalo Harbor, and took it down to New York Harbor where, nine days later, he performed the "wedding of the waters," thus joining the Great Lakes and the Atlantic. The town that now whines about government and taxes was created—indeed, New York City itself was created—by a massive expenditure of public funds called the Erie Canal. It was—whiners please note—precisely that investment of taxes that created the commerce from which the wealth flowed. Immigrants by the tens of thousands came through dirty Buffalo and its dirty waterfront, and from its docks they lit out for the West. The squalor, exploitation, prostitution, and venery of the docks started in 1825 and continued for a hundred and thirty years, until the Welland Canal opened and made of Buffalo an obsolete port. Then great and enduring panic set in. Well-intended urban-renewal projects tossed out all the poor people from the docks, and the docks themselves were dismantled. The state government filled in the last stretch of the Erie Canal and built an expressway in its right-of-way. Patronage politics lingered on and on just like in Chicago, even longer, but not so colorfully. The Erie Canal waterfront was for a hundred years a regional symbol of sin, even though it was in that very harbor, at the terminus of the Erie Canal, that the great sin of slavery was combated most effectively, for it was Buffalo Harbor that was the last stop on the Underground Railroad. Canada, which is to say freedom, is the shore just a couple of miles across from Buffalo Harbor.

So this is a place of liberation, and of possibility. Its air should ring with a joyful chatter of peace (Canadians don't have many guns) and of prosperity (Canadians make excellent beer) and of happy times, because the water is quite clean now.

And kids? Departing kids? There is this to say about kids. Kids are notoriously interested in traveling, especially to the sunny South, especially kids whose parents relentlessly inculcated in them the equation Sunshine = Good. A decade ago, I designed a political campaign for a Buffalo friend, a successful campaign, which succeeded brilliantly in getting him elected on the Keep Our Kids platform. The kids, of course, kept moving around, as kids do. So everybody got mad, and now there isn't any sport in public life in Buffalo anymore, because everybody in Buffalo is convinced that the kids are gone for good. The local ruling class picked up on this sense of defeated expectations, and now, rather than enjoying a happy chatter in which we all admit that this is the best place in the world, with good fishing, too, the loud people forever repeat the rant about taxes, and bus drivers' salaries, and lost kids. So instead of being happy about all that there is to be happy about, folks do go *on* with their bad-tempered whining about taxes—and for this I blame myself. Thankfully, there is the start of the football season.

That is when Buffalo ceases its caterwaul about its stain. The community ignores the four opportunities that the football team has had to win the Super Bowl. Hope, in September, each September, springs eternal.

So it was this past September. At noon, in a light rain, we put our slickers on, and began planting crocus and tulip bulbs in the rain-softened soil. I selfishly hoped that the rain would stop in time for me to put my single in the Black Rock Canal (the part of the Erie Canal that still works) for a good long row, a good cool fall row, before the unwelcome guest drops in from Canada and makes an ice rink of my best water. Shovel in hand, yellow slicker-clad, we listened to the pregame show on Canadian radio because it's an AM station in St. Catharines that carries the game for them and for us, too.

The other Canadian guests are most welcome, any time. The Canadians cross this way with their new strong dollars. They become indistinguishable from Buffalo people, for Canadians forsake their national insignia for toques, jackets, jerseys, headbands, and peaked caps with the blue and white bison logo of the football team. And the Buffalo people shed their own class and race and political affinities and merge into a new, happy, hopeful iteration.

Perhaps this happens only here. Perhaps it is different in Pittsburgh and Cleveland, in Detroit and St. Louis, in festering Baltimore with its amusement park waterfront and its sprawl and its Pigtown. But it can't be. We can't be alone in being a queer stranded community within which all the characteristic boundaries of class, race, national identity, and ethnic style are broken. I will ask: do all those football cities, do they too all have lefties like we do in Buffalo? Here is what ours are like: ours spend the week lamenting national politics and reiterating their credentials as devoted enemies of the skybox class, and then suddenly, on pregame Saturday, they're ready to parse the defensive secondary, and to praise the new coach's decision to go for it on fourth and three last week in New England, and to walk through the injury list, and to debate our prospects if the new quarterback can't find the short-yardage tempo he'd found in the preseason. Even the day before the home opener, the talk on the lefty radio station, as among the 8 a.m. regulars at Spot Coffee, became, because of football, the same species of manly assertions asserted in the locker room at the Country Club of Buffalo.

It's football. It's the Bills. Everybody here cares about the Bills. If football is meaningless to you, or if you hold it in contempt, I caution you to listen up anyway: in Buffalo, nobody in business, on the faculty, in the courts, at the library, or in the grocery store will bother speaking to you on a football weekend unless you have something to say about the Bills. Thus in vain will one seek contradiction of the following assertion about Buffalo: that the chatter on the mountaintop is identical to the chatter in the valley.

That would be a claim that's been made before.

It has a certain democratic ring about it.

One version of that statement was uttered about four hundred years ago, in Florence. A terribly talented public servant took a forced vacation when the Medici prince Lorenzo rousted out the incumbent Republic. The clever and experienced but nonetheless unemployed public servant went home to a place like Buffalo, to his family home, in a sort of exurb of the great city where he'd formerly had great responsibility. And there, in that exile, he did what economics compelled him to do all day long so as to keep some income coming in, so as to keep the babes fed. But at night, he described, in his letters to his friends, and in his note to his new prince, that he would doff his workaday weeds and go suitably attired into his library, there to meet his true peers for his true labor, which was to write an extended essay of advice for the new head of the new regime, with the help of all the authorities he could marshal from all his bookshelves. This he did because he, the competent discard, rather hopefully, albeit naively, believed in his own virtue, and believed that he still had much value to offer, and that the new prince ought to give him a job—maybe even his old job—just because of his record of achievement, his acknowledged and demonstrable excellence.

This person was Niccolo Machiavelli, who was brilliant, and a fool.

He wasn't ever invited back in, of course. He said he'd been high and he'd been low, and so who better than he to advise the new prince?

Indeed. The new regime not only failed to offer him a job—it arranged for him to be tortured. Hung him up by his thumbs, behind his back, and hoisted him up high because some other advisor to the new prince had decided that depriving Machiavelli of income and of occupation was insufficient punishment for his mistake, which was to have served the old regime.

Machiavelli was shocked that he was so abused. He wrote a letter to his noble friend in the new regime, one Vettori, rather in the way that a mouse asks a cat for love. "I've done everything you've asked," he said. "I'm virtuous," he said. Vettori was a politician. Vettori would not invest his own power to assist his friend, and so Vettori had no good news for Machiavelli.

Nevertheless, Machiavelli wrote on, and while he worked, ever hopeful, he worked like one who was being rewarded. For his labors he received, eventually, a few coins while he yet lived. He also received some accolades for the work that he did for himself—especially for his book about the Roman author Livy, and for another, smaller work, about how to fight a war. Then, after he passed, came a few centuries of vilification. His reputation for insight was then and is yet untarnished, but it didn't get him a job in the new regime, and all his talent purchased him neither love nor good repute.

From the mountain, from the valley: that sounds like a good resume, doesn't it? But of course the continents where the common folk dwell are all flatlands, paved over for parking so that eighty thousand of us can drive out to the stadium in all kinds of weather and shout for our team. The well off mix with the unkempt on that blacktop prairie at the pregame Sunday ritual of the tailgate. Charcoal-grilled Sahlen's hot dogs, Weber's mustard, hot Italian sausage from Mineo & Sapio, marjoram-and-garlic kielbasa from Wardynski's, and two brands of Canadian beer are the sacred foods at this Seder. The classes mix, and all talk Bills talk. Then when game time approaches, the elite break away from the flow of humanity moving in through tunnels to the stadium, for the elite have their own viewing rooms there, their skyboxes.

The company pays for these set-apart spaces high above the valley. These specific mountaintops are warm. There's a potty. There are televisions for reviewing replays. There are trays of snacks. There are great wide sliding windows that open up to let in the bright autumn air, or, in December, a jab of winter. Their seats are leather, and padded. The seats outside are hard plastic, but you knew that.

Machiavelli never was the prince. When he wrote that dedicatory preface to the essay that was his plea for reinstatement, he erred: he never, ever should have claimed to Lorenzo the Magnificent that he'd been high as well as low. Lorenzo was and always had been of the peak and not of the plain. So to the question: did the Prince Lorenzo di Medici read this unemployed Machiavelli's letter, and heft Machiavelli's little book in his jeweled hand, and regard Machiavelli's broken thumbs and twisted shoulders, and think, who is this person to presume he can advise me at eye level?

Knowing the vocabulary of football is the delight of the folks outside. Too much mastery, one observes, is annoying to the people in the soft leather seats; when mastery is mere competence unmarried to money, it's not mastery, it's just . . . annoying. Princes like to feel masterful. Owners of skyboxes share this characteristic: they are not your peer. You who are in the box with them are a favored peasant, not a peer. The peasants of the native villages nearby sit outside in the weather, on the hard, cold plastic seats. They sit outside, in the weather, with their expertise about football, outside with the not-princes who pay retail for their tickets out of their own shallow pockets. Natives and peasants drink beer from paper cups. They defer. They look longingly through the windows at the skyboxers, who ignore them. "Defer, Machiavelli," you mutter as your read his letter to Lorenzo the Magnificent, knowing, sadly, the ending to that story.

Come Monday, if the Bills win, everyone will pretend that we all dwell on the plain common. When they lose, it is back to loud anger over lost children, and the reinstitution of the castes, and the Canadians go back to being Canadians.

The other shore

Home here is next to Canada, which in summer becomes an extension of Buffalo. This is especially true for achievers.

In the years when Crystal Beach thrived, the reward for getting good grades was to be allowed to cross the border. One would take one's report card down to the grocery store and get tickets for rides at a great lakeside amusement park. It was five tickets for each A, three for each B, one for each C, and they could only be redeemed in Crystal Beach, in Fort Erie, Ontario, Canada. A twenty-minute ride on a vehicle that children now refer to as a Cheese Bus involved a brief stop and conference with stern-faced, uniformed officers whose boss was a lady named Her Royal Highness Elizabeth the Second, who wore a light-blue gown and who looked young and kind. Each light-standard on the Canadians' main highway, the Queen Elizabeth Way, had an open steel signature conjoining the capital letters E and R, for Elizabeth Regina, the Queen. As we drove by on our cheese bus, we knew that this was a better, more formal place. It was a clean place. We were to be on our best behavior. Yet it was a place of lawlessness, too. We knew that we weren't supposed to buy Player's Navy Cut cigarettes, and we knew (in the way young adolescents know) that there would be dire consequences due anyone who dared to smuggle fireworks back across the border into the USA, but we dared anyway. After a day of smoking Player's and Export A's, and of riding rides and of eating cones of French fries seasoned with vinegar, we bought Chinese fireworks and stuffed them under the bus seats. Riding the high arch of the Peace Bridge to the American border, the U.S. Customs officers commanded us to leave the bus. Our caches of contraband were always discovered and confiscated, but we were never arrested, only scolded; small rules, small infractions, small punishments.

And now, many years later, we are returned here, and once again cross the border.

From the house in Buffalo to the Welland Canal in Port Colborne, Ontario, is twenty and one-half miles. The westerly wind that gathers force all along the length of Lake Erie keeps a cyclist comfortable even in the last of summer, in September. It was so strong one September day it took me one hour and forty-five minutes to pedal to the Welland Canal.

It took five hours to get back.

The delay wasn't a shift in the wind or weather, or persnickety terrorist-hunting U.S. Customs officers pulling the tires off the rims. It was the visiting. So many Buffalo people spend their summers on the Canadian lakeshore that one can stop at any bay and find hospitality, because every Buffalo person who is there is an achiever, and prosperous enough to be in Canada for the summer. These Summer Canadians demonstrate their prosperity by being welcoming and generous.

The coastline between Buffalo and the Canadian canal that made Buffalo's port obsolete is a sequence of scalloped bays spaced by sand-spit points. Marching westward from the border there is Erie Beach, then Waverly Beach, then Crescent Beach; Rose Hill, Bertie Bay, Windmill Point, Crystal Beach, Bay Beach, and then the longest point in the area, big Point Abino with its white lighthouse and its killer undertow that sucked a strong teenaged boy out of the arms of his rescuer. Then Holloway Bay, Silver Bay, Pine Crest, Lorraine with its point where, if one's surname is correct, one is permitted to hunt ducks in October.

The bays are named for the roads that end at the shoreline, but this is not entirely true. Nor is it entirely true that there is a rank-ordering of bays in terms of their prestige or expense, in the way that Americans ever pursue the construction of social pyramids. Yet it is true, approximately, that the cheaper beach houses are nearer Buffalo. Past Waverly Beach, a wader cannot see the city to the east, and that seems to add value. So grand houses dot the shore at Rose Hill, cluster at Bay Beach, and utterly dominate at Point Abino, but they recede among the big numbers of merely handsome dune-top houses in Silver Bay and the beach-level cottages at Pine Crest. The big money retakes the sands and the dunes at the arc of Lorraine Bay before the incongruous lakeshore industrial plantation just the other side of Lorraine Point. The big nickel-smelting plant for which Nickel Beach is named takes the other side of the last sand spit that thrusts out into the lake before the Welland Canal. So in Canada, the stretch of beach is all fun and leisure, a new bike path on an old rail-bed, pretty golf courses, working farms, and English hedgerows. On the American side, there's no nice bicycle path on a former railroad right-of-way, but there is a right-of-way, flanked by wild roses, full, in September, of bursting milkweed and bounding goldfinches and reddening sumac just like in Canada. It is the same lake-plain topography, the same geology, wildflowers, colorful seasonal birds. But on the American side, the beach is not immediate; on the American side, the city gives way to brownfields and then to ten miles of defunct steel factory before the beachfront begins. In Canada, approached from the big American city, peace and calm and nature and water occur immediately and run for twenty and one-half miles before the apparatus of wealth-making reappears, which is to say, brute industry and transportation infrastructure, tankers and freighters, giant machines that lift cargo from boats and place it onto belching trucks whose drivers have thick arms and who smell of sweat and cigarettes.

For those twenty and one-half miles from the border to the canal, the focus is the beach. There aren't many simple shore-side bungalows anymore. But the steady progress of evolution from simple to grand is a lurching thing, if linear. The big new development of the old amusement park grounds of Crystal Beach, just east of Bay Beach, is, in Bay Beach terminology, the "Vinyl Village." This is not a compliment. I know a deca-millionaire who has a brand-spanking-new vinyl-clad four-story place there. He should be in Bay Beach, or in Lorraine, or tucked away at the end of Rose Hill Road, amid the towering *chan wakan*, hereabouts known as cottonwoods. He says he can't be bothered with an old house, and his kids want to ride their little bikes in that little tangle of streets and to see their friends without having to make play dates all along the ridgeline of dune-top houses.

So for the rest of the shore to both the east and the west of the Vinyl Village, the beach houses are in single file. For all the shore, all of it, the style is what one was brought up to call shabby genteel. It was defined by three generations of WASPs. It is a rumpled shirt and khaki trousers and sneakers made of canvas. These are the Buffalo-born playwright A. R. Gurney's people, literally and by literary figure as well. John Cheever wrote about their Long Island kin before he collapsed into narcissism; Gurney, ever the reporter, never has.

Anthropologists call it culture. Historians who wish they were anthropologists cite the late Clifford Geertz, and then call it culture, because access is not about bloodlines anymore. Access to the Canadian shore has for fifty years or more been open to the Catholics and Jews of Buffalo's business and professional classes, more recently also to the

South Asian Muslim bankers and doctors who have arrived in Buffalo, and to the various Commonwealth transplants to Canada as well, all of whom have discovered this stretch of shore, all of whom buy their way in just the same way that the WASP sons of Civil War profiteers and Erie Canal merchants did. The only difference is that their purchases are more recent, and mainly from the shabby genteel scions of the WASPs who are now, after three or four generations, so shabby that they can no longer afford Canadian shore summers.

Then there are the visitors, like me. I cycle to it, and back, on warm weekend days. I am invited to simply everyone's because of my minor celebrity status as a local official. Those who are prosperous enough to reside there, in season, expect cold drinks and hors d'oeuvres to be expected of them.

That gives the Summer Canadians much opportunity for display and demonstration. The houses are money pits. They are old. The development at Lorraine, farthest from Buffalo and closest to the Welland Canal, celebrated its centenary recently; Lorraine is where the duck-hunters are allowed to hunt if their surname is that of one of the founding families. Most Lorraine houses are Yankee white-clapboard frame houses or cedar-shake shingle houses because this is the westernmost extension of Yankee culture. In Lorraine as in every bay, it is work to be a Summer Canadian. Labor is required, and money: there are sea walls to maintain, and boat hoists to secure, and staircases that every year are pounded to splinters by the violent Lake Erie storms and by the plate tectonics of Lake Erie ice. Roofs need shingling more often because of weather and because of the forest, the famous Carolinian forest, of stormwater-loving *chan wakan*, walnuts, ash, beech, oak, maple, tulip magnolia, and more, which drop copious tonnages of catkins, nuts, florets, and helicopters, which collect, and sprout, and trap water in eaves, and create ice jams, and cost—just as new kitchens cost, just as new lakeview windows cost, and as new siding costs, and landscaping, and fallen-tree removal, and taxes, and the ever-advancing value of the Canadian dollar all cost.

This calm culture of easy hospitality and clapboard houses and khaki trousers is a display of wealth as sure as any peacock's. Money is on display, as surely as money is on display in the Hamptons, Florida, Kennebunkport, Cape Cod, the Vineyard. The first demonstration of financial comfort in Buffalo may be admission to a downtown club. The next is residence on the Canadian shore.

There is a domestic version of all this, for Lake Erie has a U.S. as well as a Canadian shore. South and west of Buffalo, past the defunct steel plants and before the Cattaraugus Indian Reservation at the county boundary at Cattaraugus Creek, there is the American lakeshore. It is middle-class 1950s-vintage split-level frame houses from Hamburg Beach south to the formerly seasonal community of Wanakah, where there is an abrupt discontinuity. Where in Canada there are Yankee clapboard frame houses set atop dunes, on the American shore there is a ten-mile row of lakefront mansions set atop gray shale cliffs. Where the old lake highway splits from the new, which is where the old road takes the name Old Lake Shore Road, is the expensive and still-exclusive Wanakah Country Club. A very modest Episcopal Church is at that intersection, and in it has ever been the Episcopal class distinction: inlanders are workers, Old Lake Shore Roaders are aristocrats. (In Canada, beach people are Americans, inlanders Canadians.) This church used to be the summertime church of the aristocrats from Buffalo, who knelt at their city Trinity under the glow of Louis Comfort Tiffany's colorful windows; at this Trinity, the low-church ways of the year-rounders is the way. The architecture is the theology: no stained glass, no incense, no season but servitude. The city Trinity was the high church of liturgical near-Catholicism and King James English; the shore Trinity is the low church of American Protestantism in the American vernacular.

Old Lake Shore is mansion row on the lake side. There are estates with names. There are garages with turntables that still hold American-made Duesenbergs and Pierce-Arrows. There are walled gardens, tennis courts surrounded by century-old hedges, vast lawns that slope gently to the cliffside. There are iron fences backed by screening shrubs and by mature forests hundreds of yards deep. There are high stone walls. All along that stretch, there is a beach, but it is far, far below the top of the shale cliffs until the cliff diminishes at Sturgeon Point, which is approximately across from Point Abino in Canada. Up to Sturgeon Point, there are the cliffs of gray shale. Past Sturgeon Point are the dunes and the wide sand beaches and the flat-stone shingle shoreline. But until that shift of geology, beaches are a sometime thing; what lasts through storms and through winters of ice mountains and open water alike is the tall gray shale cliff. The people who still care to touch the water, rather than just look at the sun setting over it, must maintain long metal staircases that either telescope out of winter's way, or that terminate with ends made of big oil-barrel pontoons that float on the surf when the season ends and the water rushes all the way in on the westerlies. Frank Lloyd Wright designed a clifftop mansion here called Graycliff for a Buffalo millionaire for whom he also designed a city house. There are houses as big as

Newport "cottages" here, built for tycoons of steel and railroading and shipping and banking of that same age when Vanderbilts and Pierponts and their like reigned farther east. Some of these places remain in the possession of such families. Two big estates whose builders were Catholic gave them to the Church, and those estates have for decades been retreat houses for orders of religious. Graycliff itself was for almost fifty years the North American home of a priestly order known principally in Poland, Hungary, and Spain. One mansion that had been a religious house was purchased by a new tycoon, who demolished it and has now built himself a new mansion, behind new iron gates that open automatically for the owner and stay closed for the rest.

This is the other culture of the waterfront. It is permanent, not seasonal. It is American, not bi-national. But on either shore, the shore means testosterone. Access to water means money, conspicuously displayed, unambiguously demonstrated. Power, not goodness or intelligence or wit, is what's demonstrated. The more power, the less the obvious effort. On either side of the border, everyone with a water view adheres to the rules set by the WASPs. There's no sweat, no effort, no exception. You either own or you're entertainment—admitted for a while because of some entertaining attribute, other than money, that is.

On the American shore, it's enclosed real estate. The power on display there is the power of mountains. In Canada, American money on display is much more accessible: it is an assertion of success, each high-maintenance clapboard house is, but more so, it is a demonstration of adherence to the tribal code of a tribe now revered, now maligned, ever aped, in manner, dress, demeanor, however obsolescent or moribund it may now be as a class or tribe or moiety among tribes. The Canadian shore is a self-refreshing assertion of WASP culture.

All that is what occurs on the beach. Canada itself, where the British live, is inland. Only a few hundred yards in from the shore, the southern Niagara Peninsula is a calm latticework of straight roads that reach through pastures and past dairy farms, roads that are superb for cycling. My favorite is Nigh Road. It starts in a postwar Canadian subdivision, but in its westward course, it's a farm road.

On the September ride to Port Colborne, I ride past tracts of the damp Carolinian forest in which so much variety of bird life thrives. I ride past mown hayfields, and fallow fields, and fields still growing their crops of beans and sugar beets and cabbages and corn. Here and there are big new suburban-style "country" houses, set up in aggressive limestone blocks, that have been set down between working farms—inland versions of the lakeshore houses that are built-out net-worth statements—but mainly, there are farms. There are hedgerows, too, in which there are yellow warblers, red tanagers, red cardinals, brown doves, muddy chipping sparrows, plain robins, and occasional and always astounding bright-blue Indigo Buntings. I have no doubt that within those coverts there are grouse, I have heard but not seen them there. Above these breaks of trees, sitting about twenty feet up on the overhead power lines, are shrikes and hawks, and swooping and diving all around are swifts and swallows, the kind with orange breasts and the kind with gray, too. The tumbledown old horse sheds smell sharply of fresh manure. The onshore breezes of the later afternoon bring the mixed scents of rotting lakeweed, fresh-cut hay, slow ditches, beef-cattle pies drying in pasture. The tough westerly against which cyclists struggle on the way out to see the Welland Canal become wicked cross-breezes on the way back, but there is all that quiet presence of the persisting preindustrial native realm to engage eye and soul.

The long climb up the Peace Bridge incline is a struggle in any season because it is a mile at a 10 percent grade before it flattens at its very crest, precisely above the Black Rock Canal. It's a short coast of only some dozens of yards to get to the Customs shed and the ritual of producing cards that one's sweat and one's stretchy shorts and one's wheels and helmet make ridiculous, because it's a lunatic's thought that anybody with miles under his ass is a threat to anything American but a barstool.

Cyclists race the storms across the Niagara River. It's good to beat them, and to return through the disheveled streets of the West Side of Buffalo, where the two-story clapboard houses that Yankees built to house themselves are like the two-story clapboard houses that Yankees built to amuse themselves. On the homeward side of the bridge, these houses are hand-me-downs, first to the immigrants from Sicily who until Nixon dominated the bridge neighborhood, and now, in just the past decade or so, to immigrants from Puerto Rico. The Sicilians had their gardens and their wallpaper. The newcomers have adjusted those Yankee clapboard houses with flags and with hues of blue and coral and yellow paint that one would never, ever see on a beach house in Canada.

The idea of the city

Terry Cooke is a marathon runner, the head of the Canadian Urban Institute, and the former elected head of government in Hamilton, Ontario, that nearby industrial city where they still somehow manage to operate a big port and make steel. Hamilton was on the way to becoming Buffalo—a sprawled-out, deindustrialized former rail-head—until local leaders like Cooke and an engaged electorate transformed the place into a stabilized and now growing regional city with a merged city-county government. Last week, Cooke gave out a lifetime achievement award named for a legendary urban theorist, writer, and activist who came to fame in 1960s Manhattan when she rallied a neighborhood to prevent Washington Square Park from being turned into an expressway. The Jane Jacobs award went to Bill Davis, the former Ontario provincial leader who joined Jacobs, who had moved to Toronto in 1968, in stopping an expressway project that would have ripped Toronto in half.

Sadly for Buffalo, Jane Jacobs bypassed Buffalo on her way from New York to Toronto; the Kensington Expressway devoured Humboldt Parkway in 1967, the year before Jacobs took up residence in a place beyond the reach of Robert Moses and his expressway-building epigones.

Jacobs, who died a couple of years ago, has recently become a rallying icon for urban designers and planners, professions that used to ignore her. She is the guru for a new generation of pro-city theorists and writers, and for real estate developers, too. She's the neighborhood activist who beat the great Robert Moses.

Robert Moses was the planner whose name became synonymous with huge public works projects in the 1950s and 1960s. In New York City, he is known for massive projects including the Cross Bronx Expressway and the Verrazano-Narrows Bridge, but also for his defeat at the hands of Jane Jacobs. In Western New York, we know Moses not from the sorry devastation his protégés gave us in the form of city-destroying

Kensington Expressway, but from the life-giving Niagara Power Project in Lewiston, and for the parkway named after him. The power project is such a great feat of engineering and clean energy that it stands in sharp contrast to Moses's automobile-centered work: not only does it produce clean electricity, it also produces money, including an annual payment of about $9 million that goes into a fund in Buffalo, a fund which could change Buffalo's future for the better, or, in the alternative, which could be squandered on an automobile-centered project (but more on this later).

Robert Moses, in sum, engineered many massive concrete public works that had everything to do with cars, because Moses's calculations always favored cars over people dwelling in their messy, idiosyncratic, slow neighborhoods. But Jacobs beat him.

So when the Canadian Urban Institute sent the Canadian leadership class a message this past week, that message took the form of an attaboy for a beloved former Ontario premiere, and the award citation was all about retelling the story of how Bill Davis and Jane Jacobs beat a Robert Moses-style expressway. "If we are building a transportation system to serve the automobile, the Spadina Expressway would be a good place to start. But if we are building a transportation system to serve people, the Spadina Expressway is a good place to stop," is what Davis said almost forty years ago. Go to Spadina Avenue today and you'll see what they saw then: in a city almost half of whose residents were born outside Canada, Spadina is a cluttered, buzzing, crowded neighborhood whose shops' signs are in Chinese, Vietnamese, French, Portuguese, Ukrainian, and even English. There are cars on the street, but there are also streetcars on rails, and bicycles, and pedestrians. Masses of them.

The Canadians adopted her, and now they celebrate everything urban, but not only in Toronto, where adaptive reuse of old buildings has been a given for decades. Calgary's mayor won an Urban Institute award for a new waterfront park and residential development squarely inside his city. Hailing from medium-sized cities all across the country, a fittingly diverse assemblage of citizen groups, local government officials, not-for-profits, and students got recognized for various happy projects. For the Canadians, Jane Jacobs is all about neighborhoods where positive, clever people live together such that they get happier in each other's presence.

But down here among us Yanks, Jane Jacobs is becoming something of an ideological mascot-in-dispute. Principal and influential among the new Jacobs fans are the New Urbanists, who loudly claim her. Former Milwaukee mayor John Norquist, who heads the Congress for a New

Urbanism, leads an annual "Jane Jacobs pub crawl" in Manhattan, and wherever New Urbanists meet, real estate developers get it crammed into their heads over and over again that the next real money to be made is going to be made in cities—or in suburban places that are set up as dense, walkable replicas of city neighborhoods. Next are the hopeful progressives who are not in the real estate business but who write admiringly of Jane Jacobs continuously; Google her name and it's hard not to find right-thinking liberals extolling her as a model economist of the efficiency of urban density. Greens, too, love cities; green writers lionize Jacobs. And now, not to be forgotten, the Right wants her, too.

The relentlessly anti-government Howard Husock, of Harvard's John F. Kennedy School of Government, might have had very wide eyes indeed last week in Toronto at seeing how non-ideological the notion of urban density has become in a country committed to the very kind of regional land-use planning that makes American conservatives choke. Husock, writing recently in the Manhattan Institute's *City Journal*, claimed Jane Jacobs for the Right, and chided American liberals and leftists for misreading her signature 1961 book, *The Death and Life of Great American Cities*, as anything other than a paean not only to free-market capitalism, but also to the established American version of urbanization: immigrant arrives in city ghetto, immigrant makes dough, immigrant books for the burbs making way for new immigrants.

It's true that Jane Jacobs described that "creative destruction" process, and the sequencing of uses of buildings in city neighborhoods. And it's true that big bad Robert Moses was a planner, and that she hated his version of planning—which was all about cars and getting suburbanites to and from their suburbs. But in the Toronto Jacobs moved to, fought for, and stuck with, there is now a bagpiper's tattoo for all things Jacobs that are about her adopted countrymen's version of her, and in the actualized, implemented urbanism of Canada today, there is not a peep of dissension or protest against planning that has as its goal the urban density and agglomeration economics that Jacobs praised. Canadians claim *that* Jane Jacobs. But still, so do Harvard's anti-planning Americans, including not only Husock, but also the prolific young economist Edward Glaeser, who protests against things like regulations for historic preservation, claiming that they disrupt the natural, sometimes chaotic, sometimes unpretty cycles of entrepreneurship and collapse in old neighborhoods.

Cities are complex, and the great writer addressed that complexity, and as with any heroine who has competing fan bases, the debate will go on because she wrote so much that there's evidence in her oeuvre for any argument you want to make. But the anti-government ideologues have a political agenda for which they mine Jane Jacobs's work: she didn't much like welfare spending as it was practiced in New York City in the early 1960s, and said so, and thus the "free market" boys love her for that and relentlessly bold-print those excerpts. But if you believe that welfare spending is the enemy of successful urban density, check out the European and Canadian cities that Jacobs admired: their successful evolution to new levels of density, diversity, and economic complexity has come about concurrently with much, much bigger social service and income-support regimes than in America.

But let's move on: the big issue, and the big change that hinges on which of our versions of city-loving Jane Jacobs gets emphasized, is our Robert Moses issue. That is, we have some decisions to make about oil-based personal transportation and the suburban landscapes that cheap oil and the Robert Moses mentality made possible. If, as some believe, the global crisis in petroleum will inevitably cause a massive re-migration to cities and an abandonment of suburbanization, then the progressive, green, Canadian version of Jane Jacobs will prevail. If cities are going to remain occasional entertainment venues for suburbanites who need massive subsidized parking garages so that they can drop by, dispose of some discretionary income, then burn some BP oil on their way back home via the Moses expressway, then the Manhattan Institute version of Jacobs will drive our spending. And the $9 million a year that is coming to Buffalo from the Power Project relicensing will be used to build us a Robert Moses version of urban life, rather than a Jane Jacobs version. For that's what the proposed Bass Pro project is fundamentally about: constructing massive parking garages for car-driving visitors.

Most who claim Jane Jacobs seem to be thinking of the spunky mom-in-tennis-shoes activist from Washington Square Park in 1963 or Spadina Avenue in 1971, when she fought big bureaucrats to defeat plans for expressways that murder neighborhoods and kill public space, especially green space.

But how are the lessons of Toronto and New York City relevant to the little cities that Jane Jacobs leapfrogged over? And there's another question that the great urban theorist left us: before her death in Toronto a few years ago, Jane Jacobs began to have some misgivings about some parts of civilization—not the "civitas" part, to be sure—and she became a more nuanced thinker than the one who, earlier in her career, seemed to have a rule for everything urban based on her own Manhattan experience.

Maybe that's because, in the almost fifty years since her fights with Robert Moses, and forty years since beating the Canadian expressway-lovers, Jacobs, and a few others, came to recognize that the suburbs are a part of city life, too.

The American city and 1968

The test case for Jane Jacobs is the city that was lost to racism, but that, paradoxically because of the biggest of big governments, became America's most compelling example of how a new way of urban living might work—even here in the Rust Belt.

When Terry Cooke introduced the Jane Jacobs Lifetime Award, he made blunt, plainspoken reference to what the Canadians of Bill Davis's generation wanted to avoid. Back when they were fighting the Spadina Expressway, Cooke said, they were already well aware of how they didn't want their city to "go the way of Buffalo, Cleveland or Detroit, where the central city was abandoned."

Cooke could have mentioned Washington, D.C., which was similarly abandoned. But nowadays, people who love cities love much that has happened in Washington, D.C. They particularly love the way some of its close-in suburbs have developed over the decades since Ronald Reagan's "conservative" government poured billions of borrowed federal dollars into the Potomac River basin's regional economy.

It's either paradoxical or funny that Reagan's anti-Washington spirit resulted in a flowering of government-stimulated wealth that is now much, much larger than the government spending that launched it.

The hallmark program of the Reagan years was the massive defense build-up, but his borrowed billions bought us much more. Reagan unleashed a feeding-frenzy for lobbyists which has never since abated. It brought Bentleys, minks, polished English-made shoes and many glittering evenings to Washington, but it also brought dowdy downtown D.C. back from abandonment. Reagan's unprecedented peacetime budget deficits, and his tax reform, plus the monument-consciousness and preservation-mindedness of the late senator Daniel Patrick Moynihan, engendered a showy and elegant rehabilitation of Washington—much of which had been torched and abandoned in the riots that followed Martin Luther King Jr.'s assassination in April, 1968. Harvard's Edward Glaeser may gripe about how preservationists and their pesky rules are making Manhattan a destination for the rich alone, but Washington's rules about keeping buildings no taller than the Capitol spire, and about preserving the "fabric" of the city by keeping the facades of old buildings intact, attracted so many prosperous people and so much redevelopment that their very presence overwhelmed the forces of decline. The strongest, largest, and most enduringly prosperous black middle class is a major achievement of the Washington metro renaissance.

Washington is hardly recognizable since the great tax-cutter came to town. The slums of O Street, the crack-infested rooming houses of Massachusetts Avenue, and the mess that was all of the central city in the mid-1980s have been succeeded by refreshed or replaced brick and stone structures that were always there but that looked like, and were, slums. A skid-row hotel that in Reagan's reelection year hosted high school students on field trips and delegations from impoverished western Indian tribes in $21-a-night rooms has long since been charging ten to fifteen times that rate. The retail landscape, supported by a larger and steadily growing local population, is more abundant than ever in the city's history. Chinatown hums and is no longer marooned between an uncertain downtown and a self-contained Capitol Hill. The short walk from the Gallery Place Metro station to the new National Portrait Gallery encompasses local and chain coffee shops, restaurants, a multi-screen movie house, home furnishings stores, clothing and jewelry and specialty shops, the offices of architects, lawyers, dentists, accountants, and consultants of every description, and there is more of the same in every direction where, in the 1980s, there was only riot wreckage and Georgetown somewhere off to the west.

Yet forty years since King's death and the great conflagrations, there remain great stretches of unreclaimed territory, which is another way of saying that the urban racial and class divide lives on even in one of the richest of America's metros. Capitol Hill has been expensive for some time, but H Street Northeast, immediately behind the handsomely polished and happily functional Union Station, is a commercial strip that limps in the seemingly perpetual gloom of that dismal history, as does much of the rest of Northeast Washington. Only inches from the prosperity and renovation of the classic rowhouses with their tiny neat yards and Easter Egg pastel colors, the body language of this street shrugs "boundary." It's still a broken territory. Urban pioneers do their pioneering in places like H Street Northeast; in Washington, as in Brooklyn or even in Buffalo, that means young professionals, but first, it means immigrants. There are refugees from Ethiopia's harsh politics and wars and droughts who have escaped all that, and who are happy, and proud, to operate a coffee shop named for the owner's home province. Men from the Ethiopian taxicab associations visit it on Sundays. Across H Street Northeast, a conspicuously Caucasian yoga studio proudly proclaims its first anniversary with a fabric sign anchored on the empty storefronts to the right and to the left.

But the plywood enclosures sealing the windows of those vacancies have been there through more than one season—they have, according to locals, been there for a generation. The upstairs offices, shop fronts, and apartment buildings are largely unredeemed by tenants, and the farther from Union Station, the emptier. The growth outward from Capitol Hill is indeed occurring: there are more owner-occupied rowhouses than a decade ago, and fewer storefront churches. The sense of the street is that the four decades of abandonment, poverty, isolation, and street crime will linger on, if not for a fifth decade, then at least a while longer.

This is, however, paradise regained compared to the great swaths of Buffalo, Detroit, Chicago, and other cities that burned in the 1968 riots—because at least in Washington, new activity is right next door. Speculation on H Street Northeast still makes sense even after the real estate crash. It's coming this way—you can feel it. H Street Northeast will be next to "come back." And another 600,000 souls are projected to enter the Washington metro over the next decade.

Not so in the burned cities of 1968. Many, many square miles of those cities are still barely, if at all, touched by the investment of capital and of hope that restores the density of dwellings and commerce, the density of plural human life that we used to call "civilization."

Toronto: the un-hollowed city

Jane Jacobs moved from New York City to Toronto in 1968 when Toronto was a haven for young American men who liked this continent better than Vietnam's. Toronto was then the polyglot and dense urban affair that it is today, only much smaller and much grayer. Toronto had a big university and big banks right downtown, to be sure, and it was in 1968 a growing port city that was actually benefiting from the Saint Lawrence Seaway. That's the project that had been imagined as the great public work that would, at its completion in 1957, catapult Buffalo and other Great Lakes cities back into the first ranks of American cities. The August 15, 1955 issue of *Newsweek* featured a cover story on Buffalo's rosy economic future, a future that, the magazine shouted, hinged upon the Saint Lawrence

Seaway. Business moguls, planners, and politicians were all quoted to the effect that Great Lakes cities, but especially Buffalo, would thrive as never before because the new system of locks and canals would open the world to American exports, and Buffalo to a new era of prosperity.

By the mid-1970s, when Buffalo's and the other Great Lakes cities saw their middle classes flee in the wake of Rehnquist's Supreme Court decisions on school desegregation, Buffalo and the other Great Lakes cities also saw the collapse of their industrial economies—and the Saint Lawrence Seaway helped them not. Instead, it was Toronto that had experienced the growth, and it was Toronto that received the trade, and a lot of Vietnam War protesters, and with them, Jane Jacobs. Toronto became Jane Jacobs's favorite city—full of the life, the street romance, the inexact and idiosyncratic texture that she had observed as life-creating energy in small sections of Boston, of Washington, D.C., of New York City and of the other places she had celebrated in *The Death and Life of Great American Cities.*

That book had made Jane Jacobs famous. It became her platform for the decades of the 1960s through the 1990s. It is hard to imagine today, when there is a stampede to out-Jane each other, that her hypothesis was largely spurned by the profession of planners. For those four decades, American students and urban-oriented thinkers thought of urban life and dreamed of urban renewal, and even invented "new urbanism" to characterize some of their ersatz-urban development projects hatched far from old cities—but the planners and developers lived with the rest of Americans, in a nation whose Caucasians had abandoned cities, out in the automobile suburbs.

As Jane Jacobs left the USA, white folks abandoned cities. The watershed year was 1968. The watershed events were those post-assassination riots. Whites abandoned cities out of fear of black violence. But whites also abandoned cities at the insistence of and with the active urging of every level of government. With subsidies and with new Kensington Expressways, federal and state and county and town governments enabled rapid suburbanization and the low-density sprawl that threw North American humanity into the thrall of automobiles, subdivision developers, and suburban politicians.

Buffalo, New York is a prime example of the new geography of Caucasian dispersal from city to suburb. Until 1960, just over half of the one million people in the 1,000 square miles of Erie County lived within the 40.5 square miles of the city of Buffalo. By 2000, 70 percent of the county's population was outside the city limits. Of the 130,000 African Americans in Erie County in 2000, all but 10,000 lived inside city limits. Of the 800,000 whites in Erie County, more than 600,000 lived outside the city limits. Back in 1950, when the city of Buffalo was almost 600,000 strong, more than 90 percent of the people living inside the 40.5 square miles were white. In short, the white population fled while the black population stayed. The tax base moved a few miles north, a few miles south, a few miles east of the municipal and school-district boundary, and the suburban jurisdictions added population, but the population of the region stagnated. This happened in Buffalo, in Rochester, in Syracuse, in Pittsburgh, in Cleveland, in Cincinnati, and in dozens of other metros in the Great Lakes states. It's the same story.

It is not the story, however, of Toronto.

Toronto had a different experience of 1968. Toronto in 1968 was amused by all the new American boys showing up. It was brightened by the first few coffeehouses and youth-oriented saloons and shops in the rowhouse streets just north across Bloor Street from the university. But Toronto never had crowds of angry African Canadians torching their substandard housing and looting their neighborhoods' commercial areas in protest over yet another murder of a beloved leader. Toronto was peaceful, staid, "diverse" in the sense we mean that term now, with calm saloons for men closed on Sundays as all the shops did, and with restaurants that were required to maintain separate entrances, away from the bar, for women.

Then Toronto suddenly changed. In 1970, political crisis in Montreal, which had been the financial and cultural capitol of Canada, hit hard. Prime Minister Trudeau declared martial law after Quebec separatists kidnapped and killed a government minister. Capital fled. That is to say, big English-speaking commercial banks and insurance companies and industrial concerns abruptly began expanding their operations in English-speaking Toronto. Within a few years, some of the power and the money of Montreal, if not the cultural sophistication of Montreal, shifted to Toronto. The political and cultural self-awareness and assertiveness of French-speaking Quebec was a bonanza for the gray city of Upper Canada. By every measure of population (size of workforce, per-capita income, educational attainment, number of enterprises created), of infrastructure (housing units constructed, lane-miles of road, miles of public transit, water, sewer, and utility systems constructed) and of activity (tons of freight handled, number of enterprises incorporated, taxes collected), Toronto's growth after 1970 was positive and sustained. And because of the focus by Toronto and Ontario government planners—a focus on keeping the infrastructure compact and city-focused rather than allowing the sprawl that characterizes American urban regions—the city grew in density and still grows in density. Adaptive reuse characterizes every old brewery, storehouse, distillery, and factory not still (or again) utilized for its original purpose.

It all made Jane Jacobs happy.

Yet in her last book, *Dark Age Ahead*, Jane Jacobs complained. She complained about, oh, this and that. She restated her ancient gripe about traffic engineers, whose antipathy to the scientific method she'd decried back in the fights over traffic-calming in Manhattan in the early 1960s. Traffic engineers had made messes in Toronto, too. In all her years in Toronto, even after the great victory over the Spadina Expressway, she nurtured a specific hatred of the lakeshore's Gardner Expressway.

But in her last book, she also shared her happiness about the new phenomenon of "import replacing"—the not-so-novel fact that local urban density in Toronto has created a market robust enough to support local manufacturing of furniture and other items that used to be imported. Jacobs hailed the fact that local money circulates better locally, because products that for so very long had been imported from overseas cheap-labor producers are now, in dense Toronto, being produced and sold locally.

The happy urbanist Jane Jacobs warns, in her last book, of a "dark age" precisely like the cliché of post-Roman Europe of barbarians and illiteracy and chaos that we learned about in high school. The bad times coming are not coming due to some shortfall in Toronto's urban success. The darkness descending on us, she says, is descending due to true science being abandoned, and self-policing by the learned professions ending, and families being so stressed that they erode, and cultural memory being obliterated, and taxes disconnecting from local needs.

This is not the book for which we should remember Jane Jacobs. Her gripe about the decline of science and of standards among professions, and her contradictory gripe about municipal government change in the province of Ontario, are gripes writ larger than gripes should ever get writ. (She liked local government, and wanted Toronto to be governed as a city-state, then got mad at the government she'd advocated for.) She got angry with some engineers, planners, bank economists, and other educated elites and then wrote this book, in part, to warn that it was their blindness that was dooming civilization. Some of those very local, very fleeting controversies should have been edited out of her tome.

It is when she speaks of cultural loss, though, that a chill of universal recognition descends. We have read elsewhere, especially in Jared Diamond's *Collapse: How Societies Choose to Fail or Succeed*, about societies that forget. Jane Jacobs warns that we are forgetting about what it means to live in cities.

That's the warning we need to heed. Driving through the sprawl of Generica—the suburban landscape that is precisely the same in suburban Buffalo as it is outside Chicago, outside Washington, outside every city, one sees what Jane Jacobs loathed and what some (but not enough) young people now flee—the automobile-based roadside culture that depends upon endless supplies of imported energy, and that some well-meaning people now want to import into urban centers.

What the Canadians have figured out is that their taxes stay low when their cities sustain density. Spadina Avenue is all about locally owned enterprises. The density that works there and in the great cities comes about when new immigrants come in and create sustainable economies by lots of small-scale enterprises, and that happens most effectively when public infrastructure moves people around in vehicles other than cars.

If the small- and medium-sized cities are part of the same civilization that the great cities lead, then Jane Jacobs is indeed the right guide for us all. What Jane Jacobs contributed to our cultural discourse, a contribution that will long outlast her, is a warning that civilization is about cities—places where people live in close proximity, where they have a sense of shared identity, where they interact (shop, play, study, work, date) near where they live, and it ain't about municipal boundaries. This is the point that her last book idiosyncratically makes. As she passed, she took a parting shot at all the Robert Moseses she could think of, refighting old fights. I doubt that a new urbanist, or an old urbanist, or even an ideologue could mine any one of Jacobs's texts to find support for the idea of building parking garages for suburban day-trippers. Yet if that's what keeps happening to public money in America, civilization will stay north of us. We will not only forget who we are: we will forget that we ever knew.

Flags

Tampa, Florida, has a Buffalo connection. But now that the Sons of Confederate Veterans have put up a 139-foot flagpole from which they're going to fly the Confederate Stars and Bars, I have no desire to visit Tampa any more.

Tampa has been attracting the winter-weary from Buffalo since about the time a Buffalo engineer named Willis Carrier earned the first patents for air conditioning. It was air conditioning, and federal money, that stimulated the great migration of capital and people from the Union states to the states of the Confederacy, including Florida. Buffalo flocks to Tampa in the annual "snowbird" migration, in such numbers that the whole west coast of Florida has a Buffalo feel about it.

But this huge Confederate flag reminds us that Florida is not home.

Home here in the north is the place from which many of our ancestors set out to serve in the Union army in the Civil War. They returned victorious, and their victory gave us the United States, including Florida. Almost 700,000 Americans died in that war that made us one country.

I actually knew the daughter of a man who fought in the Civil War, a man who was there to see the Confederate flag lowered in defeat the day General Lee surrendered at Appomattox. The daughter of that soldier was my nana, my great-grandmother. Her father served with the 112th New York Volunteers, a regiment that helped defeat the rebellion in Florida. (His outfit also beat Johnny Reb in Georgia, the Carolinas, and Virginia, too.)

When I was a boy in the days before Vietnam, my nana and I went to parades and Independence Day events in our town. The Civil War service of those illustrious ancestors of ours was still being recognized along with the service of our World War II heroes still living. People still wore their Grand Army of the Republic insignia. Just about every town in our part of the world has a Civil War monument in the town square—a statue of a Union soldier in a forward-tilted cap, or a cannon, or an obelisk. The big city has parkways and great bronze sculptures of generals like Bidwell, and Grant, and Sheridan, and of course, Lincoln, our martyred hero.

And since the 1930s, the historical society has been erecting markers throughout the region for farmhouses and churches where local people sheltered others, on their way to Canada, people whom the Confederacy fought to keep enslaved, people whom our Western New York ancestors fought to liberate.

Perhaps the young of Concord and Lexington see the American flag and think about the Revolutionary War. Here in Western New York, the flag reminds me of Gettysburg, and of Bull Run. When I went to Arlington National Cemetery recently, which used to be General Robert E. Lee's estate, I didn't see the Confederate flag he fought under. I saw the flag my nana's father fought for.

We know what the Confederate flag is these days. It's a wise-ass provocation. It's a Tom Sawyer sort of gesture, a protest against the suffocating righteousness of equal rights and civil rights. Flying the stars and bars is a political expression.

But it is not an innocent expression. The Confederate flag is the flag of losers. It is soaked in the blood of Americans who came together to put it down.

It's too bad for Tampa that all those Buffalo snowbirds who drive on the interstate will have to look at that big old loser Confederate flag on their way to the sun. I prefer the flag at Robert E. Lee's house, the flag of the victors, the flag that says, we came together, we're one people, we're in pursuit of impossible ideals of freedom, and of justice, though the pursuit has been so bloody and so difficult.

CHOOSING ICONS

The Piarists, Slawinski, and Wright

> As Frank Lloyd Wright emerged from the car parked under the porte cochere, Father Vercek hurried out to greet him. The architect was pointing his cane and shaking it at the long awkward shed-roof lean-to addition across the front of the house. "Who did this? Who made these changes? This is not my work," he sputtered, visibly upset at the mutilation of his dramatic concept. How would Leonardo Da Vinci have reacted if he had been presented with a repainted Mona Lisa without the smile?
>
> As Father Vercek recalled the incident, he then explained to Wright that they were a religious order and needed a chapel, to which Wright responded in apparent resignation, "Well, I guess, if you need it."
>
> —John Conlin, Graycliff Conservancy newsletter, August 2000

This is a Frank Lloyd Wright story of Buffalo. The great architect came back to visit one of his early works and was enraged that it hadn't been kept precisely as he'd designed it. Seeing the Graycliff estate near Buffalo as an old man of ninety-one, a few months before his death, Wright was annoyed. We do not know how Wright felt about seeing an empty lot where his Larkin Company warehouse had stood, or how he felt at seeing the partial demolition of his other Buffalo work.

Wright's relationship with the Larkin Company, his design of houses for Larkin president Darwin D. Martin, and his design of the company's headquarters itself, have been studied intensively because Wright's Buffalo oeuvre is the most significant, and most influential, of his early career. Wright's own diary entries and public statements about his work here indicate the intensity of his attachment to the Martin family. We know that that relationship endured, that the lives of patron and of artist interlaced. It was more than twenty years after Wright completed the Martin home in Buffalo that he designed Graycliff for Martin's wife Isabel. She needed light in this her summer retreat, so Wright built her a place into which all the sky and sun of the great expanse of the lake shore could enter. So when Wright visited Buffalo in 1958, over thirty years after he'd designed the place, and saw that a religious order had altered one of the triumphs of his early days, he lost his temper.

The priests of the Piarist order had built their chapel into the house at Graycliff such that the roofline, the famous cantilevered line, was, the preservationists now say, "mutilated." Wright calmed when told that what those priests had done was for a spiritual purpose, and indeed that their tenancy at Graycliff had prevented the place from falling entirely to ruin or even to demolition. Altered, yes; turned from a summer retreat to a year-round residence, yes. Preserved, imperfectly, yes, but preserved nonetheless. When, in 1999, forty years after Wright's death, a group of architectural preservationists bought Graycliff from the Piarists, the preservationists, being preservationists, decided early on to remove the Piarists' chapel, and to demolish the Piarists' dormitory. The Graycliff Conservancy's goal, naturally, was to return the estate to Wright's original design.

But Wright's was not the only art on the site. The Piarist priests had acquired Graycliff in 1951. By that time, the estate had already passed from the Martin family. The Piarists knew what they were getting: a summer home designed by a famous architect, a structure lacking a ready purchaser other than themselves, a structure in need of some change in order to make it winter-habitable. They also knew their own mission.

The Piarists are a teaching order whose founder was a seventeenth-century Spaniard named Josef Calasanz. In Latin, Calasanz is Calasanctius. Calasanctius is the name the order has given to many of the schools it has founded, including their school, now closed, in Buffalo.

The bare fact of this story is that in 1967, the Piarists commissioned a work of art to commemorate their order's 350th anniversary. The art was a mural, a *sgrafitto*, depicting St. Joseph Calasanctius and the abandoned children whom he saved from the streets of Rome, where Calasanctius and his fellow priests had gathered them up, housed them, and educated them, just as the "red priest" Antonio Vivaldi would so famously later do for the abandoned girls of Venice. Calasanz the Spanish nobleman had created a free school for the poor, and founded an order, the Scholae Pio, to carry on that mission.

For three hundred and fifty years, the priests of the Piarist order have continued that work. It is an order less famous than the Jesuits or the Franciscans, yet withal an order that had become over that time a very large presence in Europe. There are, or were, Piarist schools in Spain, Ireland, Italy, Austria, the Czech Republic, Slovakia, Poland, and Romania, but most especially in Hungary. At Graycliff, the Piarists had established their home in North America. For them, with this haven in the United States, with their successful school in nearby Buffalo, and because of the peace so many of them had found after decades of war and of calamitous anti-Catholic oppression and displacement in Europe, this Graycliff estate was a new beginning—a place to celebrate their own survival, surely, and the survival of their Calasanctius mission.

There were Poles and Spaniards among them, but most of the Piarists of Graycliff were Hungarians. Most had come to America after World War II. Some came in 1956, having been made refugees after the Soviet Union's military forces had brutally suppressed a popular uprising against Hungary's communist government. All the Piarists were teachers; some were more. Their roster included a mathematician, theologians, and a psychologist, all of whom had been educated in Rome, Berlin, and in the universities of the old Dual Monarchy of Austria-Hungary. They were of necessity linguists and translators; a few had taught at the ancient university at Koloszvar, the city that had been capital of the Austro-Hungarian empire's Transylvania province but that had, since 1918, been in Romania. (The Hungarians had called the town Koloszvar for about nine hundred years; the German speakers or Saxons of that area had called it Klausenburg for about five hundred years. The Romanians, to whom the Treaty of Trianon had given the area in 1918, call it Cluj-Napoca.)

In 1967, these émigrés commissioned a Polish-born muralist named Jozef Slawinski to put his *sgrafitto* technique to commemorating Calasanctius. Slawinski created a twelve- by eighteen-foot mural a foot thick consisting of layers of black, white, yellow, and red concrete; the *sgrafitto* technique, like fresco, requires quick work by the artist to reveal the image before the material sets.

For the ensuring thirty years, the Calasanctius mural hung on the east face of the dormitory even as the Piarist presence there dwindled. When the Graycliff Conservancy took possession of the estate in 1999, the preservationists wanted the dormitory demolished and the mural removed. There was, in the minds of the preservationists, no competition between the master architect Wright's design and what they described as the "mutilation" (i.e., the Piarists' chapel) that had been committed by an obscure group of Central Europeans whose brief presence had recently ended.

By 1999, all but two of the Piarists had died or had left for the Piarists' other American school, in Devon, Pennsylvania, near Philadelphia.

There was the issue, the lingering problem, of what to do with the mural. The Conservancy wanted the dormitory gone, but did not want to burden itself with the task of raising funds to cope with the unwanted mural, too. It took four years, until 2003, to raise enough money to remove the Piarists' mural from the dormitory, which was then demolished. It took almost two more years to relocate the mural. (The engineers who did the job were the same ones who'd moved the Cape Hatteras lighthouse.) The mural is now on the campus of Buffalo State College.

By the time it was unveiled in its new setting, it had become known as "the Slawinski mural" rather than "the Calasanctius mural" or "the Piarist mural." The keynote speakers at the installation event were the president of the college, the county executive whose money had conserved and moved it, and the president of the Polish Arts Club of Buffalo, who introduced the artist's widow, Wanda Slawinska. There were no Piarists present; there was no Hungarian spoken. And although much effort had been invested, fruitlessly, in identifying them, none of the original benefactors or patrons of the Piarists were named, because their names had been worn away by the elements.

Graycliff had been the Piarists' headquarters in the United States. They came to use it mainly as a place of rest, meditation, and religious study, and as a retirement home for priests who could no longer teach a full schedule at the Calasanctius school. Within a few miles of Graycliff along the Lake Erie shore, four other Catholic organizations own retreat houses, also formerly the estates or summer "cottages" of wealthy Buffalo families.

The estate, called Graycliff because of the sixty-foot shale cliff on which it is perched, was built as a summer place for Darwin Martin's wife Isabel. She wanted light, as much as possible, because of her failing eyes, so Wright designed enormous windows, including the first "picture window," to catch the light from the broad expanse of lake and sky at cliff's edge. Darwin Martin was introduced to Frank Lloyd Wright by Martin's brother, who, while living in Chicago, had come to know Wright's work in neighboring Oak Park. Frank Lloyd Wright and Darwin Martin would have an extraordinary, enduring, and productive relationship, starting with Martin's commission of the handsome but unimposing Barton House in Buffalo in 1903. Wright's masterwork in Buffalo was Darwin Martin's house, commissioned in 1905 and built over the next two years for the extraordinary sum of $175,000 and many, many further adjustments. The Darwin Martin House, now in the final stages of a restoration that was begun in the 1980s, is mentioned in the same terms as the Guggenheim Museum, Fallingwater, the Johnson Company headquarters, Taliesin, and the Prairie style (of which it is an exemplar) in the vocabulary of Wright's work. Graycliff, built in 1927, deserves but has not yet had the level of scholarly attention of other Wright structures; it is a handsome place, but not the overwhelming design presence or the artistic assertion of the Darwin Martin House.

The Piarists knew what they had at Graycliff. They were penniless refugees with a complex mission. That mission, that part of it concerning teaching, included their explicit effort to inculcate in their students an appreciation for art, not limited to religious art. Their school, when they had raised enough funds to open it, was an American version of a European lyceum or an English "public" school, was nondenominational. The Piarists were also men of their time, which is to say, educated men of a previous age who found themselves situated in a city with universities, colleges, diverse and significant architecture and, in the early 1960s, a set of vigorous institutions that were demonstrating progressive thinking and growth. In the late 1950s and early 1960s, Buffalo was a place of remarkable energy, especially in the immediate neighborhood of the Piarists' school. There was a brand-new college campus in the city, and next to it, there was a brand-new addition to its famous art gallery. In the city center was a brand-new central library and a brand-new county office building for the just-reformed regional government. There were plans for a massive expansion of the University of Buffalo, which had just gone from being an isolated private school to being a part of the massive public system of the Empire State under the new patrician Governor Nelson Rockefeller. Experimental hovercraft were tested in Buffalo's harbor; engineers for Bell Aerospace and other defense contractors designed and tested rocket equipment near the laboratories where only a few years before they had designed and tested the first jet engines. And Buffalo was a border community and a large Great Lakes port on the newly completed Saint Lawrence Seaway: it had the sophistication and the prospects for growth of a major regional capital.

These Piarists developed a studied affinity for this place, and chose it as the new nexus for their international brotherhood. They were persons, too, of course, beyond their membership in their order. They were immigrant veterans of the horrific recent history of Central Europe that had been, in their individual childhoods, a peaceful place of family, homeland, native language. Latin, French, and German were their languages of scholarship; English, their medium for teaching and business in this new place; but Hungarian, Polish, and Spanish were their languages of identity. The surest dimension of their collective identity was that they were men of the twentieth century, men who had known the brutal reality of having been born in a big empire that had been a collection of small nations that all had been smashed to pieces in the wars of the big powers.

Safely here, they, being mainly Hungarian, welcomed refugees from the Hungarian Revolution in 1956. The dormitory at Graycliff was built for refugees, which is to say, persons who had fled for their lives. They had left everything material, houses and furniture and musical instruments, of course; farms, title to lands, naturally; but even diplomas, credentials—the indices of individual personality and achievement. Among them were younger men who had fought Central Asian conscripts of the Soviet forces that had thrust into ancient Budapest as other Central Asians had centuries earlier. (The historic alliance of Catholic Poles and Catholic Hungarians was forged, notwithstanding the mutual unintelligibility of their languages, in their wars of survival against invasion by the Mongols and by the Turks; Poles and Hungarians regarded themselves as the defenders of Europe, and so they were.) These Budapest boys who came to live at Graycliff had fought the new invaders from the East heroically, tragically, without guns. They had faced the Russian tanks of 1956 with homemade gasoline bombs. They had thrown bricks at them. They had set up burning barricades. And they had lost, and they had fled, on foot, to Austria, to Yugoslavia, and eventually, to North America, to Graycliff. There are stories of the priests hosting young men who would slip back and forth into nearby Canada in the 1960s and 1970s, men who would go back to Europe to harass the Communists in their homeland. At Graycliff, there is access to the beach from the main house down a now-decrepit iron staircase tower, which ends on the beach at a low concrete structure which houses a ruined diesel winch for a boat hoist. The beach below the cliff narrows and widens with the seasons; there was no harbor there, nor lighthouse, but the landform itself is a beacon, because the iron staircase tower to Graycliff is but a few hundred yards from the half-mile-wide gap in the shale cliffs where Eighteenmile Creek empties into Lake Erie. From there, it is just fifteen miles across Lake Erie to Canada. Small boats make the crossing routinely.

The Piarists were casualties of the war as well as of the postwar Communist government. So was their countryman, the revered but now forgotten Joszef Cardinal Mindszenty, whom the Piarists hosted at Graycliff and at their school in Buffalo in 1971. It is now not much recalled, if at all, how much of a symbol of the Cold War the late Cardinal Mindszenty was. Mindszenty, the bishop of the ancient Hungarian royal city of Esztergom where Mathias had accepted Christianity in the year 1000, had become archbishop and then cardinal and thus a representative of the Pope. His leadership of the Catholics of Catholic Hungary is extensively credited with having kept the Hungarian government of the 1930s and 1940s from murdering ethnic and religious minorities.

The Catholic Church in Hungary (unlike the Catholic Church in Slovakia just to the north), was not allied with Nazi Germany, though the government was. Even though it had promulgated an anti-Semitic quota for university admissions after World War I, the Hungarian government had refused to kill Jewish Hungarians.

But then a new government took over in May 1944. It reorganized the local police authorities all across the country according to Nazi protocols. In that month of May 1944, the Hungarians started deporting the Jews of Hungary. Between May and July of 1944, 435,000 Hungarian Jews were deported to Auschwitz. Six months later, the anti-Semitic Arrow Cross movement took power and started the killing on home soil. When the Arrow Cross fascists came in, they jailed the cardinal of Hungary, Joszef Mindszenty, in part because the Church protested the deportation and murder of Hungarian Jews.

The Arrow Cross suppressed the Catholic Church, and rounded up the Jews of Budapest, and killed them—except for those who were saved by some truly heroic gentiles who put their lives on the line for strangers. The Swedish diplomat Raoul Wallenberg was one. So was the Hungarian Tibor Baranski, later recognized as a Righteous Gentile at Yad Vashem in Israel. So was another Hungarian, Dr. Clara Ambrus, who in 2006 was recognized as a Righteous Gentile at Yad Vashem in Israel.

Tibor Baranski and Clara Ambrus and her husband Julian Ambrus came to Buffalo after World War Two. When Cardinal Mindszenty came to visit Buffalo after his release by the Hungarian Communists in 1971, among the people who greeted him were Tibor Baranski and Clara Ambrus—for both Baranski and Ambrus were friends of, neighbors of, and supporters of the Piarist priests of Graycliff, and the Baranski and Ambrus children attended the Piarists' school, named for St. Joseph Calasanctius. The founder of the Piarist order had been canonized for having given sanctuary and educational uplift to orphans in Rome; in Buffalo, rescue and relief in this peaceful refuge was the experience of those Hungarians, Jew and gentiles alike, who came together to support Calasanctius.

Jozef Slawinski's work is of the same era and dimension as the Mexican muralist Diego Rivera's. It is public, its scale is large, its subject matter is heroic, and it is aggressively political. The simplicity of Slawinski's composition is deceptive: it seems to indicate naivete or primitivism. But to recall the artist's education in prewar Poland, and to reflect on the rapid onset of overwhelming change forced by currents in politics and in the arts in that place and at that time, is to begin to recognize his assertions. The icons of Orthodoxy are reflected in this work. Slawinski employed the planar and heroic didacticism of the Byzantine imperial style, rather than the fleshy and rounded and muscle-detailing Soviet imperial style, and in that choice of style is a political assertion. It makes a certain sense in the context of Polish art that is not so apparent this far west of where Orthodox Russia so dominated, so forcefully and repeatedly dominated, Slawinski's Catholic Poland. This struggle is there at the forefront of, and not lurking behind, the ostensible focus of the works.

Critics and art historians have had difficulty with Slawinski. To recognize the contrast between Socialist realism and its naturalism, versus the abstract and iconic presentation that Slawinski chose, is to recognize that the politics of his imagery actually becomes the subject. A local museum curator characterized Slawinski's work as "immigrant art," which is a sort of polite accusation of naivete; the comment reveals, however, both a class bias and an ahistorical consciousness.

Slawinski demonstrated his technical competence at naturalism elsewhere in his work, so the Calasanctius mural, in context, is not a naïve work, but an assertion of something else. Slawinski's austere formality looks like mid-twentieth-century realism made magical, or made simple. Slawinski's other work at first glance seems like so much of the soft American version of Socialist Realism, the kind commissioned by the Depression-era Work Projects Administration. Indeed, the public spaces in which it is shown—the main lobby of the Erie County Medical Center on Grider Street, the post office and a school in the northwestern Buffalo neighborhood of Riverside, and now outside of the Butler Library on the Buffalo State College campus—are consistent with that ethic. Public space, public art, simple stuff.

But the politics isn't socialist and secular. The politics of Slawinski's images are fundamentally different. Slawinski's subjects are subversive of secularism. The hospital mural is a filiopietistic hymn of praise to the Polish immigrant community of Buffalo and Western New York and thus is most precisely "immigrant art"; but more so, the Buffalo Polonia triptych is a documentary of Catholicism, as if to say, it's the faith that endures, and through the faith the nation. The West Hertel School mural is of the heroes of the War of 1812, as the commission had commanded, but there in the background, precursors of all the mundane activity in the foreground, are the Jesuits and Recollets; this is historically correct, because it was they, the missionaries, who in 1688 were the first Europeans to penetrate the interior of North America, via the Niagara River passage only a mile from that school. But it is also a political and a spiritual assertion as well: the Church and its soldiers are the background. Looking at Slawinski's private work for the Franciscans, politics and religion are interwoven: Mary is being crowned a queen of a medieval nation in one work, the Polish king Mieszko is being baptized in another; both of these monarchs see their conversion on the edge of the realms of Roman and Byzantine Christianity, which is the political borderland and the cultural border region that was Slawinski's native realm. The late Nobel Prize–winning poet Czeslaw Milosz spent his political and artistic life navigating these currents; he wrote essays about the "nationhood" of Catholicism, and about the transcendent religiosity of a Polish national identity that existed without benefit of a nation-state. The complexity of identity is made further complicated by those overlapping claims of—what do we call them, Catholic ethnic groups? Catholic nations? Catholic peoples?—to the same historical heroes. Stefan Batory, for one: a hero to the Poles, a prince of Transylvania, the elected king of the Polish-Lithuanian Commonwealth . . . complexity that is impenetrable and obsolete to Americans was formative to minds shaped in Central Europe in the days when Czeslaw Milosz, the Piarist priests of Graycliff, and Jozef Slawinski were young. The borders have changed, the vocabulary has been lost.

But the narrative of the image survives. The Calasanctius mural is of the Catholic priest who began free education, education as liberation and empowerment of the poor, but of course not the kind of socialist or revolutionary empowerment that was the subject of the other muralists of the mid-twentieth century. The central figure in the Calasanctius mural is the teacher. The women are iconic Magdalenes visiting from Byzantine frescoes; the doubting men of Rome look like senators of great political stature and power, but they are marginalized and dwarfed by the presence of the humble saint, whose work and subject and focus is Christ-like, and thus noble. These tensions reveal Slawinski as thus an emphatically political artist; his politics is the politics of John Paul II—the pro-labor, pro-Solidarity subversive from Krakow who understood the power of the Soviet empire, and who undermined it with his own.

Most of the rest of Slawinski's art is not available for public view except on the website of the Polish Arts Club; the largest collection of his work is confined within the Franciscan residence midway between Buffalo and Graycliff.

One work that is publicly accessible is a smaller work, a bas-relief plaque in hammered copper like a dark icon (the artist's reference to the structure of Eastern images is dramatic). This piece is hidden in an ill-lit recess of the lobby of Buffalo's City Hall. It is Slawinski's memorial to the Katyn massacre.

Katyn is a name known to Poles; Katyn was once known to the world, in the way that My Lai, Rwanda, Ground Zero, and other geographies of horror and outrage are known to the world. Katyn is the name of a forest in eastern Poland in which fifteen thousand Polish army officers were slaughtered by Stalin's secret police.

Slawinski's plaque is a grim, dignified work of mourning for a monstrous crime. In metal like an icon, it is a dark negation of any possibility that that crime can be forgiven. In metal like an icon, it is a reversal of the iconic Russian vocabulary of religious art, in which the painting of the face of the Virgin, or of a saint, is surrounded by the protective strength and richness of the metal. Here, the image of the horror is on the metal itself: the only paint is a small field of red above the central figure, red for the Polish flag.

Slawinski's mural of Saint Joseph Calasanctius was unveiled by dignitaries on a November morning in Buffalo in 2005. The artist's widow and about sixty other people attended the event. The president of the college spoke. The executive director of the Graycliff Conservancy spoke. So did the leader of the Polish Arts Club, a not-for-profit entity that had lobbied and solicited contributions for the conservation effort from various local foundations. The main donor was Erie County, whose executive read a text that made reference to the history and significance of the mural, its commission, and its subject:

> Madame President, thank you for your courage and foresight in offering this mural a permanent home on your campus.
>
> This mural is about courage.
>
> This mural is about a revolution in human history.
>
> We are standing today on a piece of public land that is dedicated to a revolutionary concept called public education.
>
> The roots of that concept are in Rome—in the seventeenth century—almost four hundred years ago.
>
> This mural is a portrait of a young man from Spain, a man of noble birth. His special mission was saving the abandoned children of the streets of Rome. Joseph Calasanctius could have been an American because he believed in the revolutionary concept—the idea that even abandoned children could be educated just like the children of the aristocracy.
>
> The religious order which he founded stayed in Italy. That order went to Poland. It went to Hungary, and to Spain, to South America, even to India. And then they came to Buffalo.
>
> The story of their presence here is for others to tell.
>
> But their concept of freedom is their gift, and our legacy—and their idea of freedom was education.
>
> How fitting, then—that this revolutionary ideal would find a home in Buffalo, New York.
>
> Buffalo is, after all, the home of a great revolutionary movement.
>
> Buffalo is the home of the Underground Railroad.
>
> Buffalo is the place that opened all of free America to immigrants like my ancestors who came here for freedom and opportunity.
>
> Just as today, kids from every corner of the world come to Buffalo State College for freedom and opportunity the Buffalo way—the Calasanctius way—through education.
>
> So this is exactly the right place for this mural.

> Because here is where we can make the connection across generations, across continents, across the span of history—a connection with a concept.

The community reaction was appropriate: aficionados applauded, employees of the college congratulated Wanda Slawinska, and the media made of it a small story.

The challenge remaining, now that the mural has been conserved, is in giving it a context.

Graycliff is now in its third phase of restoration. It is a remarkable success story in which a great many people have had a hand. Graycliff restoration will cost less than $5 million because the ongoing occupation by the Piarists between 1951 and 1999 kept the building alive, albeit imperfectly. The Darwin Martin House restoration will cost ten times as much, maybe more, including a new visitor center, because the structure was so damaged by abandonment, partial demolition, and abuse.

But there are few remaining who can still speak to the connection between Buffalo and the great historic continuity of Catholic faith, struggle, scholarship, and community. Graycliff was a refuge for Isabel Martin, whose husband Darwin Martin made commercial and architectural history as a brilliant businessman and an enlightened patron of art and architecture. A brotherhood of priests from a rich historic tradition came to Graycliff, turned it into a refuge for themselves and for young people who fought against oppression fifty years ago, when they defended the fragile civilization of the West against a monstrous despotism, and then another.

This is a hard story to tell. Mention a small nation in Central Europe and most Americans think of anti-Semitism and of mindless wars of long ago. And besides, even the Cold War is over. Teenagers do not know even approximately what Communism was—not even approximately. The Piarist priests of Buffalo are no more. Their students have moved away. The elder Tibor Baranski is dead; the younger Tibor Baranski is an attorney practicing in Beijing. Even the refugees to whom the Piarists gave refuge have moved away. The dormitory that housed them has been knocked down. A search of the database of the Buffalo and Erie County Public Library in 2006 reveals no—zero—results for "Calasanctius," "Piarist," "Father Gerencser," or "Scholae Pio" in authors, titles, subjects, or even keywords in any of the holdings.

The only physical evidence of the Piarists' former presence in Buffalo is an incongruous piece of what looks like religious art standing in an alcove behind the library of a public college. But it is a handsome work. It is powerful, even there in its curious new context. It is sheltered from the aggressions of the Great Lakes climate, which is snowy in winter, but surpassingly clement in summer, when the lake breeze moderates the heat of even the hottest summer days, which is when people from the city spend as much time as they can on the beaches, or at their summer homes perched on the shale cliffs above, enjoying the light.

The slave Daniel

On August 18, 1851, at the terminus of the Erie Canal in Buffalo, a cook on a Lake Erie steamboat docked there was attacked by a group of men wielding the power of a new federal law. A slave-catcher named Benjamin Rust, accompanied by a federal marshal and two Buffalo police officers, grabbed the cook, a former slave named Daniel Davis, intending to take him back to his former owner in Kentucky. Davis resisted. Rust hit Davis on the head with a piece of wood, whereupon Davis fell backwards down the steps into the steamboat's hold, directly onto his hot cookstove, which seared his flesh. Rust and the officers then dragged the badly injured Davis out of the boat, off the wharf and up Commercial Street to Main Street to the office of the U.S. Commissioner, and then on to the courthouse on Lafayette Square. At the hearing, in the presence of Mayor James Wadsworth of Buffalo, this cook was found, by a commissioner appointed under the federal Fugitive Slave Act, to be the legal property of the Kentucky slave-owner. As the proceedings adjourned and the court emptied onto Main Street, Mayor Wadsworth and the sheriff personally led Buffalo's police force against a mixed-race crowd of citizens that had assembled not just to protest Daniel Davis's capture, but to liberate him from a forced return to enslavement, as well.

Luckily for Daniel Davis, he wasn't turned over to the slave-catcher. Instead, Davis was put in Buffalo's jail, and Benjamin Rust was charged with assault. Bizarrely, the very commissioner who had just found that Davis was a Kentuckian's property donated $25 to help secure Davis's freedom. Meanwhile, the slave-catcher was jailed on $1,000 bail. Over the ensuing two weeks, until a dramatic resolution on August 31, 1851, Buffalo became a hot political, journalistic, and legal battleground over what was then known in the press as the case of "the slave Daniel."

Daniel Davis lost his freedom, and would eventually regain it, on a piece of real estate that was rescued by a long community campaign to preserve some of the elements that were present in the year the Fugitive Slave Act was a hot issue in Buffalo. The Daniel Davis case offers a glimpse into the history of Buffalo's harbor as a nexus of the Underground Railroad, of the American experience of mass migration, and also into the politics of abolition and in the advancement of democracy not only in America but around the world.

The two-week drama played a long-neglected role in ending the career of President Millard Fillmore. The confrontation in Buffalo undermined the legitimacy of Fillmore's Whig Party, and the New York politicians who advocated for Daniel Davis—especially governor, then senator, then Abraham Lincoln's cabinet member William Seward—created a national politics that would no longer tolerate Millard Fillmore's doomed compromise whereby some people in the United States could live as citizens while others lived as slaves.

The case of "the slave Daniel" lit this town on fire in the last half of August, 1851. In churches, in newspapers, in mass meetings, and in courtrooms, Buffalo's obscure citizens and community leaders alike declaimed about the meaning of the word "freedom" and to whom it applied. Speakers spoke ex tempore and from texts as well as to what had and what had not been intended by the men who seventy years earlier had written the United States Constitution and its first ten amendments.

Newspaper editors from the three Buffalo English-language dailies blistered each other and made no pretense to objectivity as they published commentaries, and occasionally some facts, on the principal actions and personalities in the conflict. The famous former slave and antislavery advocate Frederick Douglass followed the case from Rochester, and reported on it in his own paper, the *Liberator*. The New York City papers published items about the case. Preachers and sermonizers in Buffalo, Rochester, and Cleveland spoke and wrote about the case. Lawyers contended both in Buffalo and in the federal district court in William Seward's hometown of Auburn, New York, near Syracuse, over whether Daniel Davis was going to have a chance to live as a free citizen in a non-slave state, or whether he had been doomed by Millard Fillmore's law to return to bondage south of the Ohio River.

For two weeks, people wondered whether Daniel Davis's case, should he lose, would mean that slavery would become, in effect, legal even in states like New York, where it had been illegal for decades. A mile west across the Niagara River in Canada, the slave trade had been illegal since 1806, when Parliament had banned it in all British possessions. Members of Buffalo's nine hundred-odd African American community held meetings in which they vowed to resist being made to leave their American homes.

Though it was overshadowed by subsequent controversies in New York City and elsewhere, the case of "the slave Daniel" was the first real test of the Fugitive Slave Act, which had been signed into law by a president from Buffalo.

Today, at the restored terminus of the Erie Canal, one can visit the very place where this drama of 1851 played out. One can walk on the limestone blocks that line the Commercial Slip, where the *Buckeye State* was anchored on the day that Daniel Davis was seized. One can see the foundations of ruined buildings that had been in existence on that day. One can see what's left of the cobblestone streets that were in use then, including Commercial Street. There's a replica "bowstring" bridge that has been erected and that crosses the re-watered Commercial Slip. On the west side of the Commercial Slip, there's a new building that houses the indoor exhibits of the Naval and Serviceman's Park; the building looks like, has the shape of and the dimensions of, buildings that were in existence in the mid-nineteenth century, when Buffalo was the major port of the Great Lakes and Buffalo Harbor saw dozens of ships a day sail or steam in with lumber, grain, coal, and passengers, and sail or steam out with manufactured items, flour, livestock, and European immigrants bound for the North American interior that Buffalo's harbor and the Erie Canal had helped open.

Until 2007, many people believed that the fight to preserve that intersection of Buffalo Harbor and the Erie Canal had been lengthy, bitter, and victorious. After years of grassroots lobbying by preservationists who were opposed to a state agency's plan to pave over the site of the original Commercial Slip, newly elected county executive Joel Giambra joined with the preservationists and authored a new memorandum of understanding that ended the lawsuits, ended the acrimony, and achieved the restoration of critical historic elements of the Canal District. By October 2007, the re-watered Commercial Slip in its original site, with its "bowstring" Water Street bridge, plus a rebuilt Central Wharf and a restored historic street pattern were are all scheduled for completion.

Politics helped it happen. Seven years earlier, sensing the political opportunity, Governor George Pataki reenacted his predecessor DeWitt Clinton's "wedding of the waters" by scooping up a pail of Buffalo Harbor water to take to New York Harbor and symbolically join the Great Lakes to the Atlantic Ocean, just as Governor Clinton had done 175 years before. The governor also formally endorsed the "history-based" project to restore the Commercial Slip and the historic street pattern of the Canal District, and to rebuild the Central Wharf—the 400-foot-long wooden walkway that had stretched along the north bank of the Buffalo River from the middle of the nineteenth century well into the twentieth.

Tim Tielman and Sue McCartney, then leaders of the Preservation Coalition of Buffalo and Erie County, had been among the most dogged and vocal of the opponents to what had been called the Horizons Waterfront Commission plan to ignore the unique historical structures—including a brothel/boarding house/saloon and sometime sanctuary for escaped slaves known as Dug's Dive—whose ruins adjoin the Commercial Slip.

Emeritus Professor of History Monroe Fordham of Buffalo State College filed an affidavit in that lawsuit, in which he said, "I believe this site should be preserved and developed, and not destroyed and buried for the sake of a bogus Canal-period replica." Scot Fisher, a coplaintiff in the lawsuit to prevent New York State from failing to do an adequate historic as well as archaeological review, had gone to the 2000 Allentown Art Festival and then on to meetings all over Western New York, where he'd spearheaded the campaign that gathered over fourteen thousand signatures on petitions to "Save Don't Pave" the terminus of the original Erie Canal. In the spring and summer of 2000, columnist Donn Esmonde in the *Buffalo News* had written repeatedly about the significance of the acreage around the inner harbor and specifically about the Commercial Slip, the Central Wharf, and the historic remains of the old Canal District.

October 26, 2000 saw a community consensus as has rarely been achieved about an identity issue. Politicians of both parties actually joined with preservationists to herald an agreement that would give the community a twelve-acre site that no other community, no other city, no other country had any claim to.

In a subsequent party held in November 2000, Tielman and the Preservation Coalition awarded "Battle Stars," little star-shaped gold pins, to public officials, citizen activists, newspaper columnists and even to teenaged kids who had carried signs—and on one occasion, shovels, when, on a Saturday morning, hundreds had demonstrated, shouting to state officials, "You dig the canal or we will."

That was in 2000. Then, for seven years, work proceeded so that the community's plan could be made real. Complicated rerouting of storm-sewer pipes and of the massive Hamburg Drain was undertaken so that the Commercial Slip, which now has water in it, could be re-watered. The once-buried streets were unearthed. Foundations of old buildings were exposed, perhaps even of Dug's Dive itself.

It's a significant historic site. More immigrants came through Buffalo Harbor, traveling by canal boat, train, wagon, horseback, or foot to light out for the Great Lakes regions of Canada and the United States and beyond, than came through Ellis Island. Many of them debarked right there in that twelve-acre Canal District. The Underground Railroad, like the Erie Canal, had its terminus in the Niagara River, which is the body of water that begins at the entry to Buffalo Harbor. Between the Revolutionary War and the start of the Civil War, at least forty thousand Africans and African Americans saw their liberation when they looked from Buffalo Harbor to see the Niagara River and Canada beyond. This site is where the first grain elevator was erected, a device that transformed the agricultural economy of North America and subsequently of the other continents as well. The Canal District, and specifically the intersection of the Commercial Slip and Buffalo Harbor, was the very place where America's continental economic power was forged.

The Buffalo that Daniel Davis found in 1851 was a very busy city, especially at the intersection of the Erie Canal and Buffalo Harbor. Buffalo in 1851 was a city of about 43,000 people, including 556 African Americans enumerated in the census of 1850. The city occupied an area that today is bounded by North Street on the north (the town of Black Rock was annexed in 1853, but Frederick Law Olmsted's Delaware Park only came about after the Civil War) and Bailey Avenue on the east. There were farmsteads adjacent to the new railroad yard in the area of Buffalo, above the Buffalo River, that had for a brief time (1790 to 1838) been the Buffalo Creek Indian Reservation peopled by the displaced Senecas of the Genesee Valley sixty miles east. South of the Buffalo River, there were a few thousand people living near the confluence of Cazenovia Creek and Buffalo Creek, many of them Irish immigrants who had come in the early 1820s, when a largely Irish labor force had set the blocks of limestone for the Erie Canal.

The action in Buffalo in 1851 was downtown, near the Central Wharf. On the day that the steam-powered, 132-foot boat *Buckeye State* pulled into Buffalo Harbor with Daniel Davis and a dozen crew, and then docked at the Commercial Slip at the foot of Commercial Street, there were at least two dozen other freighters and passenger ships in the harbor. (In the shipping season, between two and twenty lake boats arrived daily.)

If one had walked the length of Central Wharf along the Buffalo River waterfront from the mouth of the Buffalo River, over the Water Street bridge, past Commercial Street to Prime Street, one would have been able to see a network of canals—including the "Grand Canal," the Erie Canal, that Governor DeWitt Clinton had inaugurated twenty-six years earlier at the place where the Commercial Slip intersects the harbor—carrying dozens of shallow-drafting, mule-towed canal boats. The towpath, itself now under the New York State Thruway, ran along the calm portion of the Niagara River to Squaw Island, where the channel becomes the Black Rock Canal, up to Day's Slip, used by rowers of the West Side Rowing Club. The original limestone blocks set in 1825 still line the east bank of the Black Rock Canal. Back in 1999, when a UB historian warned that weather exposure could cause the old limestone blocks that had been buried in the Canal District to "blast apart," many oarsmen and oarswomen had a good laugh, because from April to November, every year since West Side was founded in 1912, nobody has ever seen a block of 400-million-year-old canal limestone explode.

Buffalo in August 1851 was bigger than Chicago, bigger than Milwaukee, bigger than Cleveland, and it was also a city hot with political friction over how, or whether, to enforce the Fugitive Slave Act. The heat had been building for months, and not just among abolitionists and the small African American community. The urgency for democracy came from the tens of thousands of recent European immigrants.

In 1848, there had been a series of democratic rebellions or "revolutions" in Europe. Masses of French, German, Hungarian, and other opponents of the monarchies had found refuge and political liberty in New York—and in Buffalo. On Saint John's Day, June 24, 1851, a crowd of around three thousand German immigrants gathered at a private grove between Delaware and Main, just south of Forest Lawn Cemetery. They came out to hear August Thieme, a member of a short-lived parliament, speak about the universal rights of man, democracy, and freedom for the oppressed. Later in 1851, twenty thousand people—almost half the city's population—massed in downtown Buffalo when the Hungarian revolutionary Lajos Kossuth came to town. Kossuth had led Hungary's failed rebellion against the Austrian monarchy in 1848. Kossuth was lionized in the American press, welcomed by huge crowds in New York City and wherever else in the United States he went to deliver his message about self-determination, democracy, and the universal rights of man.

As in many other cities at the time, there was in Buffalo a "liberty pole," a tall structure erected to commemorate American independence.

From the top of Buffalo's Liberty Pole, in the summer of 1851, flew the flags of France, Germany, Hungary, and the United States.

So for the whole summer leading up to the case of "the slave Daniel," Buffalo politics and Buffalo civic life and Buffalo parties and gatherings and picnics were in many reported cases forums for debating questions of law, justice, human freedom, and human rights—questions that the "accidental" president, Buffalo's own Millard Fillmore, had tried to answer with an equivocation.

Here was the central question: Should slavery be legal in America, or should it be made illegal, as it was in Canada?

Geography alone meant that Buffalo was never going to escape this struggle. Whereas the political activists of New York, Boston, Philadelphia, and the other large cities could argue about what the authors of the Constitution had meant when they'd failed to explicitly outlaw slavery yet had written "all men are created equal," Buffalo was on the hard edge of experience, because thousands of people fled to Buffalo so that they could get free. Thousands of Africans and African Americans came to Buffalo Harbor on the last stop on their voyage to freedom in Canada. Long before Millard Fillmore signed the Fugitive Slave Act into law in October 1850, the entire length of the Niagara River on the American shore was well established as the region of the Underground Railroad's last stations. The Society of Friends, otherwise known as the Quakers, were the nucleus of the movement here, a movement that made white rural farmers in Chautauqua, Erie, Niagara, and other counties into "conductors" of African escapees from enslavement.

And as Daniel Davis would learn, the Canal District was the precise spot in Buffalo where the fight for freedom had to be won, or lost. While in faraway Auburn it was Federal District Judge Conkling deliberated Davis's writ of habeas corpus, Davis's assailant Benjamin Rust, the Kentuckian empowered by Fillmore's law, was quickly tried and found guilty of assault and fined $50. Rust made no statement reported in any Buffalo paper. What is known is that he paid his fine, and then he left.

Meanwhile, the *Commercial Advertiser* newspaper, Buffalo's staunchly pro-Democratic paper, published a letter that was about as believable as the UB professor's assertion that blocks of Erie Canal limestone would explode if unearthed by restoring the Canal District. The author of the letter, allegedly Daniel Davis, addressed "To the Colored Population of Buffalo," claimed that Davis wanted to return to slavery in Kentucky. "We are about as well off in Kentucky as you are here . . . We have plenty to eat and to wear, and are not so badly worked—this everybody knows who has been in Kentucky," the alleged Davis wrote on August 28, 1851, ten days after he was beaten, captured, and jailed.

From papers in New York City, Rochester, Buffalo, and Cleveland, the denunciations of this composition were fast and furious. The premise of the letter was judged to be absurd, but the language was not kind: the competing *Buffalo Express* opined, in very derogatory terms, that an illiterate escaped slave would never be able to write such prose as was purported to be his.

Three days later, the federal judge writing from Underground Railroad heroine Harriet Tubman's Auburn, New York, decided that there was no legal basis on which to deprive Daniel Davis of his freedom. So Davis, accompanied by his lawyers and a group of his supporters, both African American and white, left the jail, walked down Commercial Street to the Commercial Slip and the Central Wharf, where he boarded the *Buckeye State*, gathered up his belongings and immediately left for Canada, and freedom.

Curiously, the community's preservation victory in the first decade of the twenty-first century has been under assault by the most recent state commission, flush with money from a new source. What could remain a public space with historic markers and signage and the typical activities of waterfront parks was designated as a development zone for a sporting goods retailer based in Missouri called Bass Pro. In the place where liberation, migration, commodities trade, and shipping all occurred—as well as so much prostitution and criminality that Buffalo's Canal District was for decades known as one of the most crime-ridden places in the country—the plan at this writing is to make it all the front yard of a chain store.

The old story of freedom's triumph in the Davis case is nowhere celebrated, not in any of the signage, nor in any of the explanatory materials produced, at great public expense, by the new state commission that oversees the property. The preservationists who won their case in the 2000s once again prepare litigation, so as the second decade of the new century began, it was not clear whether any of the idiosyncracies of the site or of local history would prevail. The new adversary is not community interest in the place, but a notion of commerce that is centered on leisure consumption of foreign-made goods vended by merchants from the southern Mississippi River drainage. The conflict, and there will be conflict, will once again proceed.

GEOLOGY

The stream

In the westernmost part of New York State, rivers and brooks alike are called creeks. This region was all owned by the Holland Land Company after the Revolution, but there were too few Dutch present when the surveying was done to name the numerous streams, as they are known in the easternmost part of New York State, kills. Tiny three-yard-wide Clear Creek in Arcade, where the wild brook trout grow old but never more than ten inches long, is creek. Surging, various Cattaraugus Creek, which cuts through two-hundred-foot Zoar Valley and plummets down rapids that are dangerous Class Five water for springtime kayakers fitted with helmets and flotation, then broadens and flattens below Gowanda to the width of two four-lane roads and wider, is creek as well. Only two hundred years ago, they had different appellations depending on their size, because an entirely different people named them based on their close knowledge of which was river, which stream, which brook, which merely tributary. But coming upon these streams from the east, as Englishmen and then American English-speakers did just after the war that made the region American, is explanation enough for why English-speakers used a word they'd used at home for rivulets or small arms of rivers, for only a single day's walk west of the Genesee River—that north-flowing river the breadth of which Englishmen could approach from the east and know was no creek but river—a ridge is crossed and a new watershed begins, and these streams they called creeks begin their westward flow toward Lake Erie as small waters. Rills, brooks, freshets, runs, they seem diminutive, initially small no matter that they become large near their mouths. Locals who have grown to know them acknowledge differences in their stature even as they employ this diminutive: small creeks get called *crick*; bigger ones, the ones with deep gorges that expose the four-hundred-million-year-old Devonian shales, get called *crique*. Clear Creek is *crick*; Cattaraugus is *crique*. Wiscoy Creek and East Koy Creek, which flow eastward into the Genesee from points only yards east of where the westward-flowing *cricks* and *criques* begin, are, strangely, called neither: they are The Wiscoy and The East Koy, at least to fishermen who revere them for native trout. The Koys have a wholly different character: they are kills like the Beaverkill in the Catskills. They are classic trout streams. Fishers who fish there fish flies, as in the east. They flow in a county still dominated by grantees of George III, patroons as grand in their holdings as any of the Hudson drainage of old eastern New York, and their Dutch names are the last to be found before the English and Seneca names of western New York fill the maps.

The *crique* called Eighteenmile Creek divides Hamburg Township on the north from Evans Township, the more rural of the two but nowadays becoming almost as suburban. Eighteenmile ends in a low wide arc beneath eighty feet of Hamburg shale cliff and laps at a low dune of Evans sand that runs south-southeast until the rise of the Evans shale cliff. The stretch between the two cliffs is three hundred yards, surely a river's dimension. In high-water spring and again in autumn there is a Hamburg-side channel that cuts eastward almost to the Old Lake Shore Road Bridge and makes of the narrow half-mile long island in the middle of the channel a real island, but for most of the year the island is a peninsula with a shallow freestone riffle on the Evans side and a muddy hollow backwater below the Hamburg cliffs. In spring the island's massive willows and leaning groves of sassafras and solo black walnut trees and poplars fletch out high above chest-high fiddlehead ferns and a thick thatch of feral raspberries, sumac, fox grapes, and thorn apples, and tree frogs peep brightly near the grassy cutbanks across from the Evans cliffs. The island becomes muddy but rarely floods except during thaw and stream-ice breakup in late March or early April, so it is always accessible to boys who make campfires and tree houses, and to fishermen who tromp west over its mud paths toward the mouth carrying sandwiches and six-packs and hopes of lake-going lunkers. In that lowest reach of Eighteenmile the Evans channels do not shift much, but upstream, past both the Old Lake Shore Road Bridge and the Route 5 Bridge, between the shale cliffs of Hamburg and an oxbow floodplain of Evans that stretches a mile before another bend of Evans cliffs jut up, and then again at another of the stream's next series of S-curves in the mile before the now-ruined bridge at the Versailles Plank Road, the ice and the water change the streambed's shape radically year by year. Where in spring there is a dependably deep pool at the end of the short riffle just above the first bend above Route 5, by autumn and the strong and heavy waters of October's rains, the waters have rearranged the gravel such that the riffle is longer, the pool is foreshortened, and all that remains unchanged is the long low flat stretch of slate bottom six feet down that has been polished clean of the small gray and black stones, the till washed down from the last moraines of the last glaciation, till that gives trout a dappled gray bed on which to spawn and wait invisible to anglers' interested eyes.

The fishermen come in numbers all year. They clump at the Old Lake Shore Road Bridge because there is a deep channel in that part of the stream. They stand on the crushed Hamburg shale or shin-deep in the Evans mud and slash the water with endless casts and retrieves of polished-steel spoons cast right into that slit in the stream's bottom. They plunk lead-weighted skein, egg sacs, or commercially packaged pork rinds dyed improbable colors. They use garden worms and the plastic baits hawked by men from Tennessee on cable television infomercials that invite callers to call toll-free numbers. They park their mud-streaked pickups and secondhand four-by-fours along Old Lake Shore Road in that interval between the cliff-perch lakefront mansions and the inland tracts of split-levels that the fishers here would be fortunate to afford, and walk crablike across the bridge slowly, eyes turned toward the stream thirty feet below, looking for the shadows of fish in that trench. Coming upon any density of early arrivals, other fishers move downstream to the mouth of the Eighteenmile, especially in fall, because that's when the Pacific fish come in from Lake Erie. Coho salmon, chinook salmon, steelhead—the sea-run rainbow trout that become gray and huge and are called steelhead—those are the species with which revenue-hungry state game departments have stocked the Great Lakes over the past decade, to replace the yellow pike and blue pike and lake trout that were either fished out or that succumbed to the pollution that had nearly killed Lake Erie by the mid-1960s. The new fish are monsters by *crique* standards, even by lake standards, imports from Seattle that grow to twenty-five pounds, and they can be caught at the mouths of Eighteenmile and Cattaraugus, and they are the quarry of men who are there not for the polite catch-and-release angling of Catskill or Wiscoy or East Koy fly-fishers, but for food.

Yet they are sportsmen. If netting were legal, they would probably not net. If shocking the fish with electric charges were legal, these men would not make like the government stream biologists do when they're taking fish censuses, when they wade the water to jolt it with big handheld electrodes and wait for all that meat to float stunned to the surface. The fishers of the *crique* crave the catch and then the lugging of it all home on heavy plastic line threaded through toothed mouths and red gills and slung over shoulders. For two seasons, the state made legal the fish-catching technique of snagging, which is to say casting a lead-weighted treble hook with tines two inches long across the stream, and jerking the thing as hard as the plastic rod can handle without breaking, in hopes of ripping into salmon or trout underbellies and dragging the snag bloody to bank. But the bait-fishers and lure-fishers were sportsmen enough to complain to officials, and snagging was outlawed for Eighteenmile and the other Lake Erie *criques*. Meat-hunters though they be, their sentiment about fairness to the prey prevailed, and they remain fish-catchers, and fish-killers, and fish-eaters, but not fish-mutilators.

Upstream, above the Old Lake Shore Bridge, above the Route 5 Bridge and the first of the stream's sharp bends, is a pretty and calm but fishless stretch of low, wide, flat water. The Hamburg shale cliff is only fifty feet tall there, and topped by a thick thatch of maples and hickories that drop bright broad leaves in autumn, that land and float lightly on the flawless surface of that placid stretch and move only gently downstream to the riffles below. The streambed is a polished surface of slate tiles as large as the footprints of small houses, grouted with the till gravel washed down from the moraine hills upstream, painted with only a single thin coat of algae that never prevents a felt-soled wading shoe's grip. The Evans floodplain in that bow is thick with hardwoods and tangles of purple raspberry cane and thorn apple mulched with goldenrod, purple loosestrife, milkweed, and feral fescue where the sun has direct access, and thick ferns where the sun gains no purchase. That far up, the wall of Hamburg shale and its tons of fossilized bivalves, anemones, and trilobites there embedded hush the hiss of traffic from the high Route 5 Bridge, and challenge the rare wader to walk as quietly through that plain of shin-deep stream as the stream itself courses. Ahead is another sharp bend and its riffle, then the change of sides: Evans becomes the shale wall, Hamburg the treed floodplain that cannot have been flooded for many decades, for the riffle cuts a bank almost a man's height above the midstream granite boulders that are incongruous in that sedimentary geology of shales and slates.

In the quarter-mile of deep, slow, flat water above, a man with a brown ponytail and the duff canvas jacket that the men of western New York favor who work with tools stood on the Hamburg gravel, and tossed his weighted skein toward the Evans cliff, and let it settle into the trough below. Atop the cliff a suburbanite raked maple leaves; the breeze there stole a few of them, and launched them into the quiet air of the gorge to fall slowly, cutting laterally, floating like the down from milkweed long seconds before adding their brightness as gently as spent adult mayflies to the pool's surface. The man below fished the Eighteenmile way: he tossed his weighted bait, held his pole, watched his stretch of water, and waited.

Salmonids churn up that stream to that pool and, between ten miles of riffles and flats, to pools above, and surprise all with their reach into even the smallest of creeks. But their spawning is nugatory. Their flesh is firm and pink and much sought, so they seldom linger in eddies to rot and thereby nourish the water for the fry that hatch and hide in those gravelbeds until their time comes to slide downstream to the mouth and the lake beyond. Eighteenmile is not a barren Alaska river that needs the decay of adult fish to make the water habitable for fry: it is alive with crayfish and darters and sculpins and chubs, with bass and perch and suckers; its eddies fill with cattails and its shallowest reaches with pampas grass that are home to beetles and frogs and cover for herons, its bankside trees home, in two-mile intervals, to crested blue kingfishers. All eat what the lake fish spawn: all thrive better, in this stream that divides suburbs that came into being to house workers at steelworks just twenty minutes' drive north, thanks to thc imports from Seattle and Juneau. Only the older introductions, the rainbow trout, spawn productively, and their fry have gained a place in the order of stream fish. The real prize for a wait-fisher is a hen rainbow trout, full of eggs and as long as a man's femur.

One found the man's sack of salmon roe just as another young man, this one with a chest-high daughter wearing her own miniature waders, came across the riffle above and bent to watch the success he hoped to repeat, that greatest of thrills for a fisher—setting the hook, staying with a big fish that complains of the angler's trickery by jumping from the water, kicking the surface with its tail, diving low to find a sharp slate ledge or angled boulder that can dislodge the hook from where it has caught in its ridged jaw, and failing angrily. The fisher played the fish patiently, smiling at its size, grimacing at the work of holding it, worrying aloud that that colorless line that sang with the tension of the fish's resistance would break and leave him having fought and lost only yards from success, punching the water's edge with side-to-side bootsteps that splashed ripples bigger than the fish's all across the surface of that cliff-bottom pool, gaining enough purchase on the beast to crank his reel a yard, then two, then a foot, and so shorten her nylon tether that he was able to beach rather than net her with the great long-handled green net that he'd planted like an aluminum sapling into the shattered Hamburg shale.

The daughter ran up to the water's edge and squealed delightedly to see such a fish. Her father manfully clapped the victor's shoulder in congratulation and soberly congratulated the winner, whose demeanor offered the pretense that this day was no different, this catch no cause for exclamation, this event nothing but the ordinary and expected. Under the bright cloudless sky of a memorably warm November afternoon, while the smallest whisper of breeze ruffled the drying red and brown and yellow leaves of maples above that in their movement sounded like a distant audience applauding, the two men and the girl child watched the warm gold field of that great fish's back fade to the color of the khaki streambed stone, and its flank's rainbow colors dim to the hue of a well-fingered nickel coin, and as they chatted about bait and line, the stream's surface, so recently roiled by the struggle, settled again to a flat calm, all the earth to a quiet, and the water to a mirror for the white quarter-moon rising early in the east.

PALEONTOLOGY

The protector

On a June morning in 1943 one week after he graduated from Angola High School, Howard Bruce Leathe walked 260 yards from his family's rented white clapboard house at Number 10 Orchard Street to the United States Post Office, where he volunteered to go to war.

The western New York village Bruce left for the Marine Corps had already seen many of its sons leave for this new war, as earlier Angola boys had left for the Mexican War, the Civil War, the undeclared wars against the Sioux and the Cheyenne, the Spanish-American War and to the war that was still known in 1943 as the Great War. Yet Angola is an atypical Upstate New York village in one respect: it has neither village square nor village park in which is sited a monument to the Fallen of any of those wars. In scores of other villages and hamlets of that region there are monuments, most of them to the Civil War dead, for though the whole of western New York west of the Genesee River was made available to Revolutionary War veterans (such as Howard Bruce Leathe's great-great-great-great-grandfather Elias Whitney of Connecticut), and though Perry's tiny navy defeated the British in 1813 not so many miles off the Angola shore of Lake Erie, and though Episcopal and Methodist and Congregational congregations were founded in the area and in this village, too, during the Napoleonic Wars, and so there is a depth of personal connection and family relation to the whole history of the nation and to its wars, it is the Civil War that was this region's defining event, and is so treated in stone and statuary—except in Angola. But of the Civil War's impact on Angola much was evident: both Bruce's mother and his grandmother were regular participants in meetings and functions of the local chapter of the Grand Army of the Republic, whose explicit mission was to vouchsafe the memory of their fathers' and grandfathers' service to the Union. Angola's monument to its sons' wars was thus inchoate, but no less real than stone.

Angola was on the day of Bruce's volunteering a compact place, no more than 1,500 souls all told. It had been some decades since a majority of those were Yankee souls, for the great age of Great Lakes industrialization had been made possible by massive migrations to the region from the Polish-speaking parts of Russia, Prussia, and Austria, and from southern Italy and Sicily in that long interim between the Civil War and the Great War. Angola was a far-flung Massachusetts village that had become, not only at its edges but also at its center, on Lake Street, a very Catholic, especially Sicilian, place. It had become home to laborers who stoked furnaces up the lakeshore at Bethlehem Steel, tended cars for the beltway South Buffalo Railroad, shoveled coal at Chenango Ingot and made coke at Republic Steel, bent metal at the Ford Stamping Plant, all on a stretch of the lakeshore Erie Road that for most of the twentieth century was shrouded in gray air with a variously pink or yellow tinge from all the particulate iron and sulfur those works threw unrelentingly up.

This motley village of Angola is edged on the north and east, and bisected on the south by the New York Central tracks that Bruce's father had ridden in on a very individual sort of migration from Connecticut twenty years before Bruce left for the war. Howard Collins Leathe rode in with a crew of men to rebuild the trestle over Big Sister Creek after a grain freighter bound for the flour mills on the Buffalo River wrecked and turned Big Sister into a river of festering beer. Howard, youngest of ten children, picker of tobacco in those fields that edge the Connecticut River and yet today produce the wrapper leaves for cigars, had gone to work at ten after his father Charles Bruce Leathe died of lead poisoning at a paint works. Howard had left school after the third grade to join his brothers and sisters and widowed mother Jenny Collins Leathe in the seasonal labor available to women and children in rural Connecticut. At sixteen he had lit out not for the West but for the North, to the Maine forests, there to cut trees and dance logs down the Penobscot River to the stinking pulping mills whose effluent had already choked off the ages-old runs of Atlantic salmon. Military recruiters in 1918 never reached those logging camps, so Howard missed the Great War, and in his isolation missed as well the influenza epidemic of 1918 that killed four of his siblings. From cutting wood to working it, Howard developed something of a trade in carpentry, but did so casually, without apprenticeship, and worked around New England until the rail job came, which took him west, the gypsy of work he would always be, to the village where he dwelt until his death forty-six years later. Howard stayed in Angola to marry Ruth

Marion Whitney, who was sixteen in that year of his arrival 1923, and to sell what he could of his skills to the dairymen and truck farmers and infrequent home-builders of Evans township, and to raise a family in the upper flat of a two-story clapboard house sandwiched between the south Angola swing of the New York Central tracks and the tracks of the passenger trolley that ran from Buffalo to Erie. Ruth's parents, Charlotte and Elnathan Whitney, lived directly across Commercial Street in a compact two-story white clapboard house with gingerbread trim. Howard and Ruth married, of necessity, in January of 1925; Howard Bruce Leathe was born six months later, followed by Charlotte Anne Leathe in 1927, Ruthmarie Leathe in 1929, and another daughter, Barbara Jean, who lived only four days in 1930. The Angola Hotel was less than a yard east of the Leathe house; Howard and Ruth tended bar and waited tables there for Friday night fish-fries to add cash to the $5 Ruth earned checking groceries at the grocery store 120 yards east on Commercial Street. Charlotte Whitney sewed clothing and painted lampshades and Christmas cards and raised rabbits at the end of the tiny Whitney backyard; Elnathan Whitney painted bicycles at the Emblem Bicycle factory adjacent to the tracks on Main Street. To get to school, the Leathe children crossed Commercial Street, walked past their grandparents' house up the steep one-tenth-mile hill of Washington Street to St. Paul's Episcopal Church at Lake Street, and down High Street for three-tenths of a mile to School Street and the Angola Public School. Thus much of the work, worship, child-rearing, relations, and education of this family all occurred well within the one-mile square of the village of Angola.

Except for Howard. His carpentry and general construction work took him around the township. He built barns and stables and cow fences and wellheads for farmers, and concrete forms for sidewalk-pourers, and houses and porches and garages for those who had money to pay him to build such things, and in 1929 helped build the Route 20 Bridge over the hundred-foot gorge of Eighteenmile Creek at the north border of the township. To villagers he became John Leathe, the jack-of-all-trades. He tended the counter at the Shultz Hardware store four storefronts from the grocery his wife worked (Shultz owned the house he rented), and when the Work Projects Administration gave a season of work to builders, he was there to help build the brick post office on Main Street a block from the hardware store. By the late 1930s when his son was getting to have some adult strength, his son learned to build too, and to pour concrete. Howard Leathe also gave much work away, a poor man and his poor wife building a reputation for generosity. Howard built, Ruth baked. Ruth and her mother baked bread on Sundays, and were observed tossing warm loaves to the disheveled men who stole rides on freight trains traveling westbound through Angola to some hope, however distant, of work. For St. Paul's Episcopal Church, his wife's tiny church at the corner of Lake and Washington streets, just yards uphill from the village jail, Howard built a fine oak altar. Howard and Ruth Leathe's son and their two daughters ate often at the church in the years between 1931 and 1942, and much venison and squirrel and wild rabbit and pheasant, too, in season and out, because money for store meat was scarce, the Sunday "chicken" (so the Leathe children were told) from the Whitney rabbit hutches in limited supply, and because Howard had made Seneca hunting friends poor as he and even poorer than he on the Cattaraugus Indian Reservation four miles south, where the hunting was good. Cattaraugus Reservation was where the Protestant Episcopal reverend Glenn Coykendall of St. Paul's, a Columbia-educated man who had Hebrew and Greek and Latin and the rare talent to have learned Seneca well enough to sermonize in it, had enlisted Howard to build another Episcopal church in the tiny hamlet also named Cattaraugus, just down the Versailles Plank Road from Newtown. Newtown is not a town at all, but a cluster of houses, a ball field, and the site of a modest oblong building only one story high, also white clapboard, with only one room, at whose center is a stove and down whose middle are two long chipped benches set parallel for Seneca men singers who yet sit and beat small water-filled drums and shake rattles made of snapping-turtle shells at the dances that are both sacred and social in that structure known in English as the Longhouse. A slight man, quick and challenging, the Reverend Coykendall built that Episcopal church close by the center of what was then called Seneca "paganism," and with it built commonalities between the Seneca Episcopalians and the Angola Episcopalians at church socials and Youth Group square dances at which monolingual small-town Yankees and imperfectly Englished Senecas ate and danced and sang songs never sung at Longhouse and worked and worshipped and traded trips up and down the Erie Road. Modest of means as they all were (but for the few families of the Angola congregation who owned the great lakefront estates they called, thinking themselves, with good reason, like the Vanderbilts of Newport, "cottages"), the two congregations conducted drives for used clothes and for new canned foods, such as were canned in summers by Angola girls who packed summer harvests of green beans and corn and the Sicilian farmers' tomatoes and other local truck at the canning factory south of the bicycle factory on Main Street, to benefit the truly poor, the Western Indians, the Lakota of South Dakota among whom the Reverend Coykendall had missionized after his studies of ancient texts at Columbia and before his rectorate in Angola.

This compact world, defined by its general poverty, by the tenant status of his kin and yet by his family's full involvement with church and charity, defined Howard Bruce Leathe. He was a cherished son and a good boy, mainly, identified early as a talented boy, the one who in that tiny face-to-face society won First Prize in the American Legion prize contest of 1939, good or excellent at his studies, interested in music, active in church, hard-working when he came of an age to work and when there was work to be got beyond steadying a board or swinging a hammer with his father on the odd job. He worried his mother playing football, for his heart was weakened by a murmur, but he dropped athletics for the Dramatics Club and the school choir. He played the E-flat clarinet in the Angola High School marching band; this is a difficult instrument to get more than honks and squeaks from, more like an oboe than a clarinet because so much disciplined pressure must be exerted on its small reed. Bruce's clarinet is silver, and rests in a hard-shell case lined with perfect burgundy velvet imbued with a pleasant smell, that of clarinetists' treated beeswax for the cork fittings, which is kept in a capped silver thimble that fits a cylindrical depression between the reed box and the lyre-shaped music holder that screws ingeniously into the top of the instrument, unmistakably a marcher's instrument. The Whitney strain gave the Leathe children music: Bruce's youngest sister played bugle in that school marching band; Bruce's middle sister, ever the natural center of solo attention with red hair like her brother's, learned to play the piano well enough to perform Debussy's "Clair de Lune" and Chopin polonaises, and later, when the war came and tastes changed, the new stuff called boogie-woogie, from sheet music that says it cost 5 cents, but she also played church music, like her grandmother and red-haired namesake, making her Sunday morning debut on the organ at St. Paul's in 1944. Bruce turned sixteen the year the nation entered the Second War, and all the music for his clarinet was martial and patriotic and printed in that small format that fit his clarinet's music clasp. Marches; mainly Sousa.

At eighteen he was just an inch taller than his father, well muscled and slim and athletic despite his heart murmur, never very serious but there nonetheless. He worked early mornings for the Angola Dairy, in those years situated directly behind the post office, which gave him a green shirt with a red breast-pocket patch reading "Angola Dairy" and a green hat like a serviceman's dress hat. What is now termed "fitness" is readily identifiable, in photographs of the teen Bruce Leathe, as work strength. He was slim but not slight, another redhead in a family of them, his face and form favoring his father just as his younger sister Ruthmarie's did, but with that wavy red Whitney hair that Charlotte had, too, and that may have been something of the basis for a special mutuality of caring they would develop.

In his middle teens, the material conditions of Leathe life inched upward. Howard obtained employment with the electric company as a meter reader, and moved the family in 1941 to their first whole house, albeit another rental, known in Angola as the "triangle house" for its location at the point where Orchard Avenue intersects Main Street. The Leathes obtained their first electric refrigerator, and for the first time, thanks to the electric company, Howard had steady access to an automobile. When he boarded the train for Parris Island at the Angola depot in June 1943, his family had one less mouth to feed but also one less income for the household; in early wartime letters home, Bruce several times apologized for not having contributed more of his earnings to the household exchequer. But by then the war had, by Leathe standards, positively enriched them. Ruth daily rode with other newly employed women to the Curtiss-Wright warplane factory in Buffalo, twenty-five miles away, while Howard rode even further, to the Bell Aircraft plant in Amherst, aiding the war effort and their own fortunes as well.

Bruce Leathe's walk uptown in 1943, past the Newcomb-Long American Legion Post, past the big brick Congregational Church and Bus Smith's gray frame house in whose cool ground-floor sundry shop bus passengers awaited Dunkirk & Fredonia Transit buses on contoured oak window seats, past Center Street to the post office, took place in June, which in Angola is clement. He had also walked by the house that would become the Leathe's first Leathe-owned house, on whose porch the Concord grapevines were even then trellised. Those vines fledge by June, but fruit is still a long way off, never even beginning to turn from green to purple-black until after the annual Pleiades meteor shower in the final days of August. The blossoms on the catalpas and chestnuts and walnuts and plum and apple and sour cherry trees in the deep yard behind the Leathe house are in June poised for scattering by the lake breezes over the shaded grass. The tangled raspberry canes are dewy in the morning and studded with budding fruit, and the strawberries that Howard would plant and cultivate, for strawberries are a large crop in that part of western New York, and gardeners plant the crops that farmers plant, become by mid-June red, large, ready for the juice-stained quart baskets made of pine splints that farmers and gardeners alike use and reuse. The massive poplar, five feet in diameter at its amoeboid base, was then still present to drop yellow-brown seed florets that are sticky with sap in a broad irregular circle between the barn and the inset kitchen doorway. The seventeen-year locusts would have been buzzing as Bruce set out, as they do still. Ancestor generations of cottontail rabbits were enduring the worrying of their kits by Leathe housecats, of which there would always be plenty skulking around the barn's green baseboards, crouching as is all their generations' habit under the wren houses that Howard Leathe and his son Bruce made of scrap lumber when the scrap was new and which they would nail high up on the barn on the barn's south face, the face next to the hemlock tree, for barn owls were in residence in the rafters of the barn's north face, above the highest reach of the trumpet vines, and thus the north face was not a fit wall for wrens, which are owl food. June in Angola has the new warmth that settles on the sprouting cornfields and hayfields and vineyards and deciduous second-growth forests and native crabapple prairies of eastern Evans Township and of Eden Township five miles east and Collins Township five miles south on the alluvial plain of Lake Erie, but this village is ever cooled by the westerlies off Erie one mile and a barrier wall of tarpaper beach cottages and grander "cottages" west. Howard Leathe and Bruce Leathe had had, by June of that year, at least a month's fishing there near the lake, at the mouths of the Big Sister and Little Sister creeks, whose channels grow deeper, broader, slower between the lake dunes in that season, and, filled with the plentiful rains of late spring, still teem with chubs and spotted gar and spawning bass and slow catfish and the overgrown golden carp that long ago, Howard's legend had it, were once but little goldfish let loose from a rich man's cottage's reflecting pool. These fish grew, feral, until they were longer than a boy's reflection on the creek's surface, fat orange torpedoes gliding in schools in that silted water.

June is not a clement time in South Carolina, which is the state in which the Marine Corps training camp at Parris Island is situated. A less temperate kind of summer heat is upon that country by June, especially in the low areas away from the cooler Piedmont, which itself is infernal by Angola standards. Bruce's first of what would amount to hundreds of near-daily letters from the corps reported that he sweltered in 100-degree heat on his arrival at Parris Island, where the Marines give their recruits basic training among the pines and dunes and humid heat that settles early and does not diminish until October, when storms whip across Port Royal Sound and bash those low Atlantic barrier islands with the ferocity of bombardment.

Bruce spent part of June and all of July and August of 1943 at Parris Island, training for war in heat and humidity such as is found on the islands of the Pacific where Marines were then fighting. Neither he nor the United States Marine Corps found his heart murmur an obstacle, and neither heat nor ferocious insects nor the relentlessly exhausting training at the hands of his instructors at Parris Island killed or hurt him, so at the end of his ten weeks of constant hurrying, of mitochondria-building ten-mile runs and of hours of calisthenics, of weapons-training and inspections and of answering noncoms' bullying with shouted assents of Sir Yes Sir!, and along the way of some testing of the cognitive sort (which determined that Bruce had some aptitudes the corps could use), he was sent north, over the line that splits the Carolinas, to the Marines' Camp Lejeune. Not very much of his red Whitney hair had been permitted to grow back, and not very much in the way of change emerges from those letters home: he was still the teenager, apologetically writing home to ask for a few bucks, infected with enthusiasm for war, an eighteen-year-old corpsman-in-the-making preparing for war at a time of war and of dire national emergency, brimming with a boyish eagerness to ship out and join the fight as the fierce warrior that boys then aspired to be. Being a Marine was becoming important to him. There was this in a special note to his mother, an admonition that there was indeed some new thing about him: "I know you meant well, Mom, but I'm not a soldier, I'm a Marine." He could as well have asserted, "I am no longer a boy." But of course, he was.

At Camp Lejeune he trained as a signalman. He went to radio school and learned how radios worked and how to repair them. He learned how to send and receive code using tappers not significantly advanced, except in that their pommels are black Bakelite rather than wood or bronze, over the instruments Samuel Morse had introduced ninety-nine years before, in time for President James Knox Polk to receive news of his election. He continued to write home almost daily, reporting how he reached eighteen words-per-minute, then twenty-two, twenty-four, as high as thirty-seven words-per-minute proficiency in receiving and transcribing code. He sweated his tests, tested well, groused good-naturedly about not making 100 percent and half-crowed, half-griped about keeping his test-score average above 90. ("I should be scoring 100 percent on these tests, Mother.") He rode three days on a train home for a week's furlough in the fall of 1943, which gave him the chance to see his mother's growing scrapbook of Marine memorabilia, and to drink beer with his Angola friends and with his Erie relations who had ridden up to Angola on the trolley, who were all either trending toward or already in uniform. After returning to his barracks on the New River, he described Camp Lejeune as "a swell camp." He sent home a printed Christmas dinner program from Mess Hall 325, which claimed that Christmas dinner consisted of Roast Tom Turkey, Candied Sweet Potatoes, Pumpkin Pie and twenty-six other dishes including an unfortunate innovation termed Snowflake Potatoes. On Christmas Eve Bruce attended Midnight Mass at the Protestant Chapel, and had the full-bellied leisure to take pencil to an illustrated souvenir program produced by the camp and write out supplementary captions for photographs of his commanding officers and of his haunts on base. "This is my CO." "This is where we ate Christmas Dinner." "This is where we attended Midnight Mass on Christmas Eve." In a photo spread about his own Signal Corps, "This is the work I do." Above a photo of attractive, smiling young women posed in military garb on a page entitled "Entertainment," he wrote, "Don't believe everything you see in pictures." And repeatedly, in a tone so unlike the bountiful and consistent expressions of love for his family that ended each of his letters, he warned sharply about the women in uniform, bristling often that his mother should *not* become a member of the Women's Army Corps or of any other female military unit.

Bruce's last Lejeune quiz put him sixth in his class of sixty signalmen-in-training, high enough to earn him promotion to corporal in January 1944. A day after sewing his stripes on, the Marines sent him to Omaha, Nebraska to spend the spring training in advanced code. Come May, he boarded another train, riding across mountains he wondered at, across deserts he slept through, to Camp Pendleton in California. There was more radio training, and bivouacs, and practice with his bayonet and with his M-1 rifle that he had named Betsy, evidently taking to heart the message of an official Marine statement, printed on card stock, that a Marine's closest companion, most reliable comrade, and best protector must be his gun. Bruce learned how to carry and clean and feed the heavy belt-fed Browning Automatic Rifle. He described practicing landings and infiltrations with live grenades and live ammunition exploding around him on the California beach, and long fifteen-mile marches and fast five-mile runs fully loaded with forty-five-pound pack and thirty-five-pound radio strapped to his slim frame.

And to both whet and temper his impatience to get to the war, nineteen-year-old Bruce Leathe was allowed a weekend of liberty in dazzling, mythic Hollywood. It stimulated him to write a letter less breezy and brief as his usual, one that is strangely discordant in that steady stream of his short posted notes concerning Marine training and camp life. Absent for once is the usual formulaic restatement of his good-natured exasperation with yet another day of training: he provides a first glimpse, in a personal version of block-letter printing touched with school cursive, that he was something other than a dutiful son inured to the small prospects and small measures of the small town from which he came:

> We decided to go to Hollywood and took a cab out to the Hollywood canteen just for the heck of it. Saw Judy Garland there . . . Went to the Brown Derby. Saw Nigel Bruce and Basil Rathbone. At the Palladium I danced to the music of Jan Garber with an MGM chorus girl. Boy was she nice! To make the evening complete we ambled across the street to Earl Carrol's. Didn't stay there long though as we were tired. We slept at the Hollywood Hotel. Would've gone to church Sunday morning but we didn't get up in time . . .
>
> Here we met two more Marines who were buddies of ours in Omaha. We all went up to the 2nd deck porch and watched the aristocrats swim and go for little strolls. It was here that we saw Hedy Lamarr drive up. Imagine, she even looked up and gave a greeting accompanied by a very pleasant smile.
>
> Gosh, Beverly Hills is a beautiful residential district. The hotel itself is very lovely and one can just smell the money. We met James Gleason there and believe it or not he invited us to go swimming in his pool. We did. What a home! He is a helluva swell guy. We had lots of fun. A couple of swabbies were there, too. One guy was from Erie and he knew Betty Perry's sister and also Pat Voght from the Lake. After our swim we all jaunted back (the 4 of us) to the Hotel. We ambled into the Polo Room for an appetizer.

> It was quite amazing. The place was filled with Army + Marine captains, majors, colonels and what have you. Even the Navy was well-represented. There we were: 4 corporals, but we acted as though this was a common-day occurrence and 50% of the place was our own interest. A waiter (the head waiter) showed us to a table and we ordered our bourbon + sodas. At the table directly next to me so close I could reach out and touch her with ease was Betty Grable. No, no autographs. I have too much pride to go around begging people for their signature. We are just as good as they only they have different jobs.
>
> At the table directly in front of me sat a couple of Marine majors and two starlets. They looked very familiar. Many faces did, as a matter of fact. What an odd sight that room was. All these very beautiful girls. Lovely faces + shapes + money, clothes, everything. And they were all accompanied or escorted by bald-headed pot-bellied old men or officers. Big names and big money . . . We were having a great time discussing how these people looked to us among ourselves. They were probably doing the same about us. We seemed to be the center of attraction, not because we were loud; we were very quiet. But because we were Corporals and they wondered who we knew.

This interlude with "aristocrats" began in a moviegoer's excitement at seeing stars, but was followed by a sharpness and forcefulness about who he had become. Bruce was ever anxious to get going, to get to the war, but in his letters from Pendleton, a new urgency sets in. There is a confidence that emerges from his letters, and the first stirrings of Marine braggadocio. At Pendleton he was at long last assigned to a unit, the Fifth Joint Assault Signal Corps, an outfit with, he wrote, a reputation for toughness, for it was toughness he had worked a year and two months to build. His bridge of love with the people in Angola was built and rebuilt with each letter, with each expression of affection and of devotion and of concern, with each gift from his monthly $50 pay to the bonds in his and his mother's name, with each admonition to his father not to join the Seabees, with each frequent fond address of sister Charlotte as Cherie, with each verbal tousle of kid sis Ruthmarie's brunette mop, each repetition of gratitude for "the best family a fellow could have," but his becoming as a Marine slowly constructed an ever higher wall of defining, individuating separateness. The folks at home could *not*, he would assert carefully, comprehend what he was about or who he was becoming.

One post-Hollywood letter contained a clipping from the L.A. *Herald* about an angry dustup among the brass. An Army general named Smith had confronted a Marine general, also named Smith, about the Marines' "cowboy style." The Marines, the Army's Smith asserted, had rushed unnecessarily to overwhelm the Pacific atoll of Tarawa. The Marine tactics had been too bloody. The Marines had needlessly thrown away too many American boys' lives. The Army way, Army General Smith said, was slower, more deliberate, but just as effective, and even if more expensive in materiel and time, it got the job done without needless American casualty. The clipping detailed the outcome of the argument: Army General Smith lost the exchange. The high command explicitly directed the Marines not to change tactics—to carry on as they had on Tarawa, as elite shock troops able to effect quick conquest. Marine Corporal Leathe sent the paper's account of this Marine triumph to his mother with a note curtly siding with the Marine General Smith's way, the tough and bloody and fast Marine way, telling Ruth Marion Leathe with that clipping not only that he was not a tourist who knew his station, the low station he and his tenant family had occupied in the small but taut hierarchy of Angola, but also that all that he was becoming was indeed new and different from what she had known—and that he was no longer her boy at all but a man with a purpose and a new status, who knew precisely what he was raring to go to: to savage places where Marines stormed and killed and were killed, but where they conquered, and as conquerors, were the equal or even the betters of civilians with "different jobs."

After a last long "problem" or exercise in September of 1944, it was with the wood-handled knife Howard Leathe had made for him in the metal shop at Bell Aircraft, with his heavy kit and his seabag, and with a coyness about his destination in that last stateside note to the family that was only partly the Navy censor's doing (for the Navy cut out or blacked out any reference at all to geography) that Bruce, now the assertive non-com, the squad leader with twenty fellows in his charge, boarded the USAT *Howell Lykes* for the Territory of Hawai'i.

It was not quite yet Bruce's time for war. "It is," he wrote upon arriving, "an impossibility to tell you where I am, but I am in no danger and still in the best of health." Yet he snuck some clear description of his destination in, with capable language about what could only be Hawaiian flora and weather and the feel of the special Hawaiian air, and signed off with a flourishing signature and Morse dot-and-dash of his name beneath.

In Hawai'i Bruce and his sergeant learned Japanese code. He took hikes into the rainy jungles just for fun, once taking two days' liberty to make a forty-four-mile hike to a mountaintop along trails of wild boar and feral sheep, exclaiming to his dad about the plentiful supply of pheasants that his every footfall flushed. Between the "problems" he and his team performed, he took other days of liberty to explore areas of Hawai'i open for such excursions, saving a menu from a restaurant at which a pork chop dinner cost thirty-five cents, saving a ticket stub from a high school basketball game, holding on to slips of flimsy paper on which his permission to walk civilian streets was authorized, and on to other slips of paper on which he wrote the names, addresses, and phone numbers of women who dwelled in Honolulu hotels. There was time for rifle range and joshing references in letters to Dad about the time Howard and his friend George had taught Bruce to shoot, about Dad always being the better shot with both rifle and shotgun, and about the leisure and tranquility he felt, enough to promise that "when I come home we'll go up to Canada and match skill on a deer; loser stakes the other to a dinner and a night of making the rounds." There was time for longer letters full of praise for Charlotte's ascension to Bruce's old chair of the Angola High School Dramatics Club and for Ruthmarie's prowess in song as Second Alto in the choir, and the briefest apology and confession of his nagging confusion on an issue he had never before addressed: the question of why he had failed to follow through on his having gained an appointment to West Point.

It is an astonishing find. For a boy of no means and no high military legacy to have won a U.S. Military Academy appointment meant that the boy had performed strongly in high school; that he had been interviewed by his Member of Congress; that he had been recommended; above all, that he had sought out the honor. But Bruce had interrupted his trajectory of success by rejecting West Point. Men who were boys then understand why he didn't accept that commission: he had eschewed rank and ring to become a warrior in that brief era when crowds of young men pushed into military recruiting stations as soon as the calendar proved that they had turned eighteen and eligible. But there is more. Angola was home to men who had been charged by MacArthur's cavalry on the Mall in Washington when they had gone there as members of the Bonus Army; the reputation of professional Army officers, who had raised their sabers to destitute footsoldiers, was not high among them. More still: for Bruce Leathe's ears, there had for years been his uncle Ivan Whitney's words, all through his adolescence, that the Marines were the only fit outfit to join. Bruce's mother Ruth would in later years smile knowingly about the Army and about the Navy: *her* son had been a Marine, a Leatherneck, not a shavetail or a swabbie. And this: men who were young at the war's beginning were not much interested in four years of training on the Hudson River campus while their classmates were off fighting Hitler and Tojo. And why seek mere rank and social position when there were acts of heroism to perform, and rank to earn? But this was the issue: in Hawai'i, Bruce had learned that his Erie cousin Fran had won his sergeant's stripes, and that an Angola boy had become a lieutenant. Reports posted in Angola about these other boys' promotions may have been accompanied by a gentle maternal query about when Bruce's would be coming; perhaps that query was ungentle enough to remind the beloved son that he could have been a commissioned officer if only he had taken the West Point appointment. But Bruce's response was mild; he expressed only the merest disgruntlement over Marine Corps sloth in turning corporals into sergeants. And with another paragraph of effusive devotion to Mother and to family, Bruce ended his short burp of remorse over the choice not taken, and West Point was never mentioned again.

Then, abruptly, Bruce Leathe's time for war came. In the last days of January 1945, he boarded the USS *Rutland* for the Pacific atoll Eniwetok, one of those hot, low, humid islands which had been captured by Marines as hurriedly and as bloodily as they had taken Tarawa. Eniwetok on February 11, 1945, the day Bruce landed there, had not yet been used to test the product of the Los Alamos labs. In February of what all at home hoped would be the last year of this war, Eniwetok was a staging and transfer point for the coming push to Japan, for this was the time when the emperor's forces had been driven, at heavy cost in American volunteer Marines' lives, at even heavier cost of Japanese conscripts' lives, out of most of the Pacific territories they had so swiftly conquered five years before. Bruce disembarked for only one night at Eniwetok, boarded the USS *Hansford* there, and then steamed for liberated Saipan with thousands of other Marines of the 5th Division.

By then Corporal Leathe was twenty years old. He had a small notebook in his kit into which he had written, in a precise hand with permanent blue-black fountain ink and with pencil as well, a list of words that could have been code words or could just as well have been the kind of words ("loquacious," "enigmatic," "contumely," "paradoxical," "adjunct," "ineffable," and three small pages more) that an intelligent young man bored from endless days on troop transports edging toward then crossing the International Date Line might write down to test his command of Latinate English. Or perhaps he was practicing for a shipboard spelling bee. Elsewhere in that notebook are notations that are patently code, the tools of a signalman:

> Kellog - 5BL - CG VAC
> First Lady - 3VF - ADC 5th Mar Div
> Culpepper - 3AH - RCT 26
> Rebel 39 - - Div. T. QM (1)
> Harlequin - 4LY - 26th Log. Con. (1) Off

After eight days of rough seas north from Saipan, as a member of Communications Team 9 of the 5th Joint Assault Signal Company of the 5th Marine Division, 27th Battalion, Bruce got to put it to use.

Sixty thousand Marines invaded the middle island of the Ogasawara or Bunin archipelago750 miles north of Guam and Saipan, a heavily fortified place with two Japanese airfields named Motoyama Airfield No. 1 and Motoyama Airfield No. 2. The island was pitted with thousands of caves concealing twenty thousand Japanese soldiers who had constructed many dozens of concrete bunkers for their mortars, their heavy and light artillery and rocket and antiaircraft weapons. The island had been so heavily fortified by the Japanese because it had grown, as the war had advanced, to singular strategic importance: it was the halfway point between Saipan and their home islands. A volcanic island with negligible vegetation, which still managed to sustain clouds of insects, it is just a ridged patch of rock merely five miles long, with black powdery pumice for beaches, called Iwo Jima.

The official Marine Corps history of the battle for Iwo Jima identifies Bruce's outfit as one of the four to hit the beach simultaneously as the first wave on the first day. The month-long battle began on a blustery Monday, the 19th of February 1945. The after-drawn confidential Marine Intelligence map of this island is stunning for its indications of the density of defensive hardware; a glance at it explains how it came to be so bloody a task for its American invaders despite the week-long program of aerial bombardment and naval shelling it had sustained before the first Marine set foot there. Survivors' accounts of the invasion, the carnage on the black beaches, the carnage among the boulders from under which burrowing Japanese defenders fired automatic weapons at advancing

Marines, are numerous and terrifying. After the war, a film starring John Wayne called *The Sands of Iwo Jima* was shown to millions in theaters and to many millions more many times since. In this era, Iwo Jima was the Marines' defining engagement.

The 5th Division's 27th Marines, Bruce's outfit, was the one that landed near the southern end of the island, on the harsh pulverized volcanic sand beach called in Japanese Futatsune, which for the Marines was divided into Green Beach, Red Beach 1, and Red Beach 2, only five hundred yards from Motoyama Airfield No. 1. The 5th Division took those beaches without resistance; but within an hour of landing they began to suffer, horribly, losing dozens, then hundreds of men, taking a casualty every fifty seconds for the next week as the Japanese defenders rained death on them from ridges just beyond those pulverized black pumice sands that afforded not even the protection of Marine foxholes hurriedly dug, because the pumice was so fine that Marine shovels merely displaced this sand briefly before more sand would slip immediately in to erase the blades' marks.

Despite this opposition, the 5th drove across to the island's opposite shore on the first day, then split. One group, Bruce's, went south to Mount Suribachi and renown via that epic photograph that was later sculpted in bronze and erected west of the cemetery in Arlington, Virginia, as the heroic erectors of the flag that is memorialized in the Marine Monument. (Ruth Leathe would ask him, later, if he were in that photo; not having seen it, he replied from his Hawai'i hospital bed that there'd been some photographers "musing around" when they'd taken the mount, and that he was "pretty sure" one had snapped him carrying a litter; "Is that the picture?"). The other half of the 5th turned northward to the first yards of a month of arduous yard-by-yard battle with entrenched Japanese soldiers hiding in almost invisible hardened bunkers, soldiers desperate to hold this speck of land against the Americans encroaching on their home islands merely 750 miles away due north across open ocean. The accounts of this part of the battle are chilling: Japanese popped up from their invisible holes and splattered Marines with gunfire, then retreated if they could, or were gunned down or bayoneted at the mouths of their caves. After taking Suribachi, Bruce would join that fight next.

Next to the inked names in Bruce's code notebook, the names of the twenty men in his team, are four penciled checkmarks, but these are not indicators of casualty, but of some deficiency in their equipment at some inspection conducted by Bruce as squad leader; knowing of the conditions of battle on Iwo Jima, it is impossible to rule in or rule out that Corporal Leathe performed these inspections effectively, or whether they were life-saving exercises or just non-com chickenshit. Tucked into those yellowing pages is a small printed outline map encompassing the coast of China, the Philippines, Eniwetok, and Japan, with "Io Shima" dotted in, on the reverse of which is typed the following guide to Bruce's life on Iwo Jima:

COMBAT JAPANESE PHRASES

KOH-SAHN SEH YOH!	SURRENDER!
KOH-ROH-SAH-NAH-EE-YOH!	WE WON'T MURDER YOU!
BOO-KEE OH STEH-ROH!	DROP YOUR WEAPONS!
TEH OH AH-GEH-ROH!	HANDS UP!
HAH-DAH-KAH NEE NAH-REH!	STRIP!
KOH-CHEE KOH-EE!	COME HERE!
DEH-TEH KOH-EE!	COME OUT!
SOO-SOO-MEH!	FORWARD MARCH!
TOH-MAH-REH!	HALT!
DAH-MAH-REH!	SHUT UP!
MAH-WAH-REH!	TURN AROUND!
AH-TSOO-MAH-REH!	FALL IN!

Back in Angola, Ruth Whitney Leathe and her husband and her two daughters and her mother Charlotte Whitney and the family of their acquaintance Jacob Seneca of the Cattaraugus Indian Reservation knew only that both families had sons in the 5th Marine Division. Navy censors had for months prevented their sons from reporting where they were, but those families did have the radio, and the *Buffalo Evening News* of Monday, February 19, 1945, which told them what they knew about the weather in western New York ("Continued cold through tomorrow. Light snow showers today and tonight. Low tonight about 10.") but not enough of what they wanted to know:

AMERICANS SECURE BEACHHEAD ON IWO;
100 SUPERFORTS ATTACK BURNING TOKYO

Below that banner in the farthest right-hand column of this broadsheet newspaper that owned the afternoon distribution for all of Erie County, from the border on the north with Niagara County where the falls is, southward to the Cattaraugus Creek's jagged line through the middle of the Cattaraugus Indian Reservation, a paper delivered to Angola via the Dunkirk & Fredonia Transit line to Bus Smith's sundry store and depot:

> 30,000 MARINES
> GO ASHORE FROM
> 800-SHIP ARMADA
> Airfield Defense Penetrated;
> Plane Center On Honshu
> Also Hit by B-29s; Navy
> Fliers Get 659 Planes

But all that extra information about American planes hitting Honshu was of no interest, because the Leathes had a son in the 5th Marine Division, and another story, Column 5, was more precisely about Iwo, where, Leathes and Senecas now knew with certainty, their 5th Division sons were:

> AIR, SEA BARRAGE
> PARALYZED IWO'S
> BEACH DEFENSES
> First Wave of Marines Put
> Ashore in 2 Minutes, Says
> Eyewitness; Jap Guns Fired
> From Concealed Caves
>
> By John R. Henry
> Representing the Combined American Press
>
> ADMIRAL TURNER'S FLAG-SHIP, Off Iwo. Feb. 19—Japan's volcanic bastion of Iwo Jima loomed out of the chill dark dawn today like a black fire-spitting dragon and tonight two Marine divisions were scrambling to an enemy airfield atop its monstrous back, 600 yards inland from the eastern beaches. American casualties were considerable . . .

There was no news of Bruce Leathe or of Jacob Seneca in that paper, nor in the papers of subsequent freezing lakeshore days, when the boldness of the first day's headlines and the large and detailed photographs of the island on the picture page gave way to smaller stories and smaller headlines and only intermittent photographs, because the confidence of quick triumph implicit in the early headlines had no objective correlative on Iwo Jima. Three days into the fight as reported, those news readers learned that 385 Marines had been killed and also that 4,168 had been wounded "thus far," and those numbers caused great grief and great anxiety and much praying in and near that village in western New York. By the battle's fifth day, the banner headline on page 1 was all about Germany, and the subhead about that unknowable place someplace west of Hawai'i and north of Saipan and so very, very close to the home islands of the emperor was telling a less hopeful story:

> Yanks Stalled in Battle for Iwo
> Airfield after Seizing Mt. Suribachi

By March, the Iwo story was no longer on the front page, for victory was at hand in Europe, and victory was a better story.

The first news of Bruce came later in March. First a Marine officer came, then the newspaper informed the rest of the county, with word that Howard Bruce Leathe had been wounded.

There is no one left to tell how the family received the news that Bruce had not been killed, but the month of anxiety ended. More than six thousand Marines died on Iwo Jima, but not Bruce Leathe.

Bruce left that place of bloodshed on the very day in March, 1945 when Iwo Jima was officially declared captured. And that Joe Rosenthal photograph, of the great long pipe that Marines had made into a flagstaff and employed to erect the Stars and Stripes over Mount Suribachi, which photograph was published and republished everywhere, gave the news-readers of home the great surge of confidence that now, soon, because of selfless sacrifice and young American men's blood and courage and martial merit, this war would soon end.

Thirty-two days of battle on Iwo Jima behind him, their airstrips Motoyama 1 and Motoyama 2 now secured and put to terrible use by American bombers for their relentless runs at the home islands and for the next horrific battle, at Okinawa, Bruce took a ship back across the

International Date Line for Hawai'i and liberty and for recovery from the wounds inflicted by shrapnel and by a doomed enemy soldier with a bayonet attached to the end of a carbine with a dark wood stock and a pocketful of letters never to be sent, but rather taken by this Angola warrior as trophies of combat, sepia ink on flimsy the paper trail of the death he and his comrades had dealt in the month that had begun in hymns and in prayer. It was aboard the USS *Rutland*, en route from Eniwetok to Iwo Jima, that Bruce had attended a religious service whose program he'd kept. He and his fellow battle-bound Marines had sung Hymn No. 125, "All the Way My Saviour Leads Me," and Hymn No. 124, "Blessed Assurance," and had read or maybe just heard the cleric's reading from the book of Acts 26:1–31, concerning Paul's colloquy with King Agrippa and with Festus his accuser. It is a strange text for the occasion, but somehow the chaplain must have decided that this particular text had some relevance to a crowd of elite shock troops about to engage fierce battle. It is the story of snide and disbelieving reaction to the Apostle Paul's telling how Christ's light had descended upon him, and how Christ's voice had spoken to him, on the road to Damascus. Festus said: "Paul, thou art beside thyself; much learning doth make thee mad."

Bruce, at that moment on that ship not then much learned in war or in death, however much he was practiced in preparations for war, left no evidence of madness—other than that he and all the rest of those men had volunteered to be there, and to the extent that madness is a subjective thing, defined by conformity with what one's community expects, volunteering to fight, endangering oneself in order to slay the enemy, voyaging thousands of miles from home was not, in 1945, madness.

Later, though, in a small way, Bruce would verge on his own version of Pauline epiphany, this: that even after his own month of firing his gun, thrusting his bayonet, stringing his wires, carrying his stretchers, and shouting at captives, there was yet more war—more preparation, more mustering of masses of warriors like Bruce for the last push from the Hawai'i of his recovery and liberty and restaurants in April and May to the Home Islands in the summer, for that was the plan.

But first, on May 8th, a full two months after Bruce emerged scathed but alive from Iwo, there was good beer to be drunk in Hawai'i, celebratory beer, rationed heavy for the Iwo Jima victors so they could enjoy the news of the Germans' surrender the day before.

This happy early summer of imminent victory, though, changed its face quickly from ease and confidence to tense preparation and much stateside anxiety and much Marine anxiety, too. Plans for troops changed. The Ryukyu island of Okinawa, tight to the home islands, took until June the 21st to conquer, and all American materiel and forces under arms were being mustered at terrible speed for the final assault on the Empire's very center. But by mid-July, the innovations of physicists and engineers in the American desert put the admirals' designs for a million-man invasion force for loosing on Japan on hold forever, for August of 1945 was when Hiroshima on August 6th and Nagasaki on August 9th were bombed with the new nuclear weapons that put an abrupt and utter end to the war. This was Bruce's experience of it:

> Fri 10 Aug 1945
>
> Dearest People O'Mine
>
> It was 0330 when I finally retired last night or more correct, this morning; due to the fact that I had a midwatch of the guard again. Then at 0550, all in the tent were awakened by the noise of shouts, cheers, etc. It was at that time we learned Japan was willing to capitulate and that perhaps the end was near. It is hard to believe that in another day or so the conflict will be officially declared secured.
>
> It was interesting to note the difference of reactions as each man accepted the gratifying news. Some ran about wildly in a state of vociferous abandon while others appeared to take the event with complete indifference yet filled with emotion inwardly. Doubt predominated the minds of many but within an hour that doubt was converted to joy. All activity ceased and our C.O. declared holiday routine the routine for this momentous day.
>
> Eleven months ago today we disembarked from the States. I will always remember this date. Though the war is near termination, we don't expect to be shipped home immediately for we know that is impossible. We can only, and do, hope for the best . . .

Indeed, his hopes notwithstanding, Bruce had more to do. Less than a month after the incinerations and the subsequent surrender, just six months less three days after he left Iwo Jima, Bruce again sailed west past Tarawa, past Eniwetok, past Saipan, past the Bunin Island of Iwo Jima, all the way to the Home Islands.

He disembarked from the USS *Queens* at Sasebo, the Imperial Navy's base on Kyushu, the southernmost island of Japan, and was greeted by ranks of silent, head-bowed Japanese men in uniform—by those who had lost, who had failed, who had been overwhelmed by American materiel and technology and by large warriors from small villages such as Angola, New York.

Bruce Leathe, conqueror, bloodied shock trooper, became on that shore the occupier, one of those tens of thousands of American soldiers brought in to occupy Japan while the lawyers, economists, and technicians who were General MacArthur's to command redesigned Japanese society. Bruce spent October and November of the year of victory up the coast from his landing point, in Fukuoka, occupying. Policing. Collecting postcards which he bundled and sent home without troubling their white counterfaces with any message of his own, as if saying Here, Here is where I am, These pictures say more about this place than I am able to. His letters were not so many from Japan, his activities there boring and arduous and extended because his skills were valuable and rare: he was a "materiel" man, a repairer of radios, a refurbisher of shattered networks. He gathered pieces of Japan and sent them home: small ceramic bowls, lacquer bowls, lacquer chopsticks, pieces of silk fabric, two small Japanese flags, a fine hammered-steel ceremonial sword with a long curved lacquer scabbard, for whose possession he received a signed permission slip stamped by Marine Intelligence. And photographs of two Japanese women which he did not send home, but did bring home with him in his trunk. One of the women was a Kagoshima widow surnamed Hiraoka; Bruce's commanders had sent him south across the bay from that city of ashes Nagasaki to Kagoshima, so different from Fukuoka:

> The city is definitely not a beautiful one—it is something like 85% damaged by air-strikes. I have seen quite a bit of Kagoshima by taking radio-jeeps out on test runs. The remaining sections of the city are typically Japanese—dirty, poor, constricted and smothered in its own foul odor. The landmark of Kagoshima stands out in the bay. It is a volcano, tall, not too old, ruggedly creviced. Occasional belches of smoke indicate its activity. There it stands, impressive, with the majesty of all volcanoes and a crumpled Japanese city, cold and starving, at its feet.

> Even though the life of these is a hard one, I cannot feel sorry for them. They aggravate me; for it is because of them that I cannot be with you tomorrow—Christmas.

Bruce Leathe's penciled itinerary of war contains but four more entries after his note of departure from Kagoshima and the woman on March 13, 1946. From Sasebo, he embarked on the USS *Comet* on the 17th; crossed the International Date Line on the 23rd, arrived in San Diego on the 3rd of April, and three days later boarded a train. Ever the documentarian, he saved the ticket stub and placed it in his trunk and returned to Angola, New York, and stepped down from the depot's steps to the waiting arms of his mother and father and his two sisters and grandparents Whitney to the bright sharp sounds of his old marching-band comrades' music that pierced the cold rain and urged spring to get a move on. The first of the Leathe generations in America to fight for this country had joined the line of serving, blooding, and homecoming that his mother's people had laid down when Connecticut private soldier Elias Whitney volunteered, fought, and won under his General Washington, and then returned to Connecticut, and then took the in-lieu-of-pay land grant in western New York 163 years before, a line those Whitneys had refreshed with their boys' blood in the wars of 1813, 1849, 1861, 1875, 1898, 1917, and now in 1945.

For a time, Bruce's homecoming was a replica of his forebears'. The customary rhythm of life as a native of small-town Upstate New York was intact, with no change of the pattern of the generations. He had as yet no mission; Bruce merely joined in his father's work. The *Evans Town Guide* of 1947 carried a spare but typographically handsome quarter-page advertisement for the firm of Leathe, Peacock and Leathe, General Contractors for Concrete, Carpentry, Roofing and Home Construction, and so it went. Bruce rejoined the building trade.

But the Coykendalls had another example for this veteran. The Reverend Glenn Coykendall had also sent a son to war, Robert, to the Navy, and Bob had returned to Angola to a different tradition: of education. Bob would take his father's path, which led again away from Angola, to Columbia University in New York City. It was, of course, a path Bruce could have paved for himself, via the appointment to the United States Military Academy at West Point. But he hadn't. Counterfactual speculation about what may have happened to a commissioned Army lieutenant (who would certainly have missed The War had he taken his engineering degree at that campus on the Hudson) ends, for the heavy hand of the national government's postwar policy was there, more real than any personal wartime epiphany, to touch Bruce Leathe and to transform him. Bob Coykendall's status was Bruce Leathe's, and that made them both eligible for the G.I. Bill. And whether Bruce made the effort at the Reverend's urgings or with Bob's or with his own sense that an opportunity once bypassed was now presenting itself again, no matter: Bruce gathered up his papers, his diploma, his Honorable Discharge, his letters, his transcripts, his citations, and made his application, and, enabled by his government, he matriculated in September 1947 at Columbia University, the first of any generation of Leathes or Whitneys or Wallers or Collinses to go to a university.

This young man had made so many abrupt transitions, many more so than had his father or mother. At eighteen he was a small-town boy, popular, cheerful, devout, but poor and of a poor family that had been poor throughout its entire existence, its entire existence traceable, once the short span of living memories is exhausted, not by visits to any works of stone or brick or even paper left behind by Leathes or Whitneys who had come before and left evidence of any energy or special gifts they may have had, but only in brief entries in census and military records. They were a thoroughly anonymous people, Bruce Leathe's; but he was, his family knew, poised to change that. At twenty-two he was a veteran of epochal conflict, now home and industrious, with experience of both the doldrums of military life and of its harshest rigors, and already well acquainted with the vagaries of mindless fate. In one of his last letters home from occupied Kagoshima, he sensed the terrible symmetry of death:

> You undoubtedly know that Kopacz was one of my closest friends since I often spoke of him in my letters. Last week while driving a jeep, he pulled over to the shoulder of a very narrow road to avoid collision with a Nip truck that turned out from a side road. The shoulder was soft and unable to support the weight of the jeep. Consequently the vehicle, with Kop, dropped down the 15 foot embankment. Kopacz fared worst—he was killed.
>
> This is a funny world. He survived an operation, the purpose of which was to exterminate as many of these people as necessary to secure Iwo. And then he was killed trying to

> avoid injuring one of them . . . Two other men from my old outfit, both good friends of mine, were injured fatally during this past month. One was scalded to death after accidentally falling into a tub of boiling water. The other, a wireman, fell from a Nip telephone pole.

That account of useless death sounds with the deadened tone of resignation. "This is a funny world," he wrote. What rage and horror Bruce Leathe must have felt in that damp smashed ruin of Kagoshima, to have lost friends who with him had endured the month of shelling, machine-gunning, sniping, grenading, bayoneting that Iwo Jima had been.

But this dutiful son reported. A year later he was in college, a College Man. Perhaps ridiculously, he transitioned again: he became a Fiji, as the members of his fraternity Phi Gamma Delta called themselves; outrageous to current sensibilities, the frat's mascot was a black-skinned thick-lipped spear-carrying bone-through-the-nose islander in grass skirts. The letters from Columbia don't survive, but other items crept into his war chest: the invitation to a holiday ball chaired by General Eisenhower, then president of Columbia, and staffed by none other than H. Bruce Leathe, steward (as he had been squad leader) of the Phi Gamma Delta house; copy upon copy of the frat's glossy monthly magazine; caricatures in pencil of Bruce and by Bruce; stationery embossed with his and his new outfit's name; lapel buttons in robin's egg blue that read Beat Harvard and Beat Cornell from the gridiron conflicts he cheered from beery grandstands and that this returned warrior may have worn on the lapel of his college coat.

But then came a crisis at home. Bruce took leave from Columbia after his junior year to tend to his mother when she fell ill and lost a kidney that same summer of 1949; in those same months, Howard Leathe suffered a heart attack and could no longer work. The construction business his father had founded with his son and with Peacock had faltered without Bruce, so Bruce came home to work for his family—his mother, his father, his now-widowed grandmother, his little sister Ruthmarie (Charlotte had gone off to Buffalo for nursing school)—and to feed it. He had already helped buy the Leathe family its first house, barely a hundred yards uptown from the Triangle House, at 166 Main Street—the white clapboard place of New England style verging in that year on one hundred years old already. It was the place with the grapevines on the porch, and the trumpet vines on the barn, and the barn owls and the wren houses, the cats and rabbits, the great poplar tree in back, the tangles of heavy-laden raspberry canes in its deep rear yard. College man, ex-Marine, provider, buyer of the family's first-ever house, Bruce was something removed from his family; he slept not in his family's new home, but in the loft of its barn, on that nice village property but separate from his kin, demonstrating a self-denying superiority even as he took care of the rest. At night, Bruce worked for the South Buffalo Railroad up the lakeshore in Lackawanna. By day, he worked such jobs as Leathe, Peacock and Leathe had contracted to do, all through the summer of 1949 and on into the first part of the fall of what should have been his senior year at Columbia but was never to be, for one weekend evening in October of that year, on the way to court a young woman whose portrait saved in the war chest features the upswept hair and peach complexion and high bodice that made her a nice ditto of the roundest-cheeked of the three Andrews sisters of radio fame, Bruce followed not the Leathe or Whitney or Collins or Waller or even the Coykendall example, but rather the Kopacz, when he swerved his Ford onto a soft shoulder on Jerusalem Corners Road in Evans Township, the better to avoid injuring a carload of kids who'd been too young for the war, and, because that shoulder was too soft to sustain him, plunged down an embankment, and, as Kopacz had, long after the conflict that had so threatened him and then transformed him, died.

Bruce's family survived him, but not well. His sister Charlotte eloped the night of his funeral with a man who was, by all accounts, a dear and sweet man, also a veteran of battle, a Montanan who had come to western New York on a train carrying the unquenchable thirst that would soon ruin him and, later, in another Evans Township car wreck that robbed her of her beauty and of her sanity, sister Charlotte, too. Howard took some years to recover from his heart attack, but never regained his ability to work as he had before, and, after stowing the shotguns and the rifle he and his son had used to hunt deer and pheasants and squirrels, never used them or hunted again. Ruth and her mother Charlotte gathered all Bruce's letters from the war and put them in a small black deal case with base-metal hasps and a wrapped leather handle. Ruthmarie made something of a shrine to her brother, Japanning her room with paper lanterns, ceramics, the lacquerwork trophies and the war chest, and setting there Bruce's decanters with their silver hang-tags for Rye, Whiskey, and Gin, and pouring from them for her friends who had been WACs and WAVEs. Another shrine of sorts was the photograph of

Bruce in the Leathe parlor, a black-and-white portrait edging to sepia of him in his Marine uniform taken homecoming day, his long darkening red hair swept up in a style Ronald Reagan would keep through many decades, his moustache luxurious and thick but kempt, his direct hazel eyes softened by that portraitist's focus, very similar in tone and aspect to the portrait of Christ that also hung in that room, the two sets of eyes following everyone around the room forever. But a grief settled onto that household, and pervaded it, and though the deaths in ensuing years first of Charlotte Whitney, then of Howard Leathe, then of Ruth Leathe and of the sisters were all mourned quite genuinely by Angola, all the mourning for Bruce only ended when the last of the Leathes, who as a family and as a name are now gone from that village, were buried next to him in that small cemetery next to Big Sister Creek.

Obama's election

My eldest daughter came home to Buffalo, New York, to cast her first vote for a candidate for president this past November. Afterward, we drove her the sixty miles back to her college in the village of Geneseo, just east of the Genesee River. That village is not such an old place by New York standards. It is one of hundreds established just after the Revolution, after the expulsion of the Iroquois. Today it is one of those rare tidy villages; most of them are untidy and fading, but Geneseo is prosperous and lovely because the state college there provides a strong economic base that most of the Yankee villages of Upstate New York lack. Just a few miles away in Mount Morris, where our ancestor Stacy Whitney lived, the clapboard houses wilt and sag, and Main Street withers. These places all assumed their shape—clapboard houses, two-story brick and masonry commercial buildings, village commons, handsome brick courthouses, Protestant churches with five-story steeples—in Stacy Whitney's boyhood in the mid-nineteenth century. These were places shaped by the Civil War.

Ours is a family defined by that war. Stacy Whitney, my mother's grandfather's father, left Mount Morris in 1861 to volunteer for the Union army. Now, five generations later, a child of his line is nearby. Now, more than 140 years after he returned to New York State from the war, a child of his line helped elect a black man president.

North from Geneseo and Mount Morris, also on the Genesee River, up near Lake Ontario where it widens and spills into Irondequoit Bay, is the city of Rochester. Rochester is the city from which my father's great-grandfather, Richard Hollis, rode to Gettysburg with the 9th New York Cavalry. He, too, fought for the Union in the Civil War. He saw its end at Appomattox Courthouse, where he witnessed the traitor Lee's surrender.

Farther west, south of Buffalo and close to the Lake Erie shore, my mother lives in a clapboard house in a Yankee village that is just up the road from where her grandmother's father, Richard Waller, operated his smithy after his service in the 112th New York Infantry. Waller's regiment went all the way to Florida fighting rebels. Just three weeks before the surrender, Waller was briefly a captive of North Carolinians who apprehended him and his comrades on a foraging run near the Neuse River.

Buffalo newspapers of the 1850s and 1860s tell us what these men knew about the war they set out from here to fight. We can only surmise what their private thoughts were. The political messaging of the times was, however, unequivocal, because they were from the hottest of abolitionist hotbeds. Every enlistee knew, because everybody in those days knew, that the war for which they volunteered was about their own freedom, but they also knew that they were going off to fight to secure the freedom of the slaves. The slaves' freedom was important to them, because where there was slave labor, free labor was endangered. I've read the histories of each of their regiments, and have written about events of the 1850s in Rochester and Buffalo, where great dramas of the Underground Railroad occurred, dramas that were well known in the newspapers and that shaped the pro-Lincoln, pro-Seward, pro-abolitionism politics of the day. All available evidence demonstrates that our ancestors were William Seward Republicans in 1860, in the year when everybody thought it would be Seward of New York, the radical abolitionist, who would be the Republican candidate for president. When our ancestors set out for war, they knew what they were doing, why, and for whom.

Perhaps our ancestors were more concerned with the fate of the Union than they were with the fate of the enslaved. Perhaps they were bored with being young men in small-town Upstate New York. Perhaps they believed that there was personal glory to be gained by going to war. Yet withal, the rhetorical context of the small-town regiments of these Yankee New Yorkers was abolitionist, free-soil, free-labor, Protestant, and surprisingly hot, or perhaps the better word is zealous, on the question of personal liberty.

Growing up in small-town Upstate New York in the 1950s and early 1960s, I was frequently reminded of my ancestors' service in the Revolution, and in the War of 1812, but most especially in the Civil War. War was the marker of our family's generations, and the narrative of war was the story of American rightness, or more precisely, of American rightfulness. Of course, World War II was what we boys played when we played at war. I knew where my uncle and my dad had fought Japanese in their own rightful war, and though they were both gone, the elder women of our family explained, as did our community in its ceremonies and parades, that they'd joined that effort and fought on Iwo Jima and in the Solomon Islands in nothing less than a fight for our freedom. Everybody knew this. And because of the peculiar geography of western New York, I knew that this was not just a history of white guys, but also of Indians, because it was to western New York that the Senecas of the Genesee had been expelled after the Revolution. So many Senecas came to our church, and we to theirs on their reservation only four miles from home, and to the American Legion Post across the street from our white Yankee clapboard house, the post my grandfather ran, serving white men and Indians the same small glasses of beer and the same Friday-night fish fries. My uncle had gone to the Marines in 1943, turning down an opportunity to go to West Point, and he'd served with a Seneca leader's son in the 5th Marines. The Seneca boy and the white boy had taken the same bus from the same town to the same enlistment center and gone to Parris Island together, then on to Camp Lejeune, to Camp Pendleton, and then to the Pacific. I don't know what became of that particular Marine from the Cattaraugus Reservation, but I do know that when my uncle returned from the war, and from a year of serving in the occupation force in Japan, he'd reconnected. He went to Columbia, the first of his line to go to college, where he and another local boy, a white boy, the son of the minister of our church, together in that year of 1947 joined the Columbia University chapter of the NAACP.

Wars for justice were the family story. My late uncle's membership in the fight against what my grandmother called "bigotry" was part of the story, too. Of living black Americans, though, I was like every other Yankee kid in the Yankee village of clapboard houses: We had no knowledge of black Americans except from television. In our town of 1,500 souls, the Civil Rights movement was something that happened on the evening news. Only in 1967, when I left town for high school in Buffalo, was it that I saw black people on the street, and rode with them on the bus, then met individual African American persons as classmates in my new school.

It was a racial idyll, but not necessarily for the best of reasons. The shock of being in classrooms with people with more melanin than me was a small part of the terrifying newness of the school as a whole. To my thirteen-year-old mind, the real shock was the overwhelming and focusing reality of the burden of homework we were expected to do.

We were stupid Americans in a school that had been transplanted from a pre-World War II Europe, where everybody knew how to speak at least three languages, where everybody knew how to play soccer, which

I'd never even heard of, and where everybody but me knew that the first rule of life was to cease talking when the teacher entered the room, stand up and say, all together, "Laudetur Jesus Christus" to the priest with the incomprehensible Central European accent, who would shortly begin lecturing on classic texts everyone but me had already read.

Being a newbie defined everything. Even the black kids in the school were all veterans. They knew Latin. They could understand the priests' accents. Racial differences among students were as nothing when, in the first week, we newcomers were all subjected to one priest's withering contempt for our lack of Latin, and to another's thrown-up hands at our incomprehension of physics, astronomy, calculus, stoichiometry, and most of what he'd just said. Our chief refuge as students was to huddle together as fellow sufferers at the hands of people who sounded to us like Bela Lugosi's Dracula. Of much greater interest to us were the usual issues of adolescence, like aspects of personality, and the amount of one's pocket change, and whether one had cigarettes—that's what mattered in that ecosystem. I argued with students over what we were reading, and traded sandwiches with them at lunch, and played touch football between classes, and snuck smokes with the rest of them. My recollection of going to school with soccer-playing, multilingual Hungarians, with Greek Orthodox kids with different holidays from us, with blacks, with girls, with Jews, and with two tough-guy Irish kids who alternately threatened me and wheedled me for change consists of all of the above, and in about that order of importance. I can't remember the black kids standing out at all, except that the black kids and I were native speakers of English. So along with them and the Irishmen, we were more or less the regular people at that place, because none of us had come from either a displaced persons camp or from a castle recently seized by the Communists. We were just Americans.

But you know what comes next. Our idyll was not the world of the late 1960s.

We were on the ninth-grade field trip. Thirty or so thirteen- and fourteen-year-olds, a taciturn Hungarian priest, and a married pair of teachers had ridden a yellow bus down to the Everglades in the spring of 1968. On the day in April 1968 after Martin Luther King Jr. was killed, we were driving toward a Catholic school in Atlanta on whose gymnasium floor we were planning to sleep, white girls and black girls and Jewish girls on the Mrs. Teacher side of the gym, us heathen savage boys watched over by Father Mustos and Mr. Teacher on our side.

There was trouble in America as we drove north. The city of Atlanta was burning that night, as in a war, but I hadn't ever seen a war, so it was like a movie to me. I thought at first that it was a bunch of slag-pours at a long line of steel plants, because back home in Buffalo, nighttime was when they poured slag onto the ground, right at the shore of the lake, and when we drove home at night to our Yankee clapboard village, we would watch the slag-pours. It was like a lava flow, and there was fire. But it wasn't steel mills in Atlanta. I remember wondering why Father Mustos, who had spent the trip in a t-shirt, was opening up his suitcase and putting his priest collar on as we sat in traffic. There was a line of cars ahead of us, but it wasn't just traffic. We looked out the windows and saw a lot of fire, and it wasn't far away. We were being stopped at a made-up roadblock, a couple of cars narrowing the road, by some white men with clubs, men who wanted to come onto the bus to see if we had any Negroes with us. We did.

I didn't really understand what was going on when our chaperone, the Hungarian-born math teacher, bounded out of the bus, speaking sharply in Hungarian to Father Mustos, who shut the door tight behind him. The teacher went outside alone. It didn't go well. He took abuse from the men outside for refusing to let the thugs come up the steps and into the bus itself. It was unpleasant to look out the window and see a man pushing him while other men with clubs or ax-handles stood by. Then the teacher's wife was yelling, too, and kids were moving around in the bus.

Somehow, my pack-rat mother kept my notes about all this. I did not know then all that was going on, but I know now that April 1968 was only a dozen years after the math teacher had done some street-fighting, in faraway Budapest, when he'd been a schoolboy of fourteen or fifteen, just like me. I know now that our math teacher hadn't battled freckled bullies, but that he had hurled cobblestones at Soviet tanks, and had been shot at by uniformed soldiers who shot other civilians dead, and I know that he'd escaped the police dogs chasing him when he barely outran them at the Austrian border, back in November 1956, after the tanks had crushed the Hungarian Revolution. In Atlanta that night, I knew that he was in a confrontation, and made notes on it. I sensed that he was being brave. Now, in retrospect, I am awed that his bravery was so instantaneous, and so effective: The Negro-hunters didn't get on the bus, because he wouldn't let them. Meanwhile, we kids had followed Father Mustos's instructions, and had hidden Karen, Beverly, Michelle, and John under our duffel bags in the center aisle. (The priests of our school were allies of two Righteous Gentiles who made Buffalo their home, Dr. Clara

Ambrus, who lived two doors from school, and Tibor Baransky, whose sons went to our school. Those folks got Yad Vashem recognition for hiding Jews from the Nazis.) Luckily, it was dark, late, and hard to see, but we pressed ourselves up against the windows, everybody whispering, wanting to keep those guys from seeing in. Luckily, there were cars behind us. They waved us through. My notes don't record whether we slept on the gym floor that night, or kept driving.

I was a reporter in Chicago in the early 1980s when I did a ward-by-ward count of the black voting-age population, guesstimating like crazy because census tracts and ward boundaries didn't mesh well, and personal computers did not yet exist. Congressman Harold Washington later told me that my report, with the big chart enumerating the racial count in each ward, convinced him to run for mayor, and he did. Washington won after a big voter-registration drive not only on the black South Side and on the black West Side but in all those wards that everybody just assumed were solidly Richie Daley or Jane Byrne territory but which my report had identified as having small but significant populations of voting-age blacks. Washington's win in 1983 was such a validating event in my life, though I was just an observer, that I showed up at Joe and Ann Dowling's wedding in Queens with blue Harold Washington pins as my gifts to them, which they found incomprehensible. Nobody outside of Chicago much cared that a black man had been elected mayor of America's second city.

Later, my old Hyde Park neighbor Carol Moseley Braun was my client when she ran and won as the first black woman member of the U.S. Senate, in 1992. Her South African boyfriend fired all the white guys in the campaign after we'd won the primary, which was the real contest; she had no use for me as a consultant afterward, and I've not spoken to her since.

But before then, in the late 1970s and early 1980s in Chicago, I'd been so fascinated by the racial divide in Chicago that I'd decided to flout it. I reveled in being the only white reporter who regularly went to Packinghouse Hall, the union office across the street from the notoriously violent Robert Taylor Homes housing project. I'd been the first white reporter to go south of the Midway, crossing that border and leaving Hyde Park for the mysterious, unknown land beyond 61st Street, to go to then-congressman Harold Washington's office. I'd gone to dinner with the egregious Gus Savage after he'd won his congressional seat the same year

Washington had won his, and had listened to Savage excoriate me for my racism. But Gus Savage excoriated every white person as a racist. I didn't take it personally. I understood it. To him, to others, to the community, to the world, the racial divide in Chicago was everything, everything.

Once again, just as in high school, I found myself living in an idyll, which to some extent remains an idyll. It is called Hyde Park, and it is where Barack Obama's house is, and where he will live when he is not in the White House. This zone of Chicago is where the races mix, but of course the racial tension was impossible to ignore, and my time there was a time of highly publicized incidents of black-on-white sexual violence near the University of Chicago—violence that was made literature by Richard Wright in his novel *Native Son*.

Hyde Park was the neighborhood and the early 1980s the time of the famous University of Chicago professor and writer Saul Bellow's tough new novel starring race and crime, *The Dean's December*, based on local events. It was the place just down 55th Street from Washington Park, from scenes of Wright's *Native Son*, and in that place and time, Bigger Thomas seemed not to be a fictional character. It was also the place where we adventurous white twenty-somethings drank beer at actual blues bars, the Checkerboard and others, and went to the Maxwell Street market on weekend mornings in Jewtown to hear the blues, the genuine blues: Junior Wells and Buddy Guy, Sunnyland Slim, KoKo Taylor, Little Walter. I was adamant about seeing them in the flesh, before they passed away, because Howlin' Wolf had died the year after I'd arrived, and I'd missed him.

Race in Chicago then was everywhere, everything, every conflict, even anomalous ones, and there were plenty of anomalies. Before I got the reporting job, I'd worked as a typesetter at a shop that had a black Muslim newspaper as a client. Four or five of us white guys and a lone black guy did the typesetting and pasteup for *Muhammad Speaks*. I don't know how many times I either typed or corrected page proofs for Wallace Deen Muhammad's column before technology changed and they moved their business, and the organization changed and the group split into the Farrakhan faction and the mainstream American Muslim Mission with its big white mosque down on Cottage Grove. I knew where Elijah Muhammad had lived and where his son and heir still lived, slightly north of 51st Street in the curious biracial luxury of Kenwood, which is where Obama's house is; nearby, Muhammad Ali had his home, and his green Rolls Royce, in which he cruised the streets of Hyde Park, enjoying his celebrity, giving occasional lifts—quite friendly and innocent—to some of my lucky friends. Race? What about celebrity, and money? Money defined that territory more than race; 47th Street a few blocks away was poor, bluesy, alcoholic, burned-out, but south of 47th, in Kenwood and in Hyde Park, there was peace, diversity, calm commerce, famous faces, a resilient and accessible prosperity in the environs of the great university. But there was cognitive dissonance, too: A friend of mine, a former University of Chicago political science student who wrote about Hobbes and Rousseau and the notions of the social contract and how all those notions were believed by those old philosophers to have brought order to natural man, which is to say, the warring humanity of the precivilized world, told me that one of his University of Chicago professors referred to the poor black area north of 47th Street as "the state of nature."

The peculiar culture of Hyde Park, so student, so Jewish, so anti-downtown, was where such unforgiving advocates of ruthless order mixed with apologists for criminals. There had long been a notorious black gang in the area. It was variously known, after Blackstone Avenue, as the Blackstone Rangers, then the Blackstone Nation, then the Black P-stone Nation and its further iterations. I was a reporter, and I had no illusions. Whatever its name, the organization was a criminal enterprise that dealt drugs and hurt people. All the members of the gang were black, but so were almost all of the victims. The apologists were some combination of deluded, cynical, or politicized. It really was simple, and it still is. Gangsters make life hellish for everybody around them, and are the principal excuse for white racism.

The conversation about race then was, in large part dishonestly but in all aspects importantly, about crime. Nobody white would knowingly choose to take the El from Marshall Field's department store on State Street to 55th Street, and then take the bus east to Hyde Park or west to the Lithuanian delicatessens on the Lithuanian side of Marquette Park. Everybody white, and many blacks too, took the Illinois Central to Hyde Park. Only if one were a big, athletic, pissed-off twenty-something with all kinds of ancient violence in his soul would one put on a face, and pretend to be nonchalant and walk east from the El stop at 55th Street, inviting something to happen. Because in one's six-foot athletic body that sometimes happened to get into saloon scrapes, walking through Washington Park, which was and remains the dividing line between what the older folks still in those days called Bronzeville on the west and the Hyde Park enclave on the east, there was a legend waiting to unfold. It wasn't clear what that legend would have been about. I never found out, either, but I heard the ribbing or incredulity of blacks and whites at the college-kid bar Jimmy's. "Whatsa matta witch you, boy, gotta death wish?" Maxine would ask. She would shake her head, and when her shift was over, we'd drink beers, and then her young clients would walk through the sub-zero Chicago winter nights over to Ribs 'n Bibs on 53rd Street, to pick up orders of fried chicken and racks of ribs in that hot, hot sauce.

About that time, Barack Obama arrived in Chicago to start work as a community organizer. About that time, as Ronald Reagan was elected, as the steel plants of the South Side were suddenly shuttered, Chicago's conversation about race was also about politics.

After Harold Washington became Chicago's mayor, black nationalist radio host and newspaper columnist Lu Palmer challenged union man Charles Hayes for Washington's former seat in the U.S. House of Representatives. Hayes won.

The year after Harold Washington won the mayoralty, in the scorching summer of 1984, the old union man Charlie Hayes was the leading candidate to replace Washington in the special election for Washington's seat in the House of Representatives. (Bobby Rush, the former Black Panther who beat Barack Obama's challenge a decade ago, still holds that seat.) In 1984 Hayes faced a tough challenge from a black nationalist radio host named Lu Palmer, who had no use for whites, and who had made a broadcast career out of explaining that position. Black intellectuals Robert Starks and Conrad Worrill condemned the Hayes candidacy, which relied on Washington's coalition of liberal whites and a solid black base. And of course Gus Savage had no use for Hayes, either.

One breathlessly hot day in that summer campaign, I happened to be standing at the start of a parade, immediately adjacent to Palmer's open car, there to grab some quotes and then head back to the cool shelter of the newspaper. I knew all the candidates except Palmer. There was some delay, and we were just standing there with nothing to do, every man Jack of us pouring sweat. Palmer was sitting on some sort of elevated platform on a truck bed, looking uncomfortable. I looked up at him and just blurted out about how we were both geniuses to be working in conditions like this, hey Lu? Without a second's hesitation, piercing the veil, Palmer agreed. I don't recall exactly what he said, but it was just the response of a normal person, not the made-up person that was his race-focused radio persona. He might have even used bad language to describe the weather. Suddenly, white reporter and black candidate became just two uncomfortable guys waiting for the damned parade to get going. Palmer said something about he thought he'd escaped such conditions when he'd moved north. It was enough to keep me from rushing back to the office. So I walked along the parade route with him, and when there were gaps in the crowd, we talked about the race and about race. We speculated about how large a factor the whites of Hyde Park would be in a congressional election district that was more than 75 percent black. We talked about the political nightmare in which Washington had become embroiled downtown. We talked about Ronald Reagan. He and I would chat frequently after that. His radio persona, of course, never changed. It was his franchise.

Being white, it was inevitable that I was accused of racism. I was a writer, and I wrote about politics, and politics is about disagreement, and it was Chicago, so the ad hominem was ubiquitous. None of the disagreements involving white candidates and black candidates were fair or issue-based, because what was there to disagree about other than race? The language of victimization was a commonplace. Got a gripe? Blame the white guy. Lose the race? White conspiracy. Win the race? Time for redress against all whites.

The Washington victory in 1983 was the genuine precursor to the Obama victory, in that everybody in town went back to work the morning after the election; democracy happened, folks popped corks, then life went on. Of course there was a split in the Chicago City Council, with racial posturing and endless rhetoric. But to sum up some very complicated history and politics, the split of the fifty council members into the twenty-nine versus the twenty-one was more about bad-boy, old-style machine politics, patronage, and posturing than it was about race. Race was the excuse, but Harold Washington, in order to build his coalition, had had to leave his roots as a creature of the late Mayor Richard Daley's machine, and had campaigned against patronage. Washington's fight with Eddie Vrdolyak was over the spoils of victory, and Washington thundered and kept his patronage-hungry black councilmen in line by going to the "base," as the black neighborhoods were called, and threatening and reminding other elected officials about how things were going to be, and letting his formidable power over the language alternately calm and excite his crowds of supporters and activists—who, of course, all wanted patronage.

But the vocabulary of conspiracy and of victimization was widely shared in that city where Martin Luther King, Jr. had been jeered and worse over in Marquette Park only fifteen years before. A very smart historian for whom I wrote a paper or two when I was a graduate student—a paper on the self-named "New Negro" movement of early twentieth-century Chicago—was convinced that the two daily papers intentionally used unflattering photographs of Harold Washington, and dismissed my suggestions, based on my experience as an editor, that one uses a horizontal shot when the slot is wider than tall, and a vertical shot when the slot is north and south, and it's a miracle if the photo editor or anybody else does more than check to see that the image is in focus. But my professor wouldn't hear of it. He couldn't hear of it. He, and every black Chicagoan, was too protective of Washington, and tended a deep well of anger on his behalf.

I heard that anger when I would take my notebook and my tape recorder to the Saturday morning meetings of Operation PUSH, where Jesse Jackson and so many of his fellow South Side pastors held forth. These were community meetings, political meetings, mini-rallies, sometimes press conferences, but mostly an amalgam, with some churchly doings framing it all—quite different from Yankee clapboard-village Episcopalian services and tea with the vicar afterward.

On Saturday mornings in the early 1980s, I walked west to the edge of Washington Park and north along Martin Luther King Jr. Boulevard, and sat my lonely Caucasian self in a pew of what had only a few years before been a great synagogue, and what was then, and now, the Reverend Jesse Jackson's place. There I imbibed that language of protest, and witnessed many a loud outburst as scornful or hurtful or hurt as any of Jeremiah Wright's. But I also found myself in the home of the parable, and of the rhythmic performance from the sacred text, and of the homely analogy to rural practices of the common Southern home, and in those years of frequent Saturday morning sessions of two hours or more apiece, I heard much more than protest. I heard English informed by Caxton's bible, and by Shakespeare. I heard a cultural conservatism in this sense: These descendants of slaves, liberated and moved north to Chicago, emphatically embraced an oratorical tradition of their ancestors' making, which was partly a tradition of my own ancestors' making, and they measured the worth of their orators' performances by how well and truly the speakers demonstrated knowledge of the text, surely, but also by how capably the exegists handled literature, law, Latin, Greek, poetry, and more. The tradition of learned speaking, of the declamation—that antique American discourse of the educated, pre-electronic culture of the nineteenth century—was on display at Operation PUSH on Saturday mornings in Chicago in the early 1980s. But it was on display to the folks from the neighborhood. It was the home culture of the black church, there for the body of the faithful and of the community. It was not some performance at a cultural festival, and it was most assuredly not a performance for the benefit of uncomprehending reporters from downtown.

But that's how those utterances were portrayed for the wider audience of the regional media market. Downtown reporters, who were occasional intruders into this community space, would roll up in their vans and trundle their cameras and microphones down to the front of the pews and stay for a bit and then leave. Reporters then were the unschooled simplifiers that they were and still are, not a bunch of history majors or classics or English majors or anthropologists there to hear and note and nod. Reporters were unattuned to issues of grave importance to that audience—like a certain pastor's insistence on referencing only and solely the Old Testament prophets whenever he thundered on about justice, so different than Jackson's appeals from the New Testament—"Did you hear Reverend Clay Shaw talk about Jeremiah this morning, but Jesse sticking with John? Did you hear that?" was the conversation in the pew, for the difference between the pastors was the subject of much colloquy among the grayer heads in the pews, because there are cognoscenti and connoisseurs of the discipline of preaching, and an understanding that the preacher who references the Hebrew prophets is sending a different message altogether from the one who cites the language of love and of forgiveness from the New Testament.

But this essential difference was entirely lost on the downtown reporters. They literally could not see what was happening in front of them. They were there, with the enhanced sensory equipment of the camera and the microphone and the recorder, but were blind and deaf to all that. Their selections for broadcast and quotation were ever of the angriest, the "blackest" oratory—the growling preacher, the call-and-response from the crowd, the strongest finales, the loudest ovations when the subject was justice for folks stuck in rotten public housing or folks losing their jobs at Wisconsin Steel, that sorry, suddenly shuttered plant among whose betrayed ex-workers the young Obama started working just about then. The story that the media told was about black anger.

The story is about to be about black, and general, celebration. My kids have never seen any of that angry racial strife of the anguished years of

Johnson, Nixon, Reagan, nor will they. Now, here in our urban idyll of race-neutrality or race-commonality, my kids in the first decade of the new millennium are coming to consciousness long after all that—long after the civil rights war I'd but glimpsed at night in Atlanta, long after the segregated but celebrated culture of the blues had so brightly flourished in Chicago in the 1960s, long after the school-desegregation decisions had prompted white flight from the Northern cities in the 1970s, long after Harold Washington's stuttering but triumphant rise to storied success in the 1980s, even after their dad's role in Carol Moseley Braun's great triumph in 1992 and after her almost immediate postinaugural missteps once she got to the Senate. What they missed was all that had come before the long emergence of Obama; they'd missed, too, the great hope for a University of Chicago–educated African American woman from Hyde Park, and they'd missed the great letdown. Here, now, my kids are growing up in a world where people succeed or fail. My kids are colorblind in ways that are striking and joyful to me, yet everywhere in our lives the racial divide yet yawns. It yawns in the very landscape, our very streets. It is still everything.

I've been struck by how my deep personal experience in the empowerment struggles of blacks and of Native Americans has given me a perspective that my white friends find incomprehensible. I've confronted pride, jealousy, smallness, psychological gamesmanship, and, yes, sometimes greatness and sometimes even deeply moral behavior, whereas my white friends don't like or want that kind of complexity, preferring instead the warmer glow of appreciation for the symbolism we all see now that Obama has been elected. Our raveled national sleeve is now knit, they think.

Some cannot fathom why I, the veteran of the medicine lodge rituals of the northern plains, a onetime frequent sweat lodge man, too, a white guy who can actually, if clumsily, speak a native North American language—why I would be such a racist as to have taken the municipality I served into federal district court to stop the Senecas from opening a gambling casino in downtown Buffalo. I've actually been asked, "Why are you being such a racist?" Sometimes it is tiresome to try to explain. Sometimes one just cannot rebut the charge of racism if one is white and male. One sighs, and hopes that the court case gets decided the right way.

Now, perhaps, there will be fewer occasions for such accusations, because so many white Americans voted to elect a black man our president. Not enough, mind you; Obama did not win a majority of white votes. The white candidate won most of the white votes. And no doubt when Republicans oppose President Obama, there will be black Americans who shout as angrily and as loudly as any old Civil Rights–era protester, in the hurt and angry language of protest, that the merits of the issue are meaningless, that opposition to the black president is exclusively a matter of racism, that Republicans are racist, no matter that ancient dead Republicans from near Geneseo and Rochester and Fredonia went into battle to liberate themselves and slaves, too.

But yes, I too share the peculiar American relief that finally, after all the insanity of hundreds of years of race-based abuse, our riven country has a black leader who is a calm, intelligent, careful speaker; that finally, the amended Constitution's principles of representation are realized, and the old, outdated, superseded Constitution's race-based faults are utterly obsolete; that finally the politics of division and resentment are trampled asunder. So my American narcissism is good. I smile. O virtuous nation ours!

So now what?

I write in my weekly columns about the policy choices that the tough-minded no-drama Obama will have to courageously make in order to reverse the decades of rot that racism caused in our old city of Buffalo and in every other northern city. I note with sadness that on the day of Obama's victory, a black female judge who lives right near the Obama home on the South Side of Chicago was muscled hard and injured by a young black man who stole her pocketbook; this behavior is a reality for cities, a problem for whose solution there is now a more searing urgency.

Reversing the rot will require courageous desegregation; courageous reurbanization; courageous confrontation of the lingering anger of the pummeled Right to make of this country a more peaceful and just place. There is so much anguishing poverty right around me—my kids walk to school past abandoned houses, on streets walked by men who have been unemployed or marginally employed most of their lives, in an area where almost 50 percent of the black male workforce is either out of work, in jail, disabled, or too old to work and thus serve as exemplar to the school kids. There is so much urban dysfunction here and in the other Great Lakes cities that solving the problem will require an assault on the legal and economic structures that got those places and people abandoned.

Is Obama powerful enough? Is he focused enough? Brave enough?

One hopes that the answer is yes. One hopes that the forces of the market, of lobbies, of international economics, and of armies identified and yet unidentified will yield to the power of a newly empowered virtue, a civic virtue. Cities are, after all, where humanity's achievement of civilization has occurred.

One hopes. Meanwhile, I applaud the fortunate confluence of events—a dismal incumbent, a disciplined candidate, a competent street organization, a political success, and, for as long as he succeeds, a good feeling abroad in our land and validation of what Abraham Lincoln called "our best selves."

May vanity, arrogance, and narcissism not impede Barack Obama. I am inclined to believe that he will do well, disinclined to believe that he is a miracle worker, able to imagine him succeeding, or failing, as a man—no modifier. That would be his achievement, I think, and ours.

THE ALLURE OF WHAT'S ANCIENT

Tree of life

Blood that drips down the chest from a Medicine Lodge piercing tickles. There wasn't much blood, because we didn't do it Sioux-style. The scalpel blades were from Chicago; the cuts from the holes that an old man cut with them were clean, and the two short wood pegs, bison-sinew tethers looped around the ends, clean, shoved into the chest. Assiniboine dancers clench the eagle-bone whistle between the lips and brushes of sage in clenched fists, and dance looking at the pole at the center of the Lodge. The way the Sioux boys do it is very dramatic indeed: they lean back hard, putting their whole weight on those cords. It's not the cords that break, it's the skin that was pierced, the pectoral area. The skin rips out. Sioux blood doesn't drip, it cascades. One year a Blackfeet dancer danced that way too, at the Assiniboine Lodge. The preferred rips are symmetrical. They heal up like big burns the width of fingers, big old raised welts. Assiniboines don't do it that way, with the big drama of the big blood all down the chest. It's no quieter at an Assiniboine Medicine Lodge than at a Sioux Sun Dance, but there's less blood, less chest-ripping. Piercing is sacrifice enough.

Ever after, the sight of a pole brings back the feel of that blood-tickle.

In Akron, I saw a pole—an erect oak log—called the Grant Club Pole. It is like a bare telephone pole, and about as tall. The blue New York State historical marker explains that it's the third pole in that place. The first was erected by the Grant Club of Akron, New York, the political organization that supported Ulysses S. Grant's campaign for president. My home village of Angola, New York, never had such a pole even though it and all the other villages on the lake plain were all in Grant country too. Grandmother's mother's brothers and her father, too, had all fought for the Union in the Civil War, which means that they served under

General Grant. Great-grandmother herself had been born during Grant's first term as president. On a summer's day one hundred and forty years later, I'd stopped my car to look at a campaign poster dating from her childhood in a rural Yankee village in upstate New York.

The original pole lasted fifty years or so, then its replacement needed replacing. The current Grant Pole looks sturdy. It stands straight.

The pole demands a context. It's as incongruous as a single marble Doric column standing in a desert. Old pictures of these old campaign poles and of "liberty poles" always include crowds. The crowds were there for the campaign—to hear speeches, to celebrate, to give voice. Today there's just a bare pole about 30 feet tall. It sticks up out of a little patch of grass. Somebody's retail business goes on in the background, and the main street of town passes along in front of it, linking the highway and the village center. The pole itself is a leftover from an event that would have overwhelmed the village center, which is a leafy common across the creek bridge and up the road a bit. The common is the square the like of which is in every village in New England and New York, for the white folks who made a village here came from New England, organized their governments as in New England, their villages, their clapboard houses, their Congregational and Episcopal churches, their kin networks, their farms. This pole was erected outside the village center, though; this pole was a rally point at which there were bonfires, march-band music, soldiers, hot rhetoric.

I could not pass this pole by because of other poles I stopped to investigate twenty years before when I was driving on Route 2 in Montana, the road they call the High Line, along the north shore of the Missouri River. The bare nude standing poles I saw there were an abandoned Medicine Lodge, what the Assiniboines call Tibi Tanga. Those poles were from the year before. The Assiniboine men who made the Medicine Lodge put those poles up for an event, and then the event was over, and the whole construction stood there in the weather. An old Medicine Lodge looks like the skeleton of a carousel or merry-go-round in the daytime, a bare carousel stripped of colored lights, without ponies, without a stamped-steel floor. It's just a circle of man-high logs with the forks pointing up, with smaller logs resting in the forks, bridging the uprights, all circling a big forked center pole. And here's how they make a sort of a roof: into the fork of the center pole they rest the leafy untrimmed tops of long, long, skinny saplings laid atop the bridges of the man-high logs that form the outer circle. It looks like a carousel without a continuous roof, but with this big pile of brush at its apex. When the event is on, there are people all around, inside and outside this circle of standing forked logs. From outside one can't see inside because the space between the uprights is fenced with the leafy branches of the cottonwood tree that was ritually felled, attacked and dismembered by the men who made the Medicine Lodge. At night, there's a fire inside this structure, and voices declaiming or singing or just talking, and it's a living structure. It's all about life, actually. It recapitulates the structure of the cosmos. That's why the men put it up. "*Heca hena oyate ki ni pi kte no*," said the old man whose grandfather had actually visited General Grant, and who'd had his picture taken with him in the Indian Treaty room of the Old Executive Office Building. "We do this that the people may live," he said, or, because the word *oyate* signifies "nation," too, "We do this that the nation may live," all centered on that tall trunk of a cottonwood tree, the one with the cottonwood leaves bunched at its fork.

That's what the texts of the speeches have always been about back in Akron, too: we do this for the nation. There are brown photographs and grey photographs in the Erie County Historical Society. It's not work to hear the speeches that accompanied the Grant Club pole as the election of 1872 approached. We Americans all study that history in school. That was the election in which men waved the bloody shirt—literally stood up on platforms and held aloft their bloodstained Union Army uniforms—to remind their fellow men to vote for the party that had gone to war to save the Union, as had the men of the 112th New York Volunteers from all those villages of the lake plain there in Grant country. This was Yankee Protestant Republican territory. These were the villages that gave their young men to General Grant's army. They went south to destroy Secession and to preserve the Union. Their own ancestors had fought the British in the 1770s, in the Revolution; then the sons of the Revolutionary generation had fought the British in 1812 to win Western New York back again. They'd fought Senecas both times, Senecas and other Iroquois allied with the King. Come the Civil War, they fought under a Seneca named Ely Parker, from a mile upstream of the Grant Club Pole.

In 1872 when they put up the first Grant Club Pole, General Grant was President. He'd been the warrior who'd led the nation to victory over Secession. He and the warriors from Akron and Angola had gone to war and saved the Union, the nation.

They had also, incidentally but not primarily, triumphed over sin. They'd ended slavery. Western New York State and these specific villages of the lake plain had been far more than merely hospitable to abolitionism: they had hosted the last stations on the Underground Railroad. Their church undercrofts, their barns, their farmhouse attics, their sheds had all sheltered runaway slaves. Roads from the south and from the east and the Erie Canal's own tow-path were traveled by those who had escaped and who were bound for Buffalo and for its harbor, from whose Central Wharf one can still see freedom's beacon, in the form of a lighthouse on Canada's south shore, just a short sail away.

But when they went into Grant's army, the boys from Akron and Buffalo and Angola were going off to save the Union, mainly. The Union was the sacred trust violated by Secession. Preserving the Union was Grant's great message when he was first elected president, which is when he'd appointed Ely Parker, the Seneca from Akron, as his Commissioner of Indian Affairs. In his second term, Grant was again the brave commander, again leading a generation of young men to righteous conquest, this time a conquest of the tribes of the plains, especially the Sioux of the Sun Dance and also the Assiniboine of the Medicine Lodge, because Grant's goal was so to create a continental union and bind coast to coast. Grant electioneered in 1868 as a hero and deliverer, and he did it again in 1872. And it was only ten years after when, with Grant dead of cancer, Grant's Republican Party would be thought of as corrupt, and his own presidency as inept, and his war as historic and no longer politically current, except in Akron. The Democratic mayor of Buffalo, who was also the sheriff of Akron's county and then the governor of Akron's state of New York, the stunning political phenomenon named Grover Cleveland, might sweep into the presidency ten years after this Akron pole was first erected, but Akron stayed then and now as Republican as the day when Akron erected the first Grant Club Pole.

Akron still stays Republican. Akron keeps the pole. When the original fell, Akron replaced it. When it fell, Akron replaced it. Doubtless will again.

It was a cool and lovely July in Buffalo, New York, where Akron is more exotic and more distant from the city than is Canada. Buffalo borders Canada. Buffalo rides bicycles over the Peace Bridge to Canada, over the river that the Senecas and the British crossed in 1813 when they burned Buffalo. Buffalo now rents cottages on the beach there, just across from Buffalo harbor; prosperous Buffalo owns beach-houses on the Canadian shore. Rowdy boys pile into cars and brassily tell Customs Canada exactly where they're headed on a Friday night, which is to the naughty Canadian bars with the naughty girls who "dance" nude for them, sliding up and down their brass poles. After Grant defeated Secession and saved the Union, rowdy Buffalo boys who hated Queen Victoria piled their Irish selves into boats and crossed the Niagara River into Canada in what Americans call the Fenian Raid. They marched around provoking Victoria's citizens because those Buffalo rowdies were Irish and they wanted the Queen out of Ireland. Victoria's subjects fought back, threw them out, and demanded that she give them their own country to run and go and run Ireland herself without involving the Canadians any more. Every July, the Canadians celebrate Canada Day, the day Victoria gave Canadians Canada. The Assiniboines used to call Canada *Ina Tamakoce*, Grandmother's Land, recognizing Victoria.

In Canada across the way from Buffalo in July, at a party at the summer home of a prosperous friend, I saw another pole. No tickle this time. This pole was the great huge wide stump of a 150-year-old cottonwood tree, new. It had a tablecloth on it.

Ancient towering cottonwoods frame my friend's view of Lake Erie from the dune on which sit the beach-houses. His house is in New England white clapboard; it could be a house in Akron, or in Angola, or in Vermont. His slope of lawn slopes to a tennis-court-sized patch of sand, which gives way to an acre of lake-edge reeds, cattails and marsh, also framed by cottonwoods. This landscape is half a mile from freedom's beacon, the lighthouse at Point Abino, just west along the Canadian shore; Buffalo Harbor is clear and visible east, just across this end of Lake Erie, so close that Buffalo's own old lighthouse is in clear view, and the indefinable beginning of the channel called the Niagara River is just off to the left, past those trees. On either side of this lakeside lot are groves of cottonwoods and maples and catalpas and tulip magnolias, impossibly big walnuts, straight basswoods and beeches, and small trees, nut trees and sumacs and elderberries of the native Carolinian forest of which so little is left on the U.S. shore but of which Canada has a surfeit. Herons croaked in high roosts among them. Widgeons and teal and mallards and black-duck gabble and splash around in the rocky shallows at their feet before settling down in the twilight. Beyond the reeds and the trees is the lake. In 1688, a deer or a grasshopper or a Seneca saw this same slice of shore, and the Sieur de la Salle's sailing ship, the Gryphon, the first-ever sailing-ship in North America, sailed past this very place, the first ship ever powered here by wind.

And on this slice of shore my countryman had hewed down a towering cottonwood—16,000 pounds, so the tree-man had told him, of tree. Eight tons. A cottonwood. I already said that. I did indeed shudder, like a horse shudders.

Cottonwoods cut down and placed in the correct manner, in a circle around a big forked trunk, linked each to another and all to the center pole, become special objects. The Assiniboine call it *chan wakan. Chan wakan*, "sacred tree," is what a cottonwood becomes when it is cut down by two men who are veterans of combat, then hauled to the place where a shaman will direct a *Ti Jax Wachib*, or "house-building dance," or Medicine Lodge.

I shuddered at the stump in Canada. The feeling was something like grief, looking at that stump, and at the chunks of trunk and of the big branches which now served, variously, as drinks trolleys, end tables and stools for the Canada Day party. Even as the night came in and the soft fog of wine descended, I was at a wake for that great tree and for a piece of the sacred that had been put down.

It was too great a tree ever to have served as the center pole for a Medicine Lodge. I can report that the *chan wakan* that was felled for the 1985 Assiniboine Medicine Lodge was back-breakingly large, much larger than the cottonwood we'd cut in the previous year when I first became a Medicine Lodge-man. But it was no giant like this Canadian one. We were strong men then, but even in our strength this giant was too big, too big ever to be cut down for a Lodge. In Canada in July, I drank more wine, and mourned the cottonwood that had been too big even to be yard décor.

Back home in Grant Country I saw poles. The alabaster obelisk in Niagara Square in Buffalo is the monument to McKinley, the president who defeated Grover Cleveland, and who then came to the world's fair in Grover Cleveland's home town of Buffalo and was shot by the anarchist Czolgosz, Leon Czolgosz, stupidly, confusingly, a Pole from Cleveland. The Ohio politician McKinley's monument is an Egyptian form of pole from a place whose trees have no roots. McKinley's monument is stone, not a tree, not like the Grant pole, which is an oak from the farm of a patriotic Akron family. That family in 1988 made their contribution to Akron tradition by giving a straight oak to replace the one that had lasted since 1929, which had replaced the Akron original.

But the form is the same as McKinley's monument. It is straight, tall, single, centered, bare. The center-pole of the Medicine Lodge has a rainbow painted on one side, a thunderbird on the other.

Across the Niagara River from Buffalo, downstream past Niagara Falls and above the great whirlpool, back in Canada where my friend cut the cottonwood, is Brock's Monument. Brock's Monument is a towering pole of stone that the Anglo-Canadians erected to commemorate Brock for having repelled the American invasion during the War of 1812. That was when *our* English-born fought *their* English-born and each side fought with and against Senecas, again, over the question of which of us would hold these riverbanks and lakeshores and endless parklands, and which of us would build our identical New England white-clapboard houses here: men who hailed kings, or men who hailed presidents. We stood off, as before, but Brock got his tall pole monument when it was over, a hundred years later, when Canada needed to remind itself to be its own nation, and so needed its own pole.

In 1984 and again in 1985, I sang and I worked and I carried out the tasks of a Lodge-builder when I helped put a cottonwood pole up. When we were finished with our construction, we used what we had built. When we were finished using it, we left it. Near the border that divides Saskatchewan from Montana, there are circles of cottonwood each of these two dozen years, each with a grand cottonwood trunk in the center of each circle of smaller trunks. Those trees have been replaced annually by the Assiniboines, but none of these are monuments like Grant's or McKinley's or Brock's. There is a pole, circled by poles, for every year since my time there, and going back a few years before. The poles fade, and are replaced.

I see them everywhere.

Trees: I helped raise $60,000 for the Tree of Life playground at the Jewish Community Center.

Poles: I used to be a quite the observant Episcopalian, looking upwards to the guy imprisoned on the timbers.

Trees: My daughters and I, as many of them as will fit with me, lie back in a hammock strung between the old sap-dripping yellow pines, and we look up, not at each other, and we talk, and we hum songs, and we see the birds in the boughs way high above, and the sky beyond.

The folklorist Mircea Eliade described the myths of the cycle of life. He wrote about the shamans of Central Asia who would climb the short trees of the tundra, and from them visit the other world. Druids had their oaks, Lithuanians their groves of oaks, in which they remained pagan, unconverted to Christianity until the years when Englishmen landed in New York and in Canada, and long after their countrymen had founded universities and fought off invaders from Central Asia.

The Norse had Yggdrasil, the World Tree or Tree of Life. The Baltic peoples had oaks. Christmas trees, sacred oaks, the oak at Runnymede where the aristocrats of England forced King John to sign the Magna Carta. Germanic tribes and Lithuanian tribes and everybody else living around the Baltic and North seas muttered around in groves of big oaks.

But we Americans cut down trees and then put them back up again. Monuments here have a grain to them. A single commemorative tree-and-plaque installation has now become, along a bicycle path, two dozen trees and two dozen plaques. The monuments are all young trees with plaques at their bases like the Grant Club Pole in Akron. The trees aren't yet mighty oaks soaring like the Grant Club Pole or heavy-barked Canadian cottonwoods erected like Assiniboine *chan wakan*, but the expectation is that they one day will be. They are spaced so as to become monumental. To walk that suburban path is to stride a cemetery, except that it's linear and it's all supposed to be about life, because that's what the suburbs are—alive with young families, with students at a great suburban university, with wildlife (herons, muskrats, mallards, a white egret, fat munching groundhogs on every roadside) adjusting to the new housing and office parks under construction. All those new trees, and yet in our old house (erected in 1887 by Crane, the Lumber King)—in my old house, which is in the big city, I look into a back yard with our grove of sticky yellow pines planted when the house was built. Out my front doorway is a streetscape of linden trees only forty years old, because forty years ago, Dutch elm disease struck, and wiped out the cathedral-arches of towering elms which made of this city a forested place. The great American Elms lined Frederick Law Olmsted's parkways as well: Bidwell Parkway named for the General of the Civil War, McKinley Parkway named for the murdered president whose main monument is an alabaster pole; Chapin Parkway, Lincoln Parkway, and especially, most especially and most sadly, Humboldt Parkway, named for the princely German von Humboldt, who came into the interior of America to see the forest primeval, and the Assiniboine plains primeval—the Assiniboine plains of the Missouri River basin. He described Assiniboines. His painter painted Assiniboines.

In the 1960s, when the foresters came to fell the elms of Humboldt Parkway, the engineers followed close on, and dug a deep trench where the parkway elms had been, and put an expressway in it. And like ditches that drain a pond, the expressways drained away the city's university and the city's middle class and the city's young families, exactly in the years when the city lost its monumental trees.

But new trees grow.

Lindens are fast-growing and strong, fragrant in spring, and sturdy of branch. It was a scene from Central Asia when my tricky daughter egged me on, higher and higher, to climb with her to see what she claimed only she could see, but that I could see too, if only I would climb higher. My friend the reporter saw all this and giggled conspiratorially with her as I grasped skinnier and skinnier branches. Whenever he emails me, the subject line reads "Man In A Tree."

It is the trees that pull our eyes up into the holy. Trees bring the young back. Thus in this city, this old lake plain city, much new effort now infuses the parks and parkways. Young people eager for a new monument themselves bring new growth, and if there are no ancient elms for them to venerate, there are still ancient maples and great spreading oaks and big beeches and big copper beeches, too, with their curious bark that looks like the skin of an elephant. There are cottonwoods but this is the east, so they are not *chan wakan*. One towering maple nearby turns such a bright yellow in October that it blazes in the streetlight, all night long, until the November winds denude it. One oak in Delaware Park is so big that York, Lancaster, Northumberland, Gloucester and the rest could yet ride up and under it force a pact on a king. One cottonwood is so big that it towers like Brock's tall pole of a monument over a grove of cottonwoods, near the water, which grew from its white scattered seeds in long-ago Julys. In June they flower, and around Canada Day, they seed, and offer to remake the world.

Hunting the enemy

The following is an entry from the 1907 *Handbook of American Indians North of Mexico*, Volume II, published by the Smithsonian Institution.

> Sun dance. The sun dance was a ceremony confined to the Plains tribes. It was performed by the Arapaho, Cheyenne, Siksika, and Cree of Algonquian stock; the Dakota, Assiniboin, Mandan, Crows, Ponca, and Omaha of Siouan stock; the Pawnee of Caddoan stock; the Kiowa; and the Shoshoni and Ute of Shoshonean stock. In its ceremonial forms the Sun dance of all these tribes seems related, and it may be regarded as a summer solstice ceremony . . . Among all tribes there is a division of the ceremony into secret rites and a public performance. The secret rites, occupying 1 day to 4 days, are held in a tipi of preparation, which occupies a position alone in the camp circle . . . On the last day of the secret rites a great lodge is built in the center of the camp circle, the selection of the site being the office of a special individual and attended with rites. The gathering of suitable timber for the lodge and its erection are usually done by one or more warrior organizations. The selection of the center pole is accompanied with special rites and usually is in charge of the most noted warrior or warriors of the tribe. The lodge varies from a roofless inclosure with a tall center pole, as among the Siouan tribes, to a partially covered structure, consisting of an outer row of forked uprights connected by crossbars, from which rafter poles extend to the fork of the center pole. The lodge is from 60 to 100 ft. in diameter, and is always provided with an opening toward the E. On the completion of the lodge, generally late in the afternoon, the priests formally abandon the secret tipi of

> preparation, and reside until the termination of the ceremony in the Sun-dance lodge proper.
>
> [O]ne of the most common rites of the public performance is that of voluntary self-laceration or torture. The two most common forms of torture were (1) to attach the free end of a reata that had been fastened to the center fork of the lodge, to a skewer inserted in the loose skin of the breast, and (2) to drag around inside the camp circle one or more buffalo-skulls by a reata the other end of which was attached to a skewer inserted in the back . . .
>
> The lodge itself represents this earth, as the home of man. The altar symbolizes the essence of life or spring of fertilization. In the fork of the center pole was the nest of the thunderbird. Into the nest a digging stick was usually thrust, symbolic of that used by the woman who in the well-known tale climbed to the sky in pursuit of a porcupine and later gave birth to the Sun Boy. While the center pole itself, with its bands of red and black paint, is symbolic of earth and heaven, and typifies the supreme medicine or mystery, it may be regarded as symbolizing also, especially at the time of its capture, the common enemy of the tribe.
>
> The Sun dance, being strongly opposed by the missionaries because it was utterly misunderstood, and finding no favor in official circles, has been for many years an object of persecution, and in consequence is extinct among the Dakota, the Crows, and the Mandan, of the Siouan stock, and among the Pawnee and the Kiowa. It is still performed by the Cree, Siksika, Arapaho, Cheyenne, Assiniboin, Ponca, Shoshoni, and Ute. Its disappearance among certain of these tribes, such as the Ponca, is near at hand, for it has lost part of its rites and has come to be largely a spectacle for gain rather than a great religions ceremony.
>
> The sun dance was not only the greatest ceremony of the Plains tribes, but was a condition of their existence . . .

In the early 1980s, some young scholars traveled from Chicago for the central Northern Plains to do field investigation among the aboriginals of that area. They were all either working on their doctoral theses, or were already teaching at universities after having earned their doctoral degrees. Their lodestone was the D'Arcy McNickle Center for the History of the American Indian, an institute located in a private research library in Chicago, on the Near North Side, called the Newberry Library.

I was, at that time, one of those young scholars. We tended to organize by subspecialty, even though many toiled together on the large McNickle Center projects, especially the massive compilation of the documentary history of the Iroquois. My area was the Sioux, even though I came from, had family history with, and had personal knowledge of the Iroquois of my native Western New York. A happenstance meeting with a Lakota speaker had rekindled my interest in Native North America. When it came time to choose a dissertation topic, I chose one in Sioux because my buddy Calvin had helped me learn enough to pick through some Lakota-language manuscripts.

The Newberry was ours. We made it so. We attended lectures and conferences there, and drank beer at its post-conference parties. We would just hang around there. We scratched around in its archives. We forayed up to Milwaukee to scratch around in the Jesuits' archives at Marquette University, just for the heck of it, and for the Milwaukee beer. Milwaukee is where I found the originals of a German Jesuit's word-lists—his own handwritten notes—for his monumental English-Lakota dictionary, which I'd first found at the Newberry. I was stunned by the discovery. I read his letters to his superiors. I read reports of Indian Agents to their superiors about conditions there in the Dakotas, where the Jesuits labored among the conquered Lakota. Then I returned to Chicago and spent weeks and weeks in the Newberry getting more detail from its collections. I read chronicles of hardship: drought, searing summer heat, dead children, brutal winters, drink, exploitation, isolation. Historical loss.

But in Chicago, our contemporaries were making their way oblivious to all this. I would step out into the winter streetscapes near the Newberry Library with a head full of the difficult and distant Lakota-language formulations of those handwritten texts I was translating—and almost always run into a newspaper reporter, or somebody I knew from politics, because the *Chicago Tribune*, the *Chicago Sun-Times* and all the tv and radio stations were fairly close by. I was living a dual life then: by day a reporter, full of this world, by night a Siouan scholar, full of that.

One wanted to be one, or the other. Personal choice was not so much the question, as was this one: how will I live? Pay rent? Eat? When I arrived in Chicago in 1975, there were three daily newspapers, two big youth-oriented weeklies, the usual array of radio and tv stations plus a monthly magazine, like *New York*, called *Chicago*. Catching work as a stringer was easy. I sold stories all over. In 1977, I joined the staff of one of the weeklies and built my clip-file in earnest. The best fun was covering politics. I had fun, I made money, I moved ahead in a big profession in a big place.

Then the world changed. The *Daily News* closed. Hundreds of experienced reporters hit the streets. Newspaper Guild members with big by-lines elbowed with neophytes for jobs. Ownership of the *Sun-Times* changed, more reporters hit pavement. Recession, inflation. There was lots of room for my work, but it wasn't going to get me a further career unless I did something to expand the portfolio.

Leaving for Peoria or Bloomington or Buffalo was not an option. I had scratched my way up in Chicago, and too proud to go anyplace small. My pals were all piling up advanced degrees, so graduate school seemed a respectable and reasonable choice. A specialty in which I was actually interested seemed so, too. I won a fellowship, taught big classes, wrote my papers, translated my Lakota texts, worked on the credential while keeping current in the news business.

Then I met Tashunga Saba.

The Newberry Library had a program for bringing native elders in for visits and short-term residencies. It was a little oral history, a little theater, a little (before the term arose) 'political correctness' for those of us who were combining study in history with a study in the field and calling the result Ethnohistory. By and by, as the mores of the Ethnohistorians filtered into the scholarship business as conducted at the Newberry Library, more actual Indians would come around—mostly thoroughly-acculturated graduate students who happened to have tribally-enrolled bloodlines, but also in-from-the-field tribal historians. Most of the latter were elderly men with patronage jobs in reservation governments.

In that parade of old men with the weathered faces of ranchers, or the softened, smoothed faces of veteran drinkers, came an Assiniboine from Montana. Young amongst the old, prospective and vital among so many retirees content to give meandering talks in accented English about their lives on one range or another (causing no end of knowing glances and I-told-you-so nods of mainstream scholarly heads, and Okay, fine, they were right), came Tashunga Saba.

What he did that caught my attention was to give the first fifteen minutes of his seminar on history of the Assiniboines *in Assiniboine*. I was impressed. I was also thrilled that I understood some of it; Assiniboine is very close to the Lakota I'd been studying, as close or closer than Norwegian is to Swedish, Italian to Sicilian. After his talk, he indulged us, politely, and translated, thus: I am come to tell you the history of the Assiniboines, and I will tell you the truth, from the beginning. The Assiniboines began when Inktomi sent Muskrat diving out of his canoe, down into the flood, to bring back the mud from which Inktomi would make the earth. The history of the Assiniboines involved a great oversea migration from the north shore of *Mni Mu*, the Thunder Lake, across to land identifiable as the Minnesota shore of Lake Superior. The history of the Assiniboines involved massive death at the unseeable hand of the pox that left lodges blackened and whole villages dead.

As surely as if he were recounting the list of the kings of England, Tashunga Saba wove together the entire time-line, from creation story to the last tribal elections, in as compelling a performance as any I have ever heard, from plaintiff's counsel or senator-elect or dramatic soliloquist.

He

had presence.

He had wit and charm and a fluency with the written documents of the traders, soldiers, missionaries, historians and anthropologists that the assembled scholars could comprehend. The unique, proprietary material was bonus, and changed the nature of the event in that seminar room, for there before us was the self-aware subject, himself an investigator, and officially, as it were, designated by his own nation to keep, interpret, teach and also to *make* history both sacred and profane.

This man, I would learn at long suppers, was also a cultural revolutionary, a politician, and a shaman-in-training who, before he left for Montana, conversed easily with me in my anything-but-fluid Lakota, made interlingual puns, and invited me to participate in the profound, foreign, exotic, exclusive and arduous ritual known in Lakota English as the Sun Dance, but in distinct Assiniboine English as a wholly separate entity: The Lodge.

But I had to train.

Training meant working out in a simulated environment in Chicago.

In the polar January of 1984, a couple of scholars drove in a disheveled eleven-year-old Thunderbird down Division Street to an antique called the Russian and Turkish Baths. The place was a useful relic in a neighborhood once dominated by a big orthodox synagogue nicknamed The Glitz (it had served Chicago's Galician Jews). The march of ethnic succession in Chicago was itself remarkable: the Jews left; The Glitz became, first, a Russian Orthodox church, and then a Latino neighborhood center. The Mexican at the booth took our eight bucks apiece for flip-flops, sheaths and towels, and with a shift of his slow eyes, directed us down a corridor lined with black-framed photographs of forgotten local boxers to the locker room. We changed, then went downstairs to the hot rooms.

Brown young Mexicans, and blue-veined and pale old men with their religion carved in their tenderest flesh, sat or reclined in intolerable heat on cedar bleachers. Our leader instructed: twenty minutes in, then out for a breath of merely warm air in the shower room, then back in with the veterans, four times, timed to songs that would have been intrusive and absurd in such a place. At the time, I owned no songs anyway. I counted out minutes on my plastic watch, and watched the Aztecs fill five-gallon buckets with ice water from the tap that somehow stayed cold in that place, then douse each other. The water splashed my singeing arms, and I wanted some, but the scholar shook his head.

"We don't do that," he said. Oh. And who, by the way, is "we"?

Without the distraction of singing, that heat is exhausting. I sat on as high a step on those cedar bleachers as I could tolerate, and longingly watched the Mexicans fill and refill those chit'lin-buckets full, and smile and sputter and spit at the relief of it plastering their straight black hair down. I looked at my feet and heard the old-man voices in Polish, Yiddish, Russian and English. The young voices were Mexican Spanish. I tried translating from every language I could parse because I was desperate to hurry the clock.

It didn't work.

The best I could manage was ten minutes. There was no steam to cover my abrupt departures, only the heat that steamed my glasses. The veteran scholar was stoic, or impervious; he stayed, tapping his knee with patient fingers to the tune of a silent song.

For relief, we went to the wood-paneled sauna, which (I surmised) must have been the Russian of the two types of baths advertised. The real heat was in the Turkish room, whose walls were yellowed white enamel. With bare nubs of breath I told everybody that those Turks must be made of tougher stuff. The scholar only grunted.

Thus did we train. We did our training on Sunday mornings in a year when eight dollars was a lot. We were a couple of guys with the first bulges of what would become permanent middle-age girth, which made us fit right in with that congregation. I got so bold as to take it upon myself to open the iron door to the Turkish furnace and toss half a chit'lin bucket of cold water onto the coils, which sent the temperature even higher. Unlatching that iron door and throwing water was a way of demonstrating some mastery, and of telling all assembled that I was getting ready for the real thing. In that white room, with its dozen or fifteen strangers pushing sweat out, convinced to a man that the process is a guarantor of health, no one spoke much, or did much, or read books or the Sunday paper though the clear heat was dry enough. It was enough just to sit through it, watching my watch.

In the real thing, called in Assiniboine *inipi*, on a cool Montana spring evening, the space is dark and warm even before the fire-tender passes in the first pitchfork-full of hot lava-stones. It's close and hot and dark as the womb, and if in your mind's eye you can imagine the earth as a woman reclining, the *inipi* is a fair model of the swell of her pregnancy. There in that tiny enclosed darkness sit those white plastic buckets with their untouchable cool water and the relief you can only hope for as the men crawl through the oval orifice on the south end of the structure and breathe each other's breath and sweat buckets of amniotic sweat, but there is no relief, because it's only the shaman who touches the water, and he only with his brooms of fresh-picked sage.

Seconds after entering the *inipi* in that spring of 1984, I understood that that Muscovite refusenik on Division Street months before had done me a favor when he'd asked Please, gentlemen, to be putting heat at somewhat higher level, yes? because in Moscow we have baths where temperature is two hundred sixty degrees *Fah*renheit, and so may we now? Breathless, we acceded, and watched the man's two big sons slap their dad's back with birch boughs, to what end I still don't quite know.

But even Moscow-style heat wasn't enough preparation for the *inipi*, for which the High Plains English is "sweat lodge."

The Assiniboines take two of those five-gallon plastic buckets into their sweat lodges, but they're not chit'lin buckets. The labels say U.S. Department of Agriculture, and until religion gets hold of them, they're full of surplus—flour, or oats, or lard.

The *wichashta wakan* dips his sage hand-brooms in the water, and makes terrible burning billows of steam by shaking the brooms over fire-heated stones that are in a pit mere inches from the curled toes of men packed into that low belly of a structure. The steam is no relief: it's not the cold Division Street dousing that washes away all that your pores have given up to heat. It's heat that would drive you to hallucination, or vision, if you weren't distracted by singing.

My veteran scholar-friend from Chicago, who accompanied me to Tashunga Saba's sweat lodge, had an advantage over me. He'd been to many sweats. His other advantage was that he knew where he was. My first time out, I'd been off the Empire Builder only an hour before we'd piled into pickups and vans to drive from the center of the reservation community, which looked even poorer than the town I grew up in, yet curiously more ordered, down mud and gravel roads to a riverside glen. I'd have preferred a little more time to get my sea legs, for there were a few incongruities to assimilate—such as standing in a very suburban ranch-style house's parlor with a pretty young woman whose dark brown hair was, if I am not mistaken, in a Toni perm, in the Great American Desert 1984 suburban way that had much more to do with 1964, politely as I could do so, reassuring her that there was no problem that she was behind in making dinner for us all. Assiniboine protocol requires that food be ever-ready, but I was willing to make do with a glass of juice.

After all, she'd just come from aerobics class.

I could also have used a tipoff on the current configuration of the classical Assiniboine *inipi*.

The ethnologists' sketches I'd read at the Newberry Library had left me expecting a structure made of willow saplings bent to form something like the skeleton of a tortoise's carapace, which turned out to be true enough; and that over this framework there would be bison hides leather-side down, and Army or trade blankets. I'm sure that that had, classically, when the Army was handing out blankets brought in by rail from Blanket Town (i.e., Chicago), been the case.

But those were bookish notions.

On the north bank of the *Mnishoshe*, some dozens of miles west from where the muddy waters ease into the next state, the materials chosen for covering the frame were canvas drop-cloths, sheets of black and of royal-blue two-mil PVC tarp, and long green sections of shag carpeting, backing-side down.

We piled out of the trucks and formed a standing circle. Boys got the fire going with wood that had already been carefully stacked for the purpose. The fire-stones for the *inipi* pit were also already stacked, in with the wood.

I stripped with the other guys—a bunch of Assiniboines in their young twenties, Tashunga Saba the shaman, the scholar, and an older guy, round and white-looking except for face and forearms. These were none of them veterans of sweats. Some would be dancers at the Lodge, some Lodge-Builders, some helpers in the general sort of way that a big enterprise needs extras to make it all happen. What they really were were a shaman's recruits to a cultural revolution.

One of the boys stayed outside with the fire, now burned down a few ricks to reveal rocks glowing red. I piled into the *inipi*, moving sunwise around the interior, increasingly tense and claustrophobic as it became apparent in that dimness that *all* of us were going to sit in this thing.

A single fire-heated stone was enough to make that space suitable for yeast-rising bread. A second stone made it hot enough for baking. The first round of our *inipi* session took ten stones. With the entry of a all those air-breathing men stripped of all their club jackets, jeans, muddy sneakers and J.C. Penney cowboy shirts with the pointed collars and the faux mother-of-pearl snaps, the *inipi* was hot enough soon enough that I knew I was going to have trouble lasting through even the first round. When the tent-flap was down and the last piece of early-evening spring sky disappeared, what breath I had left me. I seized up. "Can't do it now, man," was my brilliant analysis, croaked in a voice I'd never heard before. Without hesitation, the flap flipped up, and I left the woman's belly the way I'd come into the world, and there I was again: wet, outside, cold. And *chapunga*-bait.

I'd crawled into a close, breathless darkness which was the model of all our mothers, bare-ass to the packed earth, with glowing rocks red in the pit and smooth bodies quickly transformed from dry to glistening in the tiny glow, and so I could say that I'd been in a sweat lodge, but that didn't quite cut it. The shaman had the good grace to say "He's the fire-keeper," so there was a role for me that I could handle—important, necessary, but subsidiary. A boy's role.

Bright-eyed but humiliated, the twenty hours of the train ride having worked their vengeance, I put my clothes on and listened. The tent muffled it all, and puffs of breeze made the thick arms of the cottonwoods groan as their new leaves caught wind.

The show went ahead. The shaman spoke first in English, for the benefit of the young Assiniboines who knew their people's language less well than I did, and then he called out the first prayer with the ancient formula I would soon hear so many times: *Han, mitugashi hokshi togap, unshiyana o*, which is to say, Grandfather, First Man, pity us. Taking up the gourd rattle that before the flap closed had lain on a small raised rectangle of sand between the rock-fire and the entrance, he led the men in a song I'd never heard before, in a language I'd learned some from books the Lakota of Chicago. To the accompaniment of what a dance-band audience would recognize as half a pair of maracas, the singers set about helping the shaman cure George, the whitish guy.

George was there because he was desperate for rescue from a condition of unknown cause or name. Though much past fifty and married decades to a Sioux woman (she is very like a Congresswoman I know: looks, arch manner and department-store jewelry, sweet and tough), he'd come for his first-ever sweat, because the unaccountable bruises on his back and belly had scared the reticence out of him.

Twilight. The shaman sang a verse, then the other muffled voices joined in for three repetitions. I heard brave joking and laughing and small sermons between songs, and wondered how in the hell they were able to keep it up inside that furnace.

The last verse of the fourth song was my signal: I opened the *inipi* flap to let steam and the fragrances of cedar-bark incense and sage billow out, and a chorus of sighs of relief that new and breathable air was coming in.

The respite was short. "*Ake*," came the command. Again.

Gingerly, I ladled the next stone out of the fire into the *inipi* on the tines of a pitchfork. The teenage experts, masters now, challenged my manhood for putting only one or two stones in per pass, but for Christ's own sake, it would have taken an aim only an inch off to burn shin or puncture instep. I said nothing; my next pass had four stones, and a loud-talker yelped when his inept leg-crossing put his ankle up against hot rocks. Lesson: don't screw with the firekeeper.

I closed the flap.

More songs: for this round, the same songs as the first time. I started to learn them. In my fatigue, I counted the verses with fingers, and looked around, and wanted to be a smoker again so that I'd have something to do and something to repel *chapungas*.

The round over, I flipped the flap and steam rushed out again. I was an expert now, too. I passed more stones in, glowing only red now as the heat began to leave them. But the heat and dearth of oxygen inside were costing the singers. Where in the first round there'd been an energy, even an exuberance to their singing, now there was tired duty. I wondered about whitish George: he was sitting at the right hand of the shaman, in the farthest reach of the lodge. An old, sick guy sitting in a tiny space with no light and no air and only steam held in by dropcloths and carpet-backing? My own somewhat wearied enthusiasm for this exoticism gave way to concern. And questions: how had George lived so long, married into the reservation community, without ever having joined in a sweat before? Was the racism here so abrupt and defining that it had never occurred to him to come until his current extremis?

Less steam, but not much less, issued forth after the third round. The boys near the entrance to that constructed cave leaned as far out as they could for the coolness and relief of unbreathed air. Ungrateful eyes watched my last forkfuls of hot stones go into the fire pit. I heard many hungry breaths for the last of the outside air as I lowered the flap for the last time.

The next songs were sung quickly, with all the enthusiasm of a chain gang in mid-afternoon. Then the shaman broke in for a long talk about what it all meant. About George's life, and work, and about knitting people together. About the power of the Lodge to comfort and make change in the lives of all whom it touches. About how important it was for everyone to know that George, after a lifetime of being oblivious to this power all around him, power that was ever celebrated right under his nose but without his attention, had made an offering of prayer cloths for the Lodge, cloths that their sweating and their singing tonight had blessed and sanctified.

Whether from happy anticipation that the ordeal would be soon be finished, or from inspiration, the pace of those last songs was brisk. As the last of the finger-reckoned vocables was sung, I threw open the flap to cheers. I gave a hand to unsteady drenched men slithering out of this mom-tent, wet as from their very first confinement, into that soft twilight. The scholar came, dizzy. The boys among them were restored to their old selves within minutes, rushing it of course, ready to tell everyone that they had done the first step.

The shaman pulled himself out; no forceps for him. Came then George, paler than before, unsteady but smiling, and, as he toweled off, greeted and touched by all.

Caesura

Somewhere along in the first few years of being a parent, I wrote an account of my travels among the Assiniboines of Montana, Saskatchewan and Alberta. I never wrote it all, nor will I. The troublesome fact is that to publish a word about any of this now is a betrayal of sorts. But it's twenty years on. Many of the persons portrayed are dead. Their names, and the names of people who aren't, are here rendered in Assiniboine, even if their names were only English when I got them. Place names too—now hidden by the toughest code of all, a language only infrequently written, a language now only infrequently spoken.

Over

Amtrak's Empire Builder took me there, all the way from the Union Station in Chicago, the port of the plains.

The ride was twenty hours through sleeping Minneapolis and the radiant dawn of the pothole topography of North Dakota, which is lush in spring: thick green grass, pintails and mallards dabbling, flashes of startling yellow on the wings of Plains blackbirds. Every American should take that train ride rather than a jet or a station-wagon full of bored, sticky children, because Americans need to see this country that the railroad helped conquer. They need to see it east to west. They need to see where the moisture of spring ends, just west of the Montana border, where the reservation begins.

Debarkation was at a siding with a squat gray wheat silo a few yards off the track. It is a modest town of five thousand called Tabex'a Wakpa, where the sunlight is sharp and the air clear. The shaman who met me there accepted a gift of tobacco, special cigarillos from the South Wabash Avenue tobacconist Iwan Ries. He drove me twenty miles to his residence in Easter Egg Village. His was a modest house, by now passed on to another family, one of a hundred or so in a small grid just north of the Great Northern tracks that my father's father used to ride in his capacity as an engineer on the Burlington line. Every house in Easter Egg Village is identical to its immediate neighbor. There were one-story and two-story versions, Levittown on the gumbo. Each and every one of these houses is wholly, unmitigatedly goofy and radically juxtaposed to the wrongest landscape in the world for tract houses. Each had its little tract of yard meant for Long Island-style thatches of fescue, but fescue is not an easy grow on the high plains of Montana, so the yards are bare gumbo and gravel in a not very exact replica of American suburbia. The name: it's a wisecrack become place-name. The company that makes those tablets that you drop into hot water, and then dip hard-boiled eggs in, may well have supplied the pastel turquoises, pinks, mustards and beiges that are the key distinguishing characteristics of these houses. A more fitting name I can't imagine, given that the material expression of Conqueror culture the Assiniboines get to see consists of things like Easter egg dye-kits, malt liquor, video games, Detroit cars and Saturday morning animated cartoons, the latter of which all—*all*—mature Assiniboine men of my acquaintance are inordinately, enthusiastically fond.

Especially Bugs Bunny. Maybe every American needs to see
Easter Egg Village, too.

We drove past a motley of feral dogs that loped comfortably after children on bikes. It looked like a suburb, except that the dogs that run after the children are big and unkempt and ugly, wild-looking enough that they could easily run down a straggler on training wheels just as they run down fawns.

The shaman's house was every house of every kid I grew up with, with the following difference: none of my friend's moms ever had a kitchen full tall, heavy men in cowboy shirts drinking green tea and eating bowls of tripe soup and venison stew and plates of wild turnips, *tinpsina*, fresh-dug. The men all spoke so very, very softly. The racial, historical, class clash was on.

Why, their eyes ask, why have you come?

You know why. It is to look at the pink in the centerfold. The men knew that they were specimens. Curiosities for the traveler, no matter that they were hardened by the labor of irrigation farming and ranching and oil-rig work in weather no educated white man from Back East would tolerate for more than the time it takes to walk from the parking garage to the office.

This is the United States. The traveler is a citizen. He is a scion of conquerors, of liberators. In their own kitchen, he faces the sons of the conquered.

At this point, every American should go home. The hate and grief of a century is in those eyes that say, You destroyed us. You turned us from men into objects of pity. Those eyes say, You killed our grandfathers, burned our villages, raped our grandmothers, made curios of our weapons, fetishes, clothes, buildings, beliefs.

But those soft voices said, welcome, friend. Eat. You are a friend of our friend. Did you see the one where Bugs Bunny dresses up like a *winkta* and marries Elmer Fudd? Of course I did. So I stayed, ate, told and heard stories, talked men's talk about the new Ford pickups, jeez, you hafta be *mas yuha* to even look at one. Turns out that a young Assiniboine prince, young Maza Wichashta of the famous Oda Shunga family, got stuck in the spring mud of a washed-out dirt road over near old Hubahu's house; they had to use horses and ropes to pull it through. *Ohan*, that was good news. Good news too that old Indechan from Saskatchewan will be coming this year with his songs, real old-style songs from the Canadian Assiniboines of the Plains, that are so different from the Stoney kind from the mountains near Calgary, which are so hard to understand that it might as well be a foreign language they're in, like French or something.

True

foreignness, right here in America. It was all the more jarring because the 18-wheelers carrying freight from Chicago rolled past only a hundred yards north. And into the conversation about Indechan and his songs, and his old Cree friends from Carry-the-Kettle and Red Pheasant who'd be coming too, intruded another sound: Xexaka Sha's big slow son had turned the TV on to catch the last inning of the Cubs game in the room just past the half-wall, the living room, that has the comfortable J.C. Penney Early American décor. Pure J.C. Penney, augmented by images of Indians that could have been purchased right where the furniture was. I slept under a plaster-cast miniature statue based on a famous image every American has seen, called "The End of the Trail." Slumping brave, lowered lance, horse with head down.

The next morning, the shaman retrieved his religious paraphernalia from a spotless cellar that has a sump pump that that climate will never command into action. (For Christ's sake, a sump pump, in an aluminum-sided house designed for Long Island.) The tools: a bison skull, painted with primary colors; a moose antler for chopping and mixing tobacco; a small bison hide whose hair is so short that it looks like a pony's skin; drums: the hand-drums, hide stretched over hoops of wood and sewn with gut or sinew, each with a cross of sinew in the back for ease of holding. There are beaters. There are pipes. There is a rattle. And there is a stack of pieces of cloth, cotton muslin mostly, a couple of yards apiece in red, yellow, green, white, blue, other colors of less consequence, all the pieces of solid hue.

With some of last night kitchen guys sitting or kneeling or squatting on the braided Early American rug, the shaman prays aloud just slightly faster than one can easily keep up with, using expressions or formulae not covered in the cobbled-together Assiniboine-language syllabus that a linguist got government money to write. Suddenly, an incense smell. It is sweetgrass. A dozen green and dry braids of it have appeared from the pockets of jeans jackets or from the little vinyl athletic grips, the kind that gaunt drifters and young soldiers have on their laps as they wait for the Greyhound to Minot.

One by one, men are bidden to stand. The shaman's helper holds up a little iron skillet with a sweetgrass braid smoldering in it that he set to fire with fire made from spark sparked the old way, with a fire-drill, while the shaman uses two fans made of eagle wing-feathers to brush the sweetgrass smoke over heads, shoulders, torsos, legs. All rub the smoke into clothes as if lathering up in the shower, and then smoke a long-stemmed pipe lit from the glowing end of the sweetgrass braid, passing the pipe sun-wise, clockwise, praying in Assiniboine if equipped to do so, tipping the half-yard-long pipestem to the four directions and then skyward and earthward both before and after the smoke.

The shaman thanks us in Assiniboine and in English. He tosses us each a pack of Marlboros, a little tobacco gift for we who will build the Tibi Tanga. The operative color here is red, the red of that fat inverted chevron that marks each pack, each pack a gift in return for the gift of our commitment. Reciprocity, not charity.

Then it's out to the caravan of trucks and vans and Delta 88s. Each takes up an item, a drum or a skin or a beater, and silently moves out.

Thus it begins.

Another Caesura

During the last years of Ronald Reagan's era, the poet Robert Bly wrote *Iron John*. A woman from my church shared her copy. My wife saw me reading it, and brought in a copy of *Esquire* magazine to show me. She held it up and said, "didn't you do this?" I extracted an arm from under my slurping child (got her granddad's thirst, does she), and looked.

It was a story about Robert Bly guys. There were photographs of white men nude to the waist, beating hand-held hoop drums about the size of oversized tambourines with the jingles off. Of white guys getting situated bare-ass inside what looked like a Sioux sweat lodge. Of white guys men solemnly painting each other's faces.

And this one: a shot of guys erecting a great penis-shaped log a dozen feet high in the center of a circle of bare earth.

I had read of these Men's retreats, but had never known what it was they did on them. I thought it was all talk, group confessionals, hugging.

"So now it's the fashion to be a savage," says me, and I patted my wife's big round belly that had our next daughter in it.

This is America. It's always been fashionable for white men to play at being savage.

Moreover

Our caravan drove west to a place that was no longer a place, a hill that was no hill, called Shiyobaha; the *shiyo* is the prairie chicken. *Baha* or *Paha* is hill; the linguists aren't happy with either B or P because in Assiniboine, the consonant is an unvoiced unaspirated labial plosive, and English doesn't have it. The generic Plains Indian pow-wow dancers who dance bent-over wearing bustles of spiky feathers arranged in a circle on their rumps and moving their heads in short jerks do so in imitation of the *shiyo*. Shiyobaha, which no longer existed except in the Shaman's mental atlas, was where he had grown up. I did not ask how the very structures of his youth had passed.

We dismounted and arranged ourselves in a ragged seated circle on the grass. The shaman produced the pipe-bowl and stem separately from an elaborately beaded pipe-bag made from bison hide, and smudged them with smoke from the sweetgrass burning in Firekeeper's little iron skillet. He prayed to the west, the north, the east, the south, to the sky and to the earth after filling and lighting the pipe and smoking a few puffs. The briefest of sermons: "This community does not exist any more. Those broken boards (gray, weathered planks only vaguely visible as smooth oblong places on the raw plain) of my grandfather's house are all that is left. There is no one here because we gave up. This community was destroyed by alcohol. *Han mitugashi hokshi togap, unshiyana o.* Grandfather, we ask you to pity us, for we are pitiful." He lit the pipe again with the sweetgrass braid and smoked, meditating on the dead, perhaps;

perhaps greeting them. We waited under skies uncluttered by clouds or telephone or power wires. Spring sang at us in the voices of insects, birds, the rustle of grasses just tall enough to catch breeze. Presently, he passed the pipe sunwise to Wanbli Gleshka Num, who, holding the bowl in the cup of his left palm, pivoted the stem in an elegant circle, smoked, then pointed the stem at each of the six directions in their turn the way one would aim a rifle before passing it to the scholar, who prayed and smoked and pointed his round and passed it to me, and I did my round with the sweet Chicago tobacco and dried red-willow bark filling my mouth and tickling my lungs, and I passed to Sage, and Sage his round, and Sage to Firekeeper and his round and he to the shaman, and again, thenceforth in silent meditation, three more times around. Sucking white smoke out of a tiny hole at the end of a stiff length of wood, I wondered briefly, inappropriately, at the sexual imagery that pervades this religion, but moved to theology, safer ground: tobacco, First Man's first plant, whose spirit is released when fire touches it.

Then it was back in the saddle and on some miles down straight, rutted gravel roads to a patch of buffalo grass next to a quizzical fenced horse south of Chansuda Ipa. We prayed and smoked again after a sermon about the evil *washiju*, who been received in friendship and trade, but had stayed, had broken the people's spirit, and how this Lodge was stronger than booze and stronger than the hate of the ignorant who had taken so much and left so little. Then our prancing Detroit steeds took us past the shore of a small lake dotted with white pelicans to Hudesha, where, merely fifty yards south of the High Line and only a little farther from the Great Northern's railbed, we smoked and prayed again next to the skeletons of the two previous years' Lodges, from whose poles many prayer cloths fluttered, sun-faded and wind-torn, in the light breeze.

Again, for the fourth time, as all of nature is in fours, we drove our manly trucks to a place on the plain and then stopped to pray and smoke and listen. It was the Lodge site.

The shaman told again how he had been walking alone here on land a new supporter owned. The man had wanted to make it available for the Lodge, but the shaman hadn't been sure. It was land high up on the rising country above the Mnishoshe. Range land, broad and windswept and dry, with short clumps of wild native grasses, and waves of bluish sage whose scent was everywhere, and spiky *unkcece* cactus scattered around like mines. From nowhere, the curlew had come and circled him crying "*Necha, necha, necha, necha*!" Right here, right here, right here, right here! But he hadn't understood what the bird was saying. He began to walk away and the bird pursued him screaming "*Zhecha, zhecha, zhecha, zhecha*," Back there! He went to the spot the bird directed and planted his tiny red dowel. He burned tobacco. He prayed. He tossed cigarettes around the place, the Philip Morris Corporation's sacred offering. Later, on his *hanblecheya*, he was given a song for the Lodge by this curlew spirit. "*Ned'uch, ned'uch, ned'uch no, zintka wakan omagiye no, a-heya hey, a-heya hey, ho yo yo yo, yoh.*"

Praying and smoking done, all hands went to the profane business of getting the double tipi set up for the coming all-night sing. Extra lodge-poles had to be procured from some guy who had made pledges of participation but was nowhere to be found, and there was firewood to get and chop and stack and more raking to do, and short lengths of tipi-cord to tie together for the great girth of the double, and a fire-pit to dig near the south end of the tipi, and other chores, just chores. Somebody arrived unbidden with a wobbly truck that had two turquoise Port-A-Potties and let me tell you, they were, for the hours before the motley fleet of pickups and cab-overs and low-slung old sedans began parking on the flat ground to the east of the site, the most incongruous edifices in sight. And sight at that place extended unbroken for miles.

I wanted Maza Wichashta to come, the charismatic Cree with the crew-cut and the reputation of super-shaman. On the trip to Hubxa I had been to The Superdome, as his *inipi* is called, a sweat-lodge big enough to fit twenty. Two women in gray workout suits had sweated with us there, and a jolly fat old fellow name of Fox. I had listened uncomprehending to Maza Wichashta's lengthy pipe-prayers and had detected disciplined meter and much alliteration, despite my lack of Cree. Afterward, at the secular dance-fest at Hudesha where Montana's governor had put in an appearance, I had heard his big drum's songs, six men doing bass and four women tremolo. I had felt his energy and smiled at his ready humor. Maza Wichashta had the natural charisma of a successful politician. And gray Ike-cut hair and taut skin.

And but for the shovel-shaped incisors, the extra melanin, the black-brown rather than blue eyes, he could have been my father's physical double.

We could have used his technical skills in erecting the double singing-tipi. The lodge poles went up easily enough, but we were skunked repeatedly trying to rig the canvas in the breeze that blew in. After much comedy, the structures were up, and joined, and secured. The wind would prove to be a blessing in itself: the voracious river-bottom *chapunga* were out in force all afternoon, but that alternately troublesome and saving wind blew most of them off.

I was already hungry.

The first time I'd done this, I'd thrown all concern for reputation aside, and spent the morning hours before Moving Down jamming leftover stew, eggs, commodity-surplus fatback, bread and slabs of sheet cake down the hatch, to the great amusement of the veterans taking tea in the Easter Egg Village kitchen. This year, a veteran myself, I'd been abstemious.

So had my pal, the scholar. I chanced to look over at him draining a can of Mountain Dew. He caught the glance. I patted my grumbling belly. He made a face that spelled regret that the cost of being examples to the young'uns was a great big a hole in the belly.

We returned from a Velvet run to the grocery store in Tabex'a Wakpa (there are many, many luscious things in a grocery store; it was brave and stupid to have gone there; the proving, which means testing, began in the deli section) to the general drift into the singing tipi.

The shaman, Pipekeeper, and Wanbli Gleshka Num had established themselves at the north end, seating themselves cross-legged next to the wrapped, painted bison skull. The rolled-up bison hide had been unfurled along the southeast wall of the tipi, and singers who had brought their drums and long, fresh-cut willow wands were arranging themselves around it, testing their drums for tone, setting some of them up on edge balanced on upright beaters near the fire, the better to drive moisture from the heads and thus make them more taut and of higher tone. Visitors, wives, sisters, children, men who would be dancing began to take up places on the southwest, ranging in a curl up the side of the tipi to where Pipekeeper kept the sweetgrass embers glowing and the tins of Velvet tobacco and the stack of prayer cloths.

When the sun set sometime after ten, I was outside sucking down a last can of soda and quietly inspecting the great dark bowl of the sky overturned above us, and the Milky Way washing down its middle, so unbelievably many stars, and so clear. A satellite passed like a bright marble rolled by careless giants from west to east. And a misty suggestive brush of aurora borealis played fire from the north.

The hiss of the shaman's rattle signaled that it was time to get inside, and quieted all the laughter and chatter of people happy to be there. He sang the four vocable verses of his first Lodge song solo in a clear tenor that filled the space. He moved immediately into the second song, again solo on the first verse: *Mayak'ubi no, mayak'ubi no, Tibi Tanga ne*," and the men at the hide joined in with their drums and with willow-wands slapping the inside-up bison hide in heartbeat rhythm for the refrain, *wakan chan, wakan makak'ubi no, hey hey, hey hey, hey he-hey*! And so on for the rest of the song, which laid out the four principal aspects of the Lodge: the structure itself, the *chan wakan* or sacred tree, *wahoxpi* or nest, and *tatanga*, the bison. The next song of his four: not the slow, easy pace of the first two, both of which began with a bit of rattle, but the abrupt and fast universal slapping and beating and near-shouting of four verses of his assertion that we would go out and attack the "enemy standing there." He closed with the mellow 2/4 favorite "*Ateye mak'u we*," Father give us this Lodge, this sacred tree, this nest, this bison.

The rattle passed to the next man, Ska, another *wichashta wakan* and, moreover, keeper of a sacred hand-game bundle, a short, snub-nosed Assiniboine from near Hubxa who had, in the old way, just done the old-fashioned thing, and traded wives with Maza Wichashta, with everybody honored in the process. He sang his round of four songs (of the dozens he owns) fast, in a high, creaky voice made older than his sixty-odd years by cigarettes and the rigors of much fasting. And the rattle passed again and again, down the line of drum-beaters and wand-slappers, to men who had come with songs that had been passed to them from fathers, uncles, grandfathers, relatives by affinity of temperament or of care, but not to Maza Wichashta, who had still not arrived, or to the women he always brought with him, who themselves always joined the singing but only when he sang. It was his personal style to kneel while singing; everyone else sat cross-legged. And only he would open each of his song sets with the rattle working in his hand and a long Cree prayer, different each time, until by some signal the drummers knew to drum along in at a low rolling pace that quickened to sharp staccato bumps when he moved that rattle jagged, like a beater, to begin his melody.

So the Lodge began. I sat adjacent to the singers and to the fire, keeping it stoked, keeping those drying and tensing drums upright, checking their tones, chatting loosely in English and Assiniboine with singers and visitors, singing along on refrains when the general voice of the place lifted, singing.

In breaks in the singing, there were prayers with pipe by the shaman and by some of the singers, and much passing of the pipe. Everyone smoked, everyone offered the pipe to the six directions. Magic or physics or a sense of restraint kept the pipe's tiny bowl's fuel burning for the duration of each sunwise pass from shaman to singers to the gallery and back to the Pipekeeper. Prayers were variously silent, mumbled, brief, endless, in Assiniboine but also in Cree. There is an art to the praying that I would have had to study for a very long time to get; the old veterans and shamans chant them *fortissimo* and *presto vivace*, and their chants are loaded with archaisms, and for those whose Assiniboine is good enough there were occasions for whoops of praise and solemn nods of acknowledgment and murmurs of *Ho, ho, ho, ho* at the skill and music of those texts.

The ensuing songs were equally various: tuneless and with rippling melodies, sometimes hard to follow, sung old-style deep in the throat and others sung the way *washijus* talk, forward in the teeth, but the beat was the same: the heartbeat, on hand-drums that together made muffled thunder that rolled and rolled into the night and established, in that vestibule to the cathedral, what we were there for.

This was a rare and jewel-like thing. But one does not so very easily become transformed from the simple, reactive being that one happens to be just by the presence of good vibrations. Fasting and working hard in hot sun had made me (there is no other word for it) cranky. My body had responded by shutting down the alimentary functions, more or less. I was greatly relieved that the water fast would not begin until nightfall of the second day, and that is something to be thankful for, but my mood was garbage. And I knew myself well enough to predict that the big test for me would be to keep it buttoned.

Most of us awoke the morning after the sing at about eight, quite far into the northern day. The shaman had already selected and, at dawn, dispatched two men to go scout for the *chan wakan*. When they returned, we dancers and builders were called into the singing tipi. The pipe was passed, prayers offered. The shaman bade the two men step forward with their report, and for the benefit of all new men, described these scouts, their role, our forthcoming tasks.

Both scouts were veterans.

More. They were veterans of combat. Only men who have shed blood for their people are eligible to choose the cottonwood tree. Thick-trunked, straight trees stand in spring in the slippery low muck of the earth, and seed-out with puffy balls of cottony white, one is chosen to become the *chan wakan*. Nature is sacred, yes; these are not pantheists but pan*en*theists. To release the sacred potential would take the hands and backs of men.

One scout, Billy, was a mountain of flesh, a very troubled guy with a grinding history of alcoholism, but so sweet and gentle, and so talented a painter, that imagining him a slim and deadly teenage draftee with trophy Vietnamese ears and noses on his belt was an effort.

The other was Ska, the elder shaman from Hubxa with the cigarette voice, who had done his fighting forty years earlier in sane, white, civilized Europe.

We piled into vehicles and followed Billy, Ska and the shaman back toward the river, descending the high plain to low wet land where a stand of cottonwoods rose between an untilled field and the reedy edge of a lake. The two scouts had tied a red cloth around a huge tree that stood somewhat apart from the rest of the grove.

We gathered around, boys and men, scouts, Lodge officials with pipe and fire. The shaman prayed loud. He cried over the tree. Crying tears, *ceya*, mourning, producing water: this should not be strange. The language and the metaphor are intertwined: one cries for a vision during the *hanbleceya*. Songs are cries, prayers to music, *ceyabi*. The tree about to die needed his mourning, and the tree, cut, stripped, carved, uprighted, would center the Lodge from which would rise the songs and whistles and calls to the thunderbirds to roll in with the tears of the sky, the rains, whose moisture would replenish the earth and nourish another season of birth, growth, life.

The scouts stripped their shirts off and took up axes. They positioned themselves at the north and south sides of the tree, the rest of us in a line southeast. The shaman instructed them carefully: that they must cut the tree down within the time of his singing his four songs; that the tree must fall southward; that they should make three false swings before first striking the tree "like you struck the enemy."

They were ready. The shaman took up the rattle and sang alone the four rounds of his first Lodge song. The chopping began.

It was a huge tree. Big Billy struck with great force; splinters flew like sparks. Old Ska struck with wily design, making a neat wedge; he had lived his life closer to the land, and so better knew how to handle country tools. The shaman sang slowly because it seemed so much work; though none of us spoke, I know we all worried that they would not complete the task in time.

But then the tree began to shudder like a great breathing beast. The shaman quickened the pace. The men chopped sharp strokes. It could have been the force of his song that pushed the tree off its stump just as the last verse left his mouth.

Then we attacked.

We dancers and builders rushed the tree as it fell, whooping and screaming on the run, and ripping off branches as trophies—counting coup, as of old, on the fallen enemy.

Then it was just the chore of stripping the tree of its head of hair that we set about. Red, bowed Swedish wood-saws, long-handled axes, hatchets, hacksaws denuded it. The scholar and Wanbli Gneshka Num made the big cuts, four feet up from the crotch on one of the two main branches from the trunk, six feet up the other. It took only tens of minutes to change this great tree into an object that could have gone to a sawyer.

It is an understatement that hefting the log onto a mired flatbed wagon took all of our strength. Clouds of *chapungas* threatened to take the rest of it. The easy part was slapping bugs and piling that wagon high with the "brush," as the boys called the leafy cottonwood branches.

Returned to the lodge site, we laid the fallen *chan wakan* north/south from the three-foot-deep hole dug at the place the curlew had told the shaman to put the red peg, leaving it propped on a makeshift log sawhorse for Wanbli Gleshka Num, his buck knife and his paints and brushes. He would carve it upright: a four-foot zigzag of lightning and a tricolor rainbow cut into the bark of one side, thunderbird and bison symbols on the other.

What followed was more strenuous labor than I had ever done before or since.

The *chan wakan* was twice the girth and weight of the tree we had cut the previous year. Raising the pole to slide it into the hole whose earthen sides would hold it upright demanded all the strength of the nearly twenty men who hefted it; to stop and hold it at higher and higher angles three times as the shaman sang his round of songs, holding it at higher and higher angles before it slid erect and upright into its home, was almost more than we could do. We were all gasping and hunched over, making mud of the earth with our sweat.

So it was meant to be, this stupendous labor of mimicking creation.

With such a huge center pole having demanded so much of us, the Lodge promised, or threatened, to be a huge task to complete, and completed, a great demonstration of this shaman's power, and of our own.

Chapungas, heat and testiness brought on by fatigue and hunger were there to make the testing harder. Down in the river bottom land where the cottonwoods grow, there was no wind, just clouds of *chapungas*. Up on the high plain the wind kept them at bay, and so the full-scale assault of the low country army diminished, thankfully, to random sniping in the high.

But there to replace insects was the Blackfeet, and his attitude.

I am an enthusiastic worker, and no stranger to hierarchy. I talk loud outdoors, and am not shy about organizing folks to get jobs done. My Assiniboine brethren are also enthusiastic, but it is a general trait of theirs to speak softly. Most did. Another trait: precious little hierarchy. Things are not planned; they happen, when they do, when a unanimity, or at least a commonality, of effort weighs against the task, things just sort of happen, and nobody takes credit, and everybody has had a say, and every achievement bears the signature imprints of each hand that was lifted to the task. And leaders instruct by example, not loud words.

The thirty-something Blackfeet was present on a mission: to help the Assiniboines out, to learn by doing, and then to take news of the doings back to his big home reservation in the shadow of Glacier National Park. These Assiniboines would actually hold their Lodge at Blackfeet the next year, thus restoring the ritual to a people who had been without it, thanks to the efforts of missionaries and Indian Service bureaucrats, for decades, and reinstating the ancient bonds between the two peoples, bonds reduced to threads by the conqueror.

Thus the presence of a *washiju* or two at the Assiniboine Lodge must have been threatening to this Blackfeet guest. The bombast and assertiveness of the *washiju* in directing the younger, less experienced Assiniboines must have been hard to swallow, but give me this: those boys looked to me as a leader. Robert Bly would understand. I had the legitimacy of veteran status, and enough of the language for capable (if halting) conversation with the revered elders, and the shaman's own obvious imprimatur; all that, all told, gave me status even beyond the scholar's in the eyes of some.

But the Blackfeet was reticent, or angry, or caught in racialism. I caught glimpses of it, but attributed his reserve to shyness. Then to fatigue, dehydration, *chapunga* bites. But when I offered to assist him in trimming one of the so-called crutch-logs, the intrusion must have been too great. He dropped his axe, retrieved his hat, and wordlessly returned to his pickup, where he sat for the rest of the day, staring at me sullenly from the within its air-conditioned cab.

I was at a loss about how to knit the raveled sleeve. There was, I concluded, nothing to do but work on.

And so we did, as determinedly as we could. We hacked holes in the stone-dry earth for the 14 crutch poles, slipping their 12-foot lengths in, jamming cross-pieces into their forks. The heat was unrelenting, as was our thirst. Numberless six-packs of soda pop were brought to the Lodge-builders by wives and younger brothers and old men, and we hungrily sucked them down. Such were the conditions that to have done the work without those calories, as we had done the previous year when we'd had only water for the building day, might well have left us all too depleted to continue.

I wondered if, in the old days before Mountain Dew and Squirt and Nehi, Lodge-builders suffered so much, worked so hard, dripped so much sweat in order to achieve the fulfillment of the great grand vision of an ancient shaman.

As it happened, despite the gigantic center-pole and all the labor, we did not build a 42-pole Lodge, because dark rushed in. The special dispensation reiterated by Zintkana Txo permitted the Lodge to be declared complete without the dreamed-of number of poles on top. For when the basic structure of the Lodge had been completed (the center pole erect, the crutch-poles joined by their cross-bars surrounding it in a great circle), we were laying those twenty-foot cottonwood saplings, stripped of all but a topknot of foliage, on those cross-pieces as fast as we could, but it wasn't fast enough. For so great a *chan wakan*, we were making a great "nest" for the *waginyan*: that Venus-mound of foliage that forty-two poles would have made at the crotch of the *chan wakan*.

But the night outraced us. Zintkana Txo's dispensation for twenty-one poles permitted us to finish precisely as darkness came rushing upon us. A flatbed trailer piled heavy with the roof or nest poles rolled in from the river bottom too late for its cargo to be used.

And then the storm came.

We were lashing the last poles on to the cross-bars and standing the brush up against the sides as its first breaths blew in out of the west. In that vast open land, we could see it coming for half an hour. I will not generalize about storms on the plains, only tell of this one. We could see its terrible fiery thunderbolts crackling through the darkening sky to the west. We could see that broken electricity illuminating far-off mountains, a storm big enough to turn the sky daylight for seconds on end. This was an Inktomi storm that could be powerful enough to flatten all this vain manly mimesis we had spent our best selves creating all day, and with winds to howl and whine divine laughter in our ears, at our smallness.

There was no escape. The winds that had blessedly whipped away the *chapunga* and the worst of the heat all day turned on us and threatened to become annihilators. The long leafy cottonwood branches that we wove into walls first rustled in that wind, then caught it like sails and then, unable to shift that craft that was so firmly anchored in the prairie, ripped away or fell through to the interior of the Lodge, leaving great gaps for more and stronger wind to pour through. That structure of our erecting was being blown apart.

The first of that storm's rain that fell on us was startlingly cold and sharp, a signal at least to perk up and pay attention, if not to run for cover from the violence of lightning and gales surely to follow. I remembered an anthropologist friend's story of being caught in such a spring storm on Eagle River Reservation in South Dakota, a storm that pounded and shook his car, smashed a flying branch through a door's window, flattened and scattered his campsite and imbued in him a sense of awe and a new understanding of why the Lakota thereabouts revered this expression of force. I remembered, and shuddered: there was no shelter to be had, no truck, no car, no shed.

As the great growling thunder sounded louder, I was not the only man who looked for the shaman or for others like Ska or Maza Wichashta, for some experienced authority who would know what to do.

Our shaman emerged, with thunder now crashing and bellowing all around us, from the singing tipi, and stood facing south-southwest, serenely meditative as the wind whipped rain against his face. Perhaps he was having a conversation with the storm. Perhaps he had come out only to tell us that it was time to stop work, that we had done enough.

Quite abruptly, the storm relented to a mere murmur. It wet us down lightly as we wove the last cottonwood brush for the dance fences inside, and then that storm just rolled on off to the east.

The shaman softly pronounced our work finished.

With his big arm making a slow arcing wave, he called builders and dancers to the singing tipi.

There were no tools to drop or nail-aprons to untie. We'd used our own shoulders for ladders, twigs for twine. I joined the general trend toward the singing tipi, detoured for just a few yards for what was left of a stray bottle of Mountain Dew and drank what I could, tossing the bottle aside as I entered and sat down again across from the steady fire, for this entrance was the final, irrevocable crossing of a special border: from the partial deprivations of the building period to the fullness of the fast.

I looked around at faces damp with sweat and that sharp, short rain, at heads of hair plastered down with the moisture of work and of passing weather. Men and big boys in windbreakers, jeans, muddy sneakers, ripped t-shirts pressed in close with their tired faces in each other's. We had all crossed the same meridian. We had all made this effort.

We passed the pipe in that calm and protected place, and then stood to hear an extraordinary speech.

First in Assiniboine and then in English, the shaman told that They had pitied us and sent the storm onward to the east, to the land that needed its rain so desperately, to the people whose very existence depended on the water that They gave us. It was a gift to the Lodge-builders, he said, that we had been given the wind and that small taste of the life-giving moisture it carried. He had thanked Them for pitying us and for recognizing our extraordinary efforts in building this Lodge.

And then, with his voice cracking, he said that he had a special message for us all: that henceforth, for the rest of this Lodge, and for the rest of our lives, we were all of us, to a man, his brothers.

Call it revelation, call it exercise of sacred authority. Call it politics. In that tipi's low light, three of the men who stood directly between me and my friend the *wichashta wakan* were those unacknowledging relatives of his, those Toba Wichaxpe men who had recently, only after the advent of his celebrity, taken to claiming this shaman as a brother—a claim that he himself had never made in return. This declaration was for them, but how, how it had cost them. Dear. They had finally won a reciprocal recognition, which they had denied their brother-by-blood for most of his life—a recognition which they now had to share with all of the men assembled.

This frankly political act, known as such only to the shaman, to me, to the Toba Wichaxpe men, to my Chicago friend the scholar—this act of knitting a family together, affected me profoundly. This, I thought, was what awaited beyond the frontier: inclusion after a term of labor, of testing, of validation. I was gripped with the feeling that I had begun a new and difficult stage of life. I remembered the shaman's fooling with me the year before about strong young Assiniboine women he knew who had watched my hewing of wood and hauling of brush, my enduring the fast and the labor with good cheer—good Assiniboine girls from good Wadopana families looking, inspecting the field of Lodge men, for good husbands. I wasn't about to toss my wife over, but food is not the only nourishment that looks good to a starving man. There would be women around after this Lodge, too.

But just then was not the time. With the end of the shaman's address, the nearer border to cross was from this zone of preparation into the final territory. It was time to move into the Lodge.

That group of individuals that had become a family of brothers filed slowly in single-file procession out of the singing tipi. The shaman, bared to the waist, led, carrying the painted buffalo skull by the horns, stopping at the cardinal points to cry and weep his prayer for the Grandfather to pity us all, including a sunburnt *washiju* who had become a carrier of sacred drums.

We trailed him sunwise from north all the way around the completed Tibi Tanga, then around the eastern side again to the entrance at the south, then in, ever sunwise, around the center pole, the *chan wakan*, past the low fences made of brush and small crutch poles and cross-bars behind which the dancers would do what they had come to do, past the new home of Firekeeper, and of the shaman, now become the Lodge Man, and of the bison skull, past the singing hide, in that spiral that took us to the earth's newfound center.

Sing

After we had reestablished the structure and placement of objects and people as they had been in the singing tipi, Tashunga Saba took up his rattle. The Lodge sing began.

Fact was, I was ready to join in the singing again, as I had done so, marginally and somewhat tentatively, more or less near the scholar, at the sing the night before. I owned the minimum four songs—one from Zintkana Txo, three from the wastrel Ricky—and so was technically eligible.

And, of course, I was a brother.

There was no place for me at the hide at first, nor for the scholar, and I didn't think anything of it. I knew this group with whom I had worked all day; I knew by sight and to greet some of the older men, including a newcomer, the ancient and venerable Saskatchewan man named Indechan, whose Assiniboine speech was so formal (and, *nota bene*, sounded so Lakota to me). But I was not the scholar, who had known them all for four years or more. In fact, this would be my Chicago brother's third Lodge, and the shaman's fourth as Lodge Maker. A man is supposed to "do" four Lodges. Back in Chicago, we had purchased lots of things for the *wakpamni*, the giveaway, that the scholar would conduct at the end of this Lodge in honor of our friend and host. That *wakpamni* would also announce to the Assiniboine world that the scholar was on his way, in a serious way, to fulfilling the ancient requirements of full manhood in the Assiniboine way. Thus the calculation of riches, of status: one accumulates a surplus just like an American bent on charity, but the general distribution of the goods would be to the needy and to comrades alike, and that act of denuding oneself of the components of richness is done as a direct honoring of someone *else*, and only indirectly as a brag.

I, though, was junior, on only my second Lodge. But I was a brother. The Lodge Man had said so. I was the man from Back East who traveled in the somewhat exalted circles of powerful politicians, and so had a special sort of cachet about me that even the friendly and dutiful and ever-self-effacing scholar never could.

But I never got called to the singing hide where the men with their endowments of ancient songs held forth. Not only was I not called to it, I was very subtly warned away, by none other than the Lodge Man.

Instead, I spent the evening seated in front of the dancers' fence, among visitors who would drop in and out, among wives, among the young boys who had helped gather brush but who had no status yet as song-owners, or as dancers, or as piercers. In other words, I was kept out of the company of the *men*.

Later, after the singing, I walked through the night and the wind back to my tent, and was convinced by the manifold evidence of my senses that it was time for me to leave.

Call them signals. The small one: the storm had blown my tent down, bending my aluminum pole segments into utter uselessness. Anyone, anyone at all could have explained that the collapse of my little house was a consequence of my having presumed to sing along while I'd heated and tested drums at the singing hide the previous night. The wind-crushed tent was, I thought, a warning to keep my distance. Small signals, and big: the Lodge Man had made me part of the brotherhood, but not to the extent that I had wanted. And in that state of fatigue and hunger and thirst, there was my special added burden of being an utter outsider, farther outside than even my pigmentary equal from Chicago. I was literally and metaphorically outside.

And, with a flattened tent, it looked like outside was where I was going to stay, because that holy wind didn't want to let me put the yuppie nylon Eureka thing up again.

After much effort with energy I didn't have, I gave up the fight and went as far as I could to the comfort and safety of *washiju*-land, by way of climbing into a little Plymouth. My friend the scholar was off with his wife in a tent that had shed wind like the proverbial duck's back does water. I was tired, sunburnt, hungry, thirsty, angry at having been excluded and, incidentally, pretty damned uncomfortable in the little seat that no amount of jiggering of levers and knobs could make recline.

It sucked. It got worse. I was overwhelmed with longing for my wife, of all people, who is, of all people I have ever known, the most capable colloquist, confidante, comforter. Next came a searing anger at myself: I felt stupid for being so much in need of membership in this outfit. With exasperation, I remembered my furtive prayer the day before when, left alone at the site with one of the teenagers who had been brought in for his cultural imprinting, I'd walked out onto the prairie and somewhat awkwardly asked for divine help in being a better, stronger man. What a crock of shit this all was.

In that god-forsaken, wind-bounced, uncomfortable little car, alone with my irritations, I dusted off the notes from the days I'd spent witnessing a racial confrontation on the Southwest Side of Chicago, in which the hopeful, hardworking black homesteaders had been told—you can't come here. You can't cross *these* borders. Stupid to try. Stupid romanticism.

And more.

Real poison: stupid bloody savages are doomed to failure. Doomed, irrelevant people. They should all cash their welfare checks and go get bags of potato chips and six-packs and watch Bugs Bunny till the last memories of their distinctiveness die. And then they can join those stateless refugees that crowd our cities now, join them in the test pattern that is what passes for a national cultural identity for the rest of us citizens of the United States of America.

Such heartfelt scoldings were coming at a fast pace, like some fearsome internal hailstorm, when suddenly, I was granted a reprieve.

Perhaps it was the memory of how much lousier I'd felt one rainy night in Hubxa the previous year, when I'd jammed myself into the similarly uncomfortable front seat of a van rather than stay inside with the blitzed Ricky and his pathetic and potentially violent apostasy.

I actually laughed at that thought, and at others—at Maza Wichashta's goading of all us fasters at the last Lodge. Maza Wichashta, he of Cree prayers and traded wife and steel-cut buzz cut. I remembered when he'd come round on the third arduous day of the Lodge the year before. He'd made a great show of wiping meat-grease off his lips while we sat there woozy from hunger, talking loud in English and Assiniboine too about how good that meat was.

I laughed more, remembering my first sight of Zintkana Txo, that squeezly weasly little derelict, an old wino on Division Street in Chicago, an allegedly major player here, but his appearance, wrinkly, skinny, in saggy baggy spotty pants that drooped to show his butt-crack, and some helpful guy leaning over to whisper, "He's a real *powerful* medicine man, is he," and I'd thought, Must be his chin-full of tobacco-juice drool that makes it so. I even laughed at my aching back, because the chances of getting comfy were so absolutely hopeless as to be well beyond comical, right up to the edge of absurd. And I looked out my little Plymouth's rolled-down window at the huge jewel-case of stars spread serenely against the blackness above, which was so wondrous, so incomprehensibly grand, that the last drips of bile in my poison-well evaporated in that celestial light, and I had no more left with which to burn myself or anybody else, and all worry and all care, all ire, all consciousness, slipped quietly into the softest restful sleep.

Loyalty

About membership. Groucho Marx said it best: I wouldn't want to be a member of a club that would have me as a member.

It finally dawned on me, with the dawn of the third day, that my job at the Lodge was to be useful. That the shaman was using me very carefully, as he had used the scholar before me. That by elevating the other white guy in the Lodge society, by announcing to all that They had come to the Lodge Man in a dream and instructed him to give the scholar the potent, puissant name Channumba Yuha Mani, Walks With the Pipe, and by putting him in with those song-endowed Leading Men, this shaman was taking an astonishing risk—which was to demonstrate to all his young crew of followers that it was necessary to distinguish between racist white assholes and good white men; and further, that good white men were to be distinguished by their longevity in this enterprise, and granted status and privileges as they earned them; that this shaman's power as *wichashta wakan* was such that he could not only bring back the helpful and respectful and pleasant Chicago scholar year after year, but he could also bring in another white guy, enthusiastic and learned, but still learning, and thus that his circle was growing. By driving a public wedge between the white guys, the shaman could demonstrate not only power but discernment, and he could instill confidence in the young Assiniboines that this power of his had long reach, but also that he wasn't so needful of white guys or of white-guy approval that he had to pack his Lodge with ringers.

As they say in Chicago, I shoulda seen it.

Indeed. Hadn't I spent all my adult years describing hierarchies of power and access? Tracing who was in, who out, who up, and how far? Think of the Lodge Man as old Mayor Daley in his formative years. I could have been a mayoral appointee, still on probation, from the same suspect faction from which the scholar had been recruited. It was safe to make me a deputy commissioner for a minor department, but not to have *two* full commissioners from the same clique, for to have *two* such aides would have been too much for the homefolks to swallow. They would have revolted against their leader. They would have split off to follow the faction of a lesser light, of whom there were several inside and outside the Lodge, waiting, as all political rivals wait, for their own chance to lead.

Of course.

I didn't then see the longer view that is so obvious now: that I, son of conquerors, was out there with the conquered, helping to right temples that had been knocked down during the conquest, and was only able to do so because the conquest had been so utterly complete that these onetime challengers to my forebears were so beaten, so overwhelmed, their riches of land and sovereignty so utterly alienated from them that it was safe for them to hold their Lodge, sing their songs, or howl at the moon like wolves if that's what they wanted to do, because they just didn't matter anymore.

Suppressing them with Christian mission work was useless because they simply wouldn't disappear, but instead lingered on, and I was there enjoying a conqueror's son's recreation, nothing more than that, before heading back home to the adult business of extending the conquest.

I am truly grateful that that latter analysis never crossed my mind then, for after my morning's clarity about the politics of the Lodge, about the immediate power arrangement, the Lodge became joyous for me again.

Maybe "joyous" isn't the word. I was foodless, waterless, sleep-deprived, and bone-bent tired from the endurance test that all the previous day's labors had been.

Power relations, risk-taking, public demonstrations of leaderly might: these were as certainly ingredients of the Lodge Man's cultural renaissance, as were drums, sweetgrass, rattles, songs, cloths, and all those other ritual objects themselves.

I creaked back from my walk out to the tall grass smiling, just in time to hear the shaman's call from inside the Lodge, as clear as morning church bells:

"Ziagu! Indechan! Ska! Wanbli Gleshka Num! Tate Hokshi! Wana, kuwa no! Bring your songs!"

It was an alarm clock for all those song-owners who had retired to all those campers and tents and tipis that had been set up among the parked cars out on the plain. It woke the dancers, who had slept behind that low brush fence inside the Lodge. They rolled out of their traditional Assiniboine nylon and goosedown sleeping bags into the chill of the morning, wobbled off to the Port-A-Potties to bleed their shriveled lizards, licked dew from their upper lips because that's all the water they were allowed.

And soon, we all stumbled into the sacred space to hear a full day of eagle-bone whistle, hide drum, and willow-on-hide music.

I merely sat shivering inside the perimeter of the dancers' fence where I'd sat the night before, running errands as directed by the Lodge Man, and watching the process unfold. The singing hide was the site of much intense work. Behind me, behind those short fences, more work was underway: a dozen fasting men who had been chosen by their visions or by their needs stood, naked to the waist, clutching fans of eagle feathers or bouquets of sage, with eagle-bone whistles in their mouths, dancing in place, eyes on the *chan wakan*, blowing a short burst of breath through those whistles in time with each beat of a drum.

The scholar took his place at the singing hide smoothly and naturally, if not with musical verve. There was not a hint of controversy at his presence there. I approvingly noted that this act, too, helped the Lodge demonstrate its power.

The haze of fatigue and discomfort gradually lifted from me at about the pace of the sun's climb, and gradually my body warmed up, and again I was happy to be there, at the center of the earth.

It would be a day of demonstrations of faith and of growth for the Lodge.

Many of the dancers stepped from behind their fence to submit to the piercing, under the direction of Zintkana Txo and his seven-sage medicine collected from the crop of a *shiyo*. They would lay on a bison hide near the north end of the Lodge, clutch their sage brooms, blow on their whistles as the old shaman cut slits into a pinch of their breast flesh and inserted a little wood peg, to which he tied a tether whose other end was tied to the *chan wakan*. Then the songs would start, and the men who were making this flesh offering to the Lodge, this little voluntary crucifixion for the benefit of the whole of the people, would stand in the entranceway to the Lodge, dancing their bobbing dance-in-place, blowing hard on their eagle-bone whistles.

The Blackfeet emerged from his obscurity. He pierced, but danced in the showy, macho Lakota manner, pulling free of his bonds by leaning back hard on the thong, ripping the flesh of his pectorals where the plugs had held him connected to the tethers. The Assiniboine way was calmer, less dramatic: men just danced, connected through their chests, as if they were suckling the *chan wakan* with long IV lines. When depleted, they unhooked, were replaced, and went back behind their fences.

But there were showy Assiniboine sacrifices, too. Iye Shiche, a stalwart Lodge Man in his twenties, had his piercing done on his shoulder blades, and dragged a buffalo skull around the exterior of the Lodge. A troubled kid named Tinpsina dragged two, puffing hard on his eagle-bone whistle and taking encouragement from the Lodge Man at every ginger step. The greater the need, the greater the offering, but all who danced, whether piercers or not, were worked hard by the day's rising heat.

Even I, a second-timer, was having a hard go. I was sorely tempted to go off my water fast, but didn't. Tomorrow, tomorrow. Only one more night. All those piercers and dancers can do it. So, can I.

Sword's unfinished work

Why would George Sword have given all this up to have become a *comprador*?

Sword, George Sword, was the dead man who got me into all this, the man I had studied, whose autobiography I'd translated from Lakota. I'd read it, labored over it, deciphered it, obsessed over it. Indians all night and Chicago politics all day. Maybe I'd been looking for the Lakotas' version of the revolutionary document—the kind of manifesto that South Side black activists regularly produced. The kind of document that the just-getting-going Latino political movement of the Pilsen neighborhood put together to prove that they were for real, had real demands. The kind of document that would forge a nation out of a people on the verge of final defeat.

There was no such document, as there was no such man. What there was was Sword.

He was a Lakota who described a warped circle with his life, from a horse-stealing, Crow-killing, coup-counting, old-style war-party leader and Sun Dance *wichasha wakan*—high-status endeavors for a Lakota in the days before the conquest—to a brutally effective tool of my ancestor, the conqueror.

Sword was captain of a fifty-man armed and mounted force of Indian police on the Great Sioux Reservation in the Dakotas in the 1880s. (History refresher course: the Civil War ended in 1865; Custer was defeated in 1876; the Sioux were beaten up and put on reservations a few years later.) Sword was for fourteen years the hammer's head of official United States government policy, which was to destroy the old religion, stop all dancing, extirpate the giveaway, and render to nothing the pre-conquest authority of shamans and chiefs. In his old age, pensioned off as a major, Sword became the dread old monolingual gentleman-resource for a reservation physician who sought to make a record of the Old Ways. Through this doctor Sword contributed importantly to making that record, including writing an autobiography, and much more detailed accounts of native theology and sacred practices than you will find here.

There have been George Swords throughout the history of the European conquest. The chairman of my thesis committee in graduate school penciled this note in the margin of one of my drafts, on the page in which

I noted that Sword, having thrown off traditional religion and accepted Episcopalian baptism, nevertheless divorced three of his wives the old-fashioned Sioux way, at *omaha* dances: "Sounds like a typical transition case."

Which is to say that Sword—who, because of his *comprador* arrangement with the new power, came to wield more unchallenged authority than any chief ever had—was an opportunist. While a man who was a practicing Christian might have stuck with a wife who bore him no children, Sword, ever anxious for that Sioux badge of full manhood that siring babies bestows, ditched woman after woman for a failure that, one must necessarily surmise, was his own dumb biological destiny. Sword would eventually become a father, by adoption: he took as daughter an orphan of the egregious slaughter at Wounded Knee.

Reading that longhand autobiography of his with the eyes of a political reporter, it did not take me a great long time to understand why this Indian changed from Tokic'un Wan, "Avenges Himself," to Miwakan Yuha, literally, "Has a Long Knife," that is, Sword, with the Christian name George glued on with a little Holy Water. The anthros who so beautifully edited the doctor's compilation of Sword's and other old men's colorful accounts of all those colorful antique religious doings focused on the highfalutin, the spiritual, the noble in those accounts.

Maybe I just couldn't get caught up in that eddy of the *zeitgeist* stream that still today posits Native Americans as mascots of all that is good and noble and unfairly disparaged by the mean old conquerors of this Arcadia, this State of Nature, this ecologically pristine realm that America could have remained if the (as it is said) evil Cristoforo Colombo and his followers had not found, raped, pillaged, infected, and depopulated it.

Maybe that's because I am from western New York, which was a bloody place in which the Iroquois extirpated the Eries in the mid-seventeenth century, and so had studied primitive warfare, and civilized warfare, too, not in terms of ethnic characteristics, but rather by casualty rates. Warfare that includes the slaughter of noncombatants is a characteristic of societies without courts. White folks who kill noncombatants are war criminals. So are nonwhite folks.

So it wasn't a happy illusion I was chasing, but rather, a clearer understanding of peoples and processes utterly foreign, yet domestic.

My labors led me to look past the religious curios, to the life preceding Sword's recollections in the tranquility of his retirement. I am interested in doctrine and ritual practice, to be sure; I am more interested, though, in lives.

What I saw was a man who saw an opportunity, and who reached for, and who got, and who exercised, power.

And this was my judgment: what a traitorous dog he was. I had searched for the enemy, and had, I thought, found him.

Somewhere in his twenties, Sword went on a treaty-negotiation trip to Washington, D.C., where he saw "houses that could not be moved." For this reason, he told the reservation doctor's interpreter, "I took a new name, the name of Sword, because the leaders of the white soldiers wore swords. I determined to adopt the customs of the white people, and to persuade my people to do so."

What he did, three years after his Lakota kinsmen and their Cheyenne allies bested Custer's cavalry in 1876, was take the job of captain of the Indian police. He didn't do it for the money (policemen were paid less than scouts or mule-drivers or even woodchoppers by the reservation authorities; and he and his men had to furnish their own horses), but for the blue uniform with its gold buttons and insignia of rank, and the American-style crew cut. And he did it for the power—the almost limitless power.

For the next fourteen years, he and his thugs busted up funerals, confiscated drums, suppressed dancing, ripped down Sun-Dance lodges, stopped the giveaways, arrested kinsmen for having more than one wife or for attempting to leave the reservation to search for food, to hunt, to visit old allies. His job, pursued with vigor, was to destroy the old society.

His uniformed policemen were the men who tried to arrest Tatanka Iyotake, Sitting Bull, but lost control of the situation, killed the old shaman and lost several of their own number in the fight. But he and his horsebacks were also the men who, after a decade of what one of their civilian bosses crowed was success in "crush[ing] out all attempts at rebellion [*sic*]," were powerless to stop the desperate messianic Ghost Dance mass movement that had, in the manner of the old religion, begun with a shaman's vision.

With the Ghost Dance, the hammer's-head force of Sword and his fellow compradors met its limit. The whole hammer, in the form of the Seventh Cavalry of the United States Army, was brought in to achieve what Sword could not, namely, the smashing of that revitalization movement. The army did it the old-fashioned way that conquerors have: with bloody force, that murdered in the snow at Wounded Knee most of my friend Sungmanitu Luzahan's grandmother's family except her and her little brother, who evaded the follow-up search-and-destroy mission of the Seventh Cavalry war criminals by hiding overnight in what her grandson described as a "big old badger's burrow."

And thus was our own George Sword, whom some today characterize, mysteriously, as a "traditionalist," restored to power.

This is so very sad. That a desperate people, a small people who had for a brief historical moment enjoyed a position of primacy and relative security in their homeland, had joined a desperate religious movement that promised to get the missionaries out of their homes, and return their children from the hated boarding schools, and that promised to restore the bison and to rid the land of the conqueror and his troops and his beef rations and his agents and all their works—only to be herded up in winter by their own relatives, and then shot by troops of Custer's old unit when all the power that Sword and his company wielded proved insufficient to stop the dancing.

But you know something of the rest of the story. After eighty-odd years of government by the well intentioned, and of local administration by successive generations of George Swords, those young Lakota men out of the streets of Rapid City and the state pen of Minnesota created the American Indian Movement, and led an armed rebellion against the conquerors and their compradors.

And today, despite the booze and the despair and the calumny of reservation life on the Plains, there is evidence that Sword failed. That the missionaries failed. That the agents, and the army, and the Bureau of Indian Affairs, all failed in their *mission civilatrice*, as their French counterparts in Africa termed their efforts, but only in this sense: our TV-watching, English-speaking, Delta 88–driving, boozing brown Earth Day mascots still persist in sweating in their *inipi*s, still sing ancient prayers to the hiss of their rattles and to the rumble of their unconfiscated drums, and still, every June, gather their menfolk around charismatic and politically savvy shamans to seek out the cottonwood tree to make it a *chan wakan* and around it construct a *Tibi Tanga*.

For a while in the 1980s, I visited with the rebellion. It had begun in 1973, when the Lakota boys took over Wounded Knee. The American Indian Movement emboldened the beaten-down traditionalists. It slowly recreated them as a force. The Lakotas led the way, noisily, with religious

renaissance among the Sioux being led by the grandson and great-grandson of Sword's shaman nemesis Crow Dog.
And for the Assiniboines, first Zintkana Txo and much later Ska and the Saskatchewan men, surfaced to hunt for successors.

But candidates for Lodge Men and shamans were few. There was the drunken criminal Ricky of Hubxa, who was equipped with language skills and his legacy of songs, right there in Deer Lodge state prison to be recruited, but no. There were the scions of old and respected reservation families, but they were too acculturated, lacking, utterly, the language that the spirits use.

But there was also my friend, the young guy who had come to Chicago, to the Newberry Library, and who had spoken of Inktomi, Muskrat, First Man, and the creation of the world. Big, physically powerful, handsome, glib in two languages, with that storytelling capability that a term of alcoholism seems to enhance. The weird little misfit Zintkana Txo gave this young shaman one of the two Lodges that had been bequeathed to him by the dwindling list of elder holy men. And with that Lodge, and with his political career, and with his wide travels throughout the region that was once Assiniboine, my friend the Lodge Man fomented a renaissance.

First, among the homefolks. Then, with wizened elders and a shy college kid with *washiju* problems, for the Blackfeet.

And then his allies turned rivals, and both Maza Wichashta and Ska got one Lodge apiece going over in Hubxa. And all those Assiniboines in Saskatchewan who went without any for so many years, as a result of the Canadian government's version of American charity, now have at least two active Lodge-makers holding all-night sings and conducting sweats and gathering prayer-cloth offerings and supervising groups of young men who, drawn by their own, lesser power, build Lodges.

Poor, deluded Sword. His own people now hold Sun Dances, what the Sioux call *Wiwanyag Wacipi*s (literally, looking-at-the-sun dances) all over North Dakota and South Dakota and Manitoba and Montana, and they've proselytized so effectively that Politically Correct college kids in California and Massachusetts, and utterly acculturated eastern Indians, and even Robert Bly's white-guy weekend retreats, have Lakota-style *inipi*s, and hand-held hoop drums to beat, and long-stemmed pipes to smoke, and circles to sit in. (Although what those Bly guys think they're doing with the penis-shaped log someone must sometime explain to me.)

Back

The next morning, the fourth and last day of the Lodge, the women emerged.

Women dance in the Assiniboine Lodge. They dance behind their own low fence of woven cottonwood brush, on the east side of the Lodge, apart from the men, but with the full complement of ritual materials. They have eagle-bone whistles, sage brooms in each hand, special dance clothing. They had come in the night before, walking right through the walls to their own sacred space.

This should be no surprise to you. If it is, as it is, men and boys who sing the songs and cut the *chan wakan* and build the Lodge, one might automatically conclude that it is all a male affair. This is apparently what the guys of Bly perceive: that the ritual and the effort are all about men bonding, or some such.

But does not the *chan wakan* stick up out of the earth, stiff and erect, and meet the soft leafy nest where all the regenerative force of divine nature is focused?

Does not the revitalizing moisture of Grandfather's spring rains come down on Grandmother earth?

And did not the authoritative shaman, my friend the Lodge Man, once confide to me that "we men just act like we have power; the women are where it's really at"?

The spirits' messengers, the eagles, the *waginyan tanga* or Thunderbirds, the rain-bringers to that parched land, are who are being called by all those people tweeting on whistles to the beat of men's songs, and it is to the woman-effigy nest of the Lodge structure that they are being called.

The Assiniboines know what even the old dead white guy Plato knew: that the ideal of humanity is the joining of male and female.

I saw the women first as I arrived groggy, stiff, and chilled to sit through the last day's singing. I spent what energy I had on running Lodge errands, or, rather, walking them. I tried to meditate on the sexual metaphors of this rite, and on what the presence of those female dancers was meant to convey to the known and unknown worlds, but analysis was beyond me just then. The fast was taking as great a toll on my capacity for abstract thought as it had on my physical endurance. But this, too, was part of the plan. For the fourth day of the Lodge is the time of visions.

A crowd of well-wishers and the curious gathered early, and watched the singers and Lodge-people as if at an arena through the great entranceway. Of the seven women dancers who had entered the previous night, two had to be led away because of the taboo against the presence of menstruating women inside the Lodge. Soon they had replaced their dance clothes with civvies, and were as happily involved in the Lodge, now as spectators, as any. No problem perceived, no offense offered, none taken: for they had just received confirmation of their own power as creators, their own small dram of the force that rules the cosmos, while the rest of us were doing the hard work of seeking it.

Again, I warmed with the climb of the sun. I sat inside the sacred space with my eyes closed and let the sounds of its congregants' music fill me, and do what it and fasting do to Lodge Men: I had a vision.

It was startling, and colorful, but regrettably short-lived, for us sons of drunks, ever wary of the chaos and terror and hurt that lurk, do not allow beauty or peace to last too long.

It took time, but gradually I became aware of the stirring in that rationality that fasting and music had overwhelmed. Reflexively, I glanced at my watch. And I laughed, and so awoke to the present. Because again, the Assiniboine's virtual prohibition against any kind of precise planning caused at least the beginnings of a crisis.

Nobody in particular had arranged for the rice and raisins, the chokecherries, blueberries, strawberries, and water that were the "first and last fruits," the cherished sacred food that would be required for the breaking of the fast. Nor, judging by the easy lassitude of the crowd outside the Lodge, did it seem that the traditional post-Lodge communal meal would come off.

Not wanting to let the unthinkable happen through any nonperformance of my own, I hopped into a truck and blasted off for a house in Chansuda Ipa as the dancers chirped energetically on their whistles, the end of their testing only an hour away. In somebody's kitchen, I met up with the scholar's wife and exclaimed that we'd better lock and load right quick.

We set to cooking rice, thawing frozen strawberries, and opening cans of blueberries and Mason jars of put-up chokecherries. Soon enough, joggling over the rutted roads and the trackless range, and just in time for the spectacular close of the event, we arrived back on the high plain.

To my great enjoyment, Maza Wichashta had at long last come—just as the very last round of songs was being sung. All those who had brought songs had gathered around the singing hide and were singing just one verse each of their songs, with the song-owner holding the rattle while the rest drummed and sang vocables or just drummed. Each time a singer would complete a song, the man assigned to the "countdown" would toss a peg onto the hide, and the singer would pass the rattle.

Maza Wichashta performed with Cree verve, enlivening everyone within and without the Lodge, so widely is he known and liked—as a joke-teller, as a singer, as a renowned super-faster and living example of living the old way. With the drums continuing their beat, he passed the rattle to Indechan, the old man from Saskatchewan, who somehow adapted his slow, stolid signature song to the rapid beat. Indechan passed to Ziagu, who passed to Ska, who passed to Tabex'a and around it went, including, stunningly, to me, for was I not a song-owner? And around again, with the relentless and high-tempo drumming making for a seamless transition between singers, until the rattle passed to Zintkana Txo, the old wino, the allegedly powerful old shaman with the saggy baggy pants, who had lived his life as a sacred clown/contrary/Inktomi man, and this is what the old bastard did.

He grabbed up the rattle, and called out "Inktomi ta tibi ne!"—"This is Inktomi's Lodge!"—and threw that rattle down onto the hide, and rose and walked away.

The confused drummers missed a few beats. We singers were entirely and to a man flabbergasted. Mouths gaped just like in the cartoons at this statement that this whole event was the Inktomi, and you know who Inktomi is—he's the trickster, the overturner, the chaos-maker, and Zintkana Txo had just made this his time and place.

But within a few seconds Maza Wichashta had retrieved the rattle and had given it voice again, and the singing and the countdown and the mere human order resumed. The pegs were tossed and the rattle passed, and, as if scored for an orchestra with baton-wielding conductor, the singing ended with a tidy unison beat.

A few singers and builders carried dishes with the break-fast foods up to the Lodge Maker, who prayed and smoked over them. It was the men from the singing hide who stepped forward to him, took up those enamel pots and plastic buckets and returned to their fellow singers, and then served the dancers, and, finally, passed the foods to the slavering Lodge-builders whose fast, if only by a few seconds, proved to be the longest. With berry-juice dribbling down our chins and sips of cold water tracing the course of our insides, we thus ended.

We emerged from the Lodge into a world remade. Bits of rice and berries in their own syrupy juice helped, and so did the crowd of a hundred or so family members, well-wishers, and spectators, who laid out an enormous feast in a motley of colorful pots and baskets and brown cardboard boxes.

Before anyone lifted a ladle or opened a pot, the Lodge Man spoke from the mouth of the Lodge, again using Assiniboine first. His words were received gratefully by the assemblage, who seemed to be welcoming their dancer kin back as if from war. But of course. Those boys and girls of theirs really were heroes, genuine high achievers, some with the scars to show for it and the visions to remember as proofs for themselves.

As the speech ended, the shaman pointed skyward. Four. Count 'em, four eagles wheeled lazily in the midday updrafts rising from the warming plain on which we sat.

Then (thank you, America), he picked up a Coleman cooler full of popsicles, and tossed one to each Lodge Man and Lodge Woman. Which was the signal for everyone else to get to the serious business of devouring the feast of stews of beef and bison and venison, of fry bread and store-bought bread, of *tinpsina*, of edible tripe soup and of truly foul and stinking didn't-wash-it-enough-before-they-cooked-it tripe soup, and of cake and chips and cole slaw and macaroni salad and you name it, washed down with every kind of soda pop and Kool-Aid and sugary juice known to today's smart Assiniboine shopper.

Not done yet.

After just a little bit of food filled my shrunken stomach, it was giveaway time. Various dancers' families give quilts and JC Penney housewares and dollar bills and quart bottles of motor oil away to folks in the crowd, in honor of their relative's sacrifices and service.

Then it was the white guys' turn to honor the shaman's fourth Lodge. We gave hand-painted t-shirts from the scholar's wife's dining-table workshop, and red polo shirts emblazoned with bisons I'd bought back in Buffalo, and toys for kids and placemats and packs of cigarettes, Blue Gauloises from my favorite tobacco store on South Wabash in Chicago.

And in return, for there is ever reciprocity, I was gifted by a dancer with the beaded moosehide moccasins he'd worn through this arduous Lodge. This man, my age, my size, had danced and fasted as a gesture of gratitude to the spirits who had saved his young son from Reye's syndrome the previous winter. Now, out on the plain above Chansuda Ipa, this contemporary of mine, who had come over from near Hubxa with his brother Mina, a veteran of the Iran hostage rescue mission, and with his scampering and apparently intact six-year-old, walked sunwise around the circle of seated celebrants, and without much ceremony but with many smiles from all around and my surprised handshake, bestowed upon me the shoes he'd worn for his first-ever Lodge.

Beautiful, truly.

But my fast had been productive in a way that was extremely convincing to me, if difficult for the others to comprehend or accept. For I, sports fans, had had a true Assiniboine vision, in living color, in the correct ancient language of my own kin, in whose terms someone—They, or Him, or Her, or perhaps just me—had spoken with unmistakable clarity and precision.

The vision was mine and will remain so. Its message I'll share: go home.

I did.

The Lodge ended at noon. Two hours later, several days in advance of my planned departure, I boarded the eastbound Empire Builder.

Next

For having crossed a border, one must always return, and be a prodigal, or be lost.

This is a lesson that an old school friend did not learn.

While I was off in Flyover Country with people springing back from my ancestors' conquest of their ancestors, one of my pals had gone to Japan—a border-crossing to a version of the future.

He has these many years been engaged in a bridge enterprise there, having to do with making liaisons between Japanese and American businesses via video. While in his twenties, he married a Japanese woman, and brought beautiful children into being. From afar, it seemed that his adjustment was pleasant and modestly profitable, comfortably exotic, with family trips home every couple of years, and upbeat reports from his parents. Photographs of the wedding showed all parties in kimonos, prettily Japanese.

But the culture into which Ned married and bought is not monolithic. It is thick and multidimensional, with trends, passions, minority sympathies. My old chum Ned did not marry an empress in whom lives the official essence of the society, but a commoner, as subject to passions and small tendencies as any other Japanese. She could have been a bourgeois housewife, or her country's equivalent of a yuppie, or a sympathizer with the Red Army faction, or whatever. From thousands of miles away, she was, to my unexacting and distracted eyes, merely Japanese.

As it happened, Ned's wife wasn't merely that. She was a philosophically inclined young woman who became an enthusiast of what can only be described as a utopian communal cult.

And, in the way of utopian organizations, it places some demands on its adherents.

These: nothing short of total personal and familial commitment. Divestment of all worldly goods and assets. Communal living. Relinquishment of the existing family relationship, such that the children would cease being children of their parents in favor of becoming junior citizens of this sub-society.

And all in the service of a very foreign, very foreign sort of mysticism whose goal is a transcendent Peace that is hard for Westerners to credit or fathom.

Standing at the precipice, hesitating for I don't know how long before deciding whether to make the plunge, Ned reached out to his old connections, to family, to friends, to old schoolmates he hadn't seen for decades. He sent out a voluminous letter describing this utopian group and his wife's determination to join him and the children to it, and asked for our help in plotting his future.

You have been reading my response.

Having had the vision that commanded return, I did so. I went back to the business of politics and policy imbued with a sense of, if you'll forgive the clumsiness of the construction, a special giftedness—a sense of having, like my friend and shaman and teacher, arrived at the fullness of my own maturity. Maybe even of moving a step closer to becoming my own First Man.

It was not enough to pursue a mere living. My consultancy has ever been selective. Reflecting on the model of my friend the shaman, the leader who eats last at the feast, who takes on the impossible because it is necessary to do so, I sought out and joined others who had some of his leaderly commitment to the larger good—not as purists needing defeat, as purists do, to reify their own sense of virtue, but as strivers for the better, willing to move by increments.

I borrowed a good motto: do not let the perfect become the enemy of the good. Which is to say, we should fight without measuring each stage of the battle by the ultimate goal—but we should never lose sight of it.

The ambiguities

> "The instability of human knowledge is one of our few certainties. Almost everything we know we know incompletely at best. And almost nothing we are told remains the same when retold."
>
> —Janet Malcolm, writing about Gertrude Stein's alleged callousness in regard to refugee French Jews, *The New Yorker*, November 13, 2006

The girls, especially our thirteen-year-old ballet specialist, love a TV show about models called *America's Next Top Model.* Our girls are all adolescents. They are investigating exemplars, as it is our American practice to do, as we do, when we vote. We choose as our representatives those who exemplify our best selves. I know this search well: I assist in it. In 1973, not quite twenty, pursuing the adolescent search, working late nights as a student journalist, I saw an exemplar in the person of President Salvador Allende of Chile.

Allende was an educated man who had been elected through a democratic process. In the context of the Cold War, in America's late Vietnam War days, Allende's democratic socialism was, for our president, unacceptable. To the world of American college students on college campuses, the perfidy of our government's opposition to this gentle faraway professor was absolutely obvious, untainted by any ambiguity—so much so that, two years after the Attica prison riot (or "rebellion"), a year after Richard Nixon's reelection, in the same year as the American Indian Movement's fight against the FBI in South Dakota at Wounded Knee, I tried to go to Chile to cover the siege of the Allende government but had to settle for someone else's telegrams because of the small inconvenience of my lack of a passport. The crushing of Allende was a profound shock in 1973, like the Arab-Israeli War of 1973, and the Nixon resignation in 1974, and the fiasco of the Saigon embassy rooftop in 1975, and the Carter triumph of 1976, by which time I was a working journalist in Chicago, where I met exiled Chileans from the anti-Allende coup of 1973.

The Chileans were modest men, those half-dozen of them. They were gentle people who tended not to interrupt one another as we sat together in an apartment near 18th Street. They were happy, literally happy, to be living in safe Chicago. They worked at some kinds of jobs, one of them at a lamp factory in Pilsen, the Mexican neighborhood that had been Slavic for the first half of the twentieth century. I wrote about them at the time—the copper-miners whose union had been broken by soldiers reporting to General Augusto Pinochet. My translator was a Mexican aristocrat who had studied for the priesthood and at the prestigious Collegio de Mexico, who had been radicalized by the brutality of Mexican interior minister Echeverria's repression in 1968, when Echeverria had ordered Mexican soldiers to shoot down unarmed student protesters. The Prague Spring had been in 1968, followed by the Prague summer, in which Brezhnev had had his proxy shoot down unarmed protestors. The Paris Riots were in 1968. The Poles rioted that year, too, against the Polish government that Brezhnev commanded to restore order. Tet had started in 1968, then in April came King's assassination, then Bobby Kennedy's. Then in 1969 came the landing on the moon, and in 1970, the invasion of Cambodia, and in 1971, the Attica riots and, shortly after, my draft notice.

Thus the story of our years of coming of age is like a Sioux "winter count," as when those preliterate horsemen of the Northern Plains noted each year by one significant event. There was the year of the great eclipse, which was 1815. There was the year of blackened lodges, sometime in the 1830s, when smallpox killed as immensely as the Black Plague had in the fourteenth century in Europe. The German writer Günter Grass nodded to this tradition of annualizing such horrors in his novel *My Century*. As I came to manhood in the late 1960s and the early 1970s, there was a calamity a year: Tet, Lunar Entry Module, Parrot's Beak, Attica, Nixon's reelection, Allende / Arab-Israeli War, Nixon's resignation, Saigon, Carter's assertion that he would not lie. There it is, 1968 through 1976, and in the same month I met the exiled Chilean copper-miners who had fled Pinochet, Jimmy Carter was elected, and old Mayor Richard Daley, whose last press conference I covered on my first assignment, died.

Grass made some reference to the Allende catastrophe in his 1999 speech in Stockholm at the event where the Swedish Academy awarded him the Nobel Prize in Literature. In Grass's speech, Allende's Chile of 1973 was just a passing reference. But Allende's death had happened more than a quarter-century before Grass's 1999 Nobel Prize speech—and still Grass mentioned Allende. Grass did not mention Budapest 1956, or Prague or Mexico City or Paris 1968, or Bobby Kennedy, or the collapse of the Berlin Wall in 1989. And as I read Günter Grass's speech, this year, seven years on, in the year in which he was revealed to have been a member of the Waffen-SS during the last days of Hitler's regime, I thought, My God, how I want to be angry and disgusted with this man, Grass, this Günter Grass the novelist, who for all my winters until this one was my exemplar of a literary man as a historical man, a political man, a moral man, and now, revealed to me and to his adoring fans, and to his wife, who like the rest of us didn't know, as a member of one of Hitler's most murderous organizations.

My children are uncomprehending of this, so I will grab the clicker, turn the volume down, and lecture them. Sixty years ago, before the debut of *America's Next Top Model*, the Waffen-SS was an official entity of the German government, dear ones. The German government was led by a man named Hitler and by his confederates in the National Socialist Party. We called them the Nazis. The Nazis were very, very bad people. They went house-to-house and town-to-town and killed people and took their property. They held huge rallies and burned books. Then they invaded countries like Poland, France, and Russia, and they killed millions of people, and they also made war against our country. The Waffen-SS was one of the organizations that Hitler and the Nazis used against all those people and against our country too. The Nobel Prize–winning writer Mr. Günter Grass, who was a favorite of your father's—just one more minute and then I'll give you the clicker—this Günter Grass was a member of the Waffen-SS, but he waited all that time from 1945 until 2006 to tell anybody.

Now then. By failing to tell anybody about this, was Günter Grass

A. Good? Or was he

B. Bad?

While I await their answer, let us do the math. Born in 1927, drafted in 1944, captured in 1945. Günter Grass was seventeen when he became a member of the Waffen-SS.

The girl practicing the piano in the other room, the one playing movements two and three of the Pathétique (the movements that require touch and sensitivity and not just the brute muscle and brute speed of the first movement) is sixteen. The sister who is so strong in her dancing, who most loves the show about models, is as old as Grass was during his Hitlerjugend days in Danzig before his city became Gdansk. The sister in the middle, the fifteen-year-old, survivor of school dramas, is as old as Günter Grass was in the occupied Baltic port city when he was drafted into military service by the Reich. In his speech to the Swedish Academy upon receiving the Nobel Prize in Literature in 1999, Grass did not fail to mention his military service. In the Swedish Academy's official biography of Grass, there is no failure to mention his military service from the age of fifteen until his capture by the Allies in 1945 when he was, if arithmetic serves, eighteen. The sixteen-year-old has moved on to a Bach piece that is more mechanical, the prelude in C minor, then to the first prelude, played not as Glenn Gould did so very precisely, with each note enunciated as definitively as an individually cited text, but in a kid's manner, with lots of sostenuto, and quite fast, like a velocity exercise in a Czerny book. In the other room, girls are hooting at the models on TV. Elsewhere, just a few blocks from here, kids are pursuing the drug trade as enthusiastic mules and runners. And just five miles from here, in the calm suburbs that are like the Danzig suburbs in which Grass grew up except that we are American and he was a German-speaking Pole with a mom from an ethnic enclave called Kashubia, there are children of fifteen who at this very moment wish they were the drug-running, gun-toting, rapping ghetto kids they see on TV, just a click of the clicker away from *America's Next Top Model.*

So Grass was a minor-aged conscript into a hideous entity. And now this is revealed, six or seven years after his Nobel Prize.

Ruthlessness is a characteristic that one associates with narcissism. In politics, the playground of narcissists, there is a small demonstration of ruthlessness that I have seen much of. It is the lie. Small politicians who wish to appear ruthless, who wish to demonstrate their strength, tend to lie. It's not sophisticated—indeed, the chief difference between small-time provincial politics and big-time national politics is that small-timers lie and believe that lying proves their sophistication, while in Washington (does any other political place qualify as "big"?) there is no need to lie, only to assert forthrightly, in a nuanced manner wherever necessary, but to assert nonetheless, and to do so no matter which personalities, constituencies, interests, or countries get crushed along the way.

I am making this too complicated. Rubes and provincials lie and betray, while presidents and members of Congress make alliances that simply, brutally, but quite decisively, assert.

Grass was both small ruthless and big ruthless, and he got away with it for a lifetime. What he got was fame, regard, the Nobel Prize, lots of money, and a place in the news every day. Lots of girls, too.

My hero.

My exemplar.

Contrast the war experience. In his Nobel speech, Grass says, I come from the country that burned books. He quotes a poet who said that to write a poem after Auschwitz would be obscene. German life, literature, thought, is divided into life and its works before and after Auschwitz, he says in his speech. I grew up knowing survivors of the camps. It's my privilege to know two Righteous Gentiles who secreted and otherwise prevented Hungarian Jews from disappearing in the Auschwitz deportations in the spring and summer of 1944, when, up in Danzig, young Günter Grass was a seventeen-year-old conscript in the Waffen-SS. That was precisely the year when my uncle was at Parris Island training to kill Japanese, and when my father was in Italy killing Germans. But then, Dad was older, twenty-four, and Uncle Bruce, when he went to Iwo Jima, was twenty-one, both of them old enough to vote and to sign contracts as adults.

Günter Grass, the boy of seventeen, was not an adult.

He was, however, an adult when he began his career as a published author. He was an adult through the 1950s, the 1960s, the 1970s, the 1980s, the 1990s, and in this, the first decade of the twenty-first century, now thirty years on from the day when Salvador Allende killed himself as men in the military uniform of his country betrayed their oaths.

The forceful and energetic new national politician Barack Obama addresses the ambiguity of political morality, as all our older children learn to, when he describes his mature acceptance of Thomas Jefferson as a hero, a statesman, and as a theorist of democracy—as a Founding Father—despite Thomas Jefferson's practice of holding slaves. Obama writes that he had himself to make a choice, which was whether to work to understand, or to succumb to anger, and thereby to diminish himself. There is something important about telling the truth. Truth empowers. Truth frees.

Most of what I have read of Günter Grass's lying is written as if the subject is fully formed—an object for all time, finished, like a sculpture, or a mountain. As an old man, Grass is more certainly that, completed, than is any adolescent, especially one under the duress of a dictatorship.

I have not finished with Grass, this adolescent who, with his truth-avoidance, remains for me an insightful boy. His work is yet work for me. Nor is my eye finished learning how to see.

Hates

The new reading material, begun just the day before Milosevic went lights-out in his war crimes trial cell in den Hague, is about the cowardice and moral confusion of the Europeans.

One recalls the radio story about Milosevic in 1989, the year the Berlin Wall was first breached, then kicked down, by East Germans brave enough to sense that if only they resisted the specific oppressions of the police state, they might win. They did so resist; they did win. In all those places in Eastern Europe where so many Americans have kin and connections, there was actual courage on display, thus: refusal to obey the official bullying of police who had, until moments before, been empowered to seize, to torture, to kill. Also released, though, in the general collapse of the Communist states, were old hatreds that the Communists had selectively suppressed. But of course, there was no virtue in that suppression: Communists had kept ethnic rivalries in their toolkit of intimidation. The Polish regime played the card of anti-Semitism when it suited it, as in 1968, but it didn't work against Solidarność, which was empowered by the Polish pope, whose most profound statement was "do not fear." But ethnic hates, old hates, were loosed in 1989, and clever self-promoting politicians figured it out: if I proclaim myself the stalwart defender of the group, then I will get a job for myself running things. There's money in fracturing government. So resentment of Slovak for Czech suddenly appeared, and voila—suddenly there's a Slovak republic for the first time since the Nazis created one. We saw it unfold on CNN. Generally, though, the revolutions were peaceful. In Prague, it was the Velvet Revolution. So the Slovaks wanted to break away and be their own little country? Then go, said the playwright Havel, the coolest president anywhere ever; he had had Frank Zappa and the Mothers of Invention at his inauguration. There was suddenly openness, environmentalism, tourism, and an end to the horrific intrusions of the thugs with the truncheons, prisons, and electrodes. It was the West, except that everybody there had no money.

As this docudrama played on the TV in front of our health-club treadmills, and the names of all these countries tumbled forth out of Wolf Blitzer's mouth, one learned or relearned some history. The Baltic states—can you name them? Can you tell which one of them speaks its version of Finnish and which ones speak their versions of Sanskrit? They became interesting facts. They're free now? Great! On to the next news item. Problem resolved. (Americans like problems to be resolved.) And then, some other countries that we didn't hear that much about also came onto the news.

Yugoslavia became a story. If we were expecting another liberation, well, not so fast. Yugoslavia came on the scene quite differently than the others. The six-part country across the Adriatic from familiar Italy hadn't been part of the Russian (excuse me, Soviet) empire. It had been the place that had gone its own way. A troublesome place, to be sure: World War I started there when the young Serb had shot the old Archduke. It was the part of Europe that the Turks had run for half a millennium. Quick newscast histories went quickly over the story about the plains of Kosovo Polje in southern Yugoslavia, on which the valiant young king of the Serbs was killed and his soldiers routed by the Turks just six hundred short years ago. The trouble today (why would there be trouble with all this freedom breaking out?) was that the Yugoslavs remembered the events of six hundred years ago as clearly as yesterday, and suddenly the pundits were saying, "it's always been that way, so it's always going to be that way."

But then why, then, was conflict news?

Answer: because conflict was new. It had been peaceful. Now it wasn't.

An American journalist named Robert Kaplan went there to see the ancient monasteries and shrines of the Serb nation, the biggest of the six parts of Yugoslavia. Kaplan there met elderly and also young religious officials who tended these small places. One dimly recalls the stories that make these people jump; one hardly has patience with all this, for mythology among us in the comfortable West is about movies and about songs sung by rock stars most of whose fans weren't even born when the Berlin Wall came down, much less when it was up. A sea of ignorance surrounds the knowledgeable and makes us islands, even if our knowledge is tiny. Even smart teenagers today have to be told over and over again what Communism was.

And time races, races ahead. Milosevic (who?) is dead.

He was on trial for terrible crimes against humanity committed between the time the Berlin Wall came a-tumblin' down and the time the World Trade Center got smashed by suicide terrorists. Milosevic was sitting in a jail in Holland when he croaked from a bad heart. So Milosevic is dead before his trial for war crimes was decided. And now the other members of his gang, the insane psychiatrist Karadzic and the murderous general Mladić, may never be given up to the war crimes tribunal.

Who was he? It matters enough to reflect. Milosevic was the correct sort of opportunistic thug for a time of change, is who he was. He was an opportunist, a self-promoting loud-talker, who was amoral enough to use forbidden symbols and with them unleash crude emotions about group identity. That's his relevance. Civilized Europe was tested by him at that particular time of upheaval and reorganization, about a dozen years ago, just as we in America were choosing a president of the Baby Boom generation.

Milosevic died at sixty-four. So in 1989 he was forty-nine. Bill Clinton was elected president in 1992 at the age of forty-six. So Milosevic was an old boomer. He had clambered up the greasy pole of political power after the death of the Yugoslav communist king called Tito (one can get away with calling him a king now because the Communists have all metamorphosed into whatever they are now). Tito had slammed the country together after leading the partisan guerillas who threw the Germans out. Tito had spent the 1950s and 1960s commanding his government to make a unified people out of Orthodox Serbs, Catholic Croats and Slovenes, Muslim Bosnians, Muslim Albanians, and Orthodox Bulgarian-speaking Slavs who had learned to think of themselves as Macedonians. (This was much to the annoyance of the neighboring Greeks whose own notion of Macedon had to do with Philip and with his son Alexander the Great.) American eyes glazed over; Americans barely knew where Yugoslavia was but had some notion about Tito because he was a stocky man who met our presidents, took them hunting for wild boar, and stayed apart from the Russians, which was the thing our government cared about most during all those years. Then Tito died. But Yugoslavia held together. There was a sort of international coming-out party for Yugoslavia when the wintertime Olympics were held in Sarajevo in 1984; the event had a cute little bear as mascot. One marveled at the pluralism of plucky Sarajevo, full of athletes, surrounded by mountains, with ancient onion-domed buildings, minarets, libraries full of the precious books of people who had decided to conserve on vowels, apparently, because all their names consisted of consonants like so many mortarless bricks jammed together, and Jim McKay and the ABC News team having so much difficulty doing their color pieces. But we in TV land all said Welcome to the World, Sarajevo, Yugoslavia. There was even a car, a little bitty thing called the Yugo. Cute like the little bear. The media extravaganza helped the place. Resorts on the Adriatic, ancient cities, undiscovered islands, skiing, mountain lakes for trout-fishing.

Then five years later, the news from Yugoslavia was that Milosevic was pulling his country out of the World and heading up a disaster.

How did Milosevic accomplish this?

The story dribbled out even as the happy revolutions, the liberating changes, took place elsewhere in confusing Europe. Milosevic won power by saying unmentionable things that ignored the recent past in favor of the ancient past. Thirty years of peaceful coexistence of ethnic and religious groups, albeit the peace achieved by secret police and official propaganda, were undone so that a guy and his guys could get jobs, cars, houses, guns, power.

His government looked like the regime of a gang. One recalls gangs from the South Side of Chicago: the predecessors of the Crips and the Bloods, like the Black P Stone Rangers (formerly the Blackstone Rangers, named after the street named Blackstone). As the gang got older, it got uglier and more violent. There were offshoots like the El Rukns, black drug-dealers pretending to be a sect imbued with the legitimacy of religiosity. Was that what CNN was showing us?

The experts on TV said no, that it was all ancient, permanent hatreds, nothing new. But there *had* been peace, just a couple of years before. Yes, the history was what it was: ugly, as recently as the 1940s. Then Tito made peace. In the irony of the multiethnic state, Tito used his thug-cops to try to make an American-style melting pot in that complex mountainous territory bounded on the north by the Danube River and on the south by the Adriatic. Religion in Tito's Yugoslavia was tolerated but discouraged, because religion was divisive. Tito urged his people—his peoples—to intermarry. Tito led a secular state. Tito's official ideology was Communist, and in his propaganda he chastised the Croats for having been fascists and the Serbs for having been monarchists. The king Tito's favorite subjects were the polyglot cosmopolitans of Sarajevo, who were of course the weakest. The Sarajevo cosmopolitans were too educated to be thugs. Too busy being tolerant, secular, economic. Serbs, Croats, Jews,

Muslims; the divisions were not those, but rather the ones the rest of the world knows: city folks versus country folks.

Then the king died and there was, by his design, nobody strong enough to succeed him. There was a "revolving presidency." Everybody's ambitions were supposed to keep everybody else's ambitions in check.

Then Milosevic touched the forbidden fruit. Milosevic manipulated the symbols of national identity. He went before the crowd at Kosovo, in the actual place where the six hundred years of defeat of the Serb nation had first occurred, and hinted that there might be a blood reckoning for the Serb nation.

Thus did he unleash hell. He chose the politician trick: he played on people's resentments. No job? Blame the other guy. Not enough money? Blame the other guy. Unfriendly strangers pressing up against your neighborhood? Stick with me, boys, we'll *get* them no matter what the rules say.

His message was for the Serbs. He started murdering Catholic Croatians in the north, Muslims Bosnians in the south, Muslim Albanians who had dared to populate the sacred territory of Kosovo. They all spoke the same damned language (except for the Albanians) and knowledgeable people tell me that you can't tell the one from the other, the Serbo- from the Croatian, which Catholics and Muslims and Orthodox all speak. The word "evil" started creeping into the vocabulary of learned Westerners who, in their archipelago of learned magazines and of learned Sunday morning television programs, sent each other messages about the eventual need for the United States and its allies to actually do something about this problem.

But the Western Europeans, including all the NATO members, wouldn't intervene to stop Milosevic from killing. Clinton wouldn't act unilaterally; he was criticized for "letting" Milosevic murder civilians and perform "ethnic cleansing" as the breathless and desperate reports came in daily over National Public Radio and on the evening news shows, but Clinton had people on it. They all say that he was trying to get our allies focused: Bush 41, you will recall, did not go alone into the rescue of Kuwait—he put the alliance together, and then when we went in, it was overwhelming, unified, "Shock and Awe," the correct name for the operation. Now, in Europe, the allies equivocated, dithered. The Russians let it be known that they would not tolerate Americans beating up on their little South Slav ally. Then United Nations "peacekeepers" from Holland stood by and let Milosevic's murderers murder. It got to be too much when

Ratko Mladić, the thug in the uniform of a general, murdered 7,500 men and boys in Srebrenica. In 1995—for Chrissake, this is just a few years ago—Clinton had Richard Holbrooke bring the sonofabitch Milosevic to an Air Force base in Ohio for negotiations (and why do we talk to such people? why do we have our officials break bread with them?). And there in Dayton, Ohio, everybody let the lying bastard jerk everybody around as if he were a statesman with a legitimate government, because dem's da rules. For another two years, he and Mladić and his guys went on murdering civilians, disrupting towns, separating communities into black and white, reducing the complexity of life to simple fundamentals the way political-religious hacks in America want it all reduced to fundamentals. One recalls one's anger at this charade. Finally, Milosevic broke the rules and we sent in General Wesley Clark at the head of the NATO force and he unleashed six weeks of bombing. Clark destroyed the roads and bridges and power stations that Tito had built in order to make all the little nations in this made-up agglomerated federation of nations happy about being on the road to flush toilets, warm bedrooms, kitchens with something to cook in them, roads with little cars on them and not just horse-carts plastered with the religious badges of old identities.

Of course, it was American resolve that made this occur. The educated cosmopolitan Europeans scolded Clark, scolded Clinton, prevaricated and equivocated because the Americans, at long last, had gone in to rescue civilians.

One was not impressed with Europe. One wondered why Europe would not run to the defense of civilians who were being murdered. Are the victims equivalent to the executioners? Did the victims bring it on themselves, the throat-slitting, the rapes, the lining-up of the boys and men of Srebrenica? How about the shelling of Sarajevo, when the city folks (Serbs, Croats, Muslims, Jews of every age and class) had to dodge howitzer and mortar rounds being lobbed at them by the hillbillies above—did they bring it upon themselves?

The difference seemed to be that Americans were able to distinguish victims from criminals, and the Europeans were not.

But then it ended. Milosevic was out of office, and his Serb successor turned him over to the War Crimes tribunal. The Croatians shunted their disposable mobsters off to Holland too, and the Bosniaks theirs—and the cameras didn't have much to cover down there Yugoslavia way.

In the intervening years, Slovenia, the little Slavic-speaking province of the old Habsburg empire, had become a stand-alone republic, as had Croatia and Macedonia (pardon, the Former Yugoslav Republic of Macedonia), and the tripartite Bosnia. What was left of Yugoslavia was the Republic of Serbia, the Republic of Montenegro (with something like seven hundred thousand people ruminating about their own independence) and the semiautonomous region of Kosovo, which wants independence because, notwithstanding what happened on the battleground at Kosovo Polje six hundred years ago, everybody who lives in Kosovo these days is an Albanian-speaking Muslim and not a Serbian-speaking Orthodox Christian. From united Yugoslavia to splintered mini-states; from a just-about First World infrastructure to a smashed Third World non-network of smashed power grids, smashed roads, divided towns without bridges, in just ten years. Hundreds of thousands dead, European elites still rushing to deny that one side in the conflict had inherent evil while the other had inherent innocence; ancient libraries burned, tourist-attracting walled cities pockmarked with shell-holes, little Sarajevo bear-dolls long since ground into mud in a city street that used to be paved.

Milosevic, Milosevic. Dead before his trial ended. Thankfully, not martyred by some authority that some new symbol-manipulator would use to stir up the believers again (though they will try). Surely, though, Milosevic will inspire the next nihilistic politician. Surely, he will terrify the next moral relativist for whom the greatest threat is not the knife at one' own throat but the inconvenient moral "absolutism" of someone, probably an American, who can distinguish death from life, lies from truth, criminality from innocence.

Is there another Milosevic coming?

You betcha. Quebec. Alberta. South Louisiana. All the angry southwestern states should the water run out but the desert border remain porous. Any number of inconsequential places, of course. Look for a politician who can play on the anguish of the aggrieved, who has a tight band of otherwise-unemployable hacks, and who has someone around who is adept at symbols, phrases, history, and TV, and just watch it replay.

Ties

The drama was of but a moment's duration, when the woman tending her bookshop became a daughter like one of my own when she reached forward and touched my tie.

I am near sixty, and inured to the ways of Downtown. Decades of wearing ties, these decorative silks around my neck, have made them habit. Putting them on in the morning and removing them after the workday is a way to demarcate time: public from private; on, off. I'd stopped on the way home, so it was still public time, when this unaccountable intrusion occurred.

She is about thirty, the young woman who served me. It is not so very well lit in her bookstore, which feels like poets and jeans and a time long ago, before I wore ties, before my own fatherhood. A starched shirt and a silk tie: formality, adultness, and I, browsing, a man with teen daughters, shaped by them, imagined that what she saw was her dad from long ago—her approving father, I hoped. Her seeing me drew her away from her conversation with a young man. We fathers always approve so predictably of our daughters, who are always so delighted with our love!

But as she approached me, she was severe.

She saw that I had books. Richler novels, old paperbacks. Richler is Montreal to me, and Montreal is a dream city, snowy and old, like this one, only better chronicled. Snowy, genuine, all Jews-versus-English and the sullen Francophones like wallpaper or geography in Richler's books, but the city for him is very much a character and a psychology itself, with its great university downtown like we should have had, all happily crammed into the spaces between banks and up against churches and apartment buildings. And Montreal has streets whose names signal the homes of each of the social classes, such that the gangs are street-named, and their fights are iconic clashes, like mythical warriors who fought astride named horses, swung named swords. I had Richler and a Malamud and a book of stories by someone Russian, Babel, or Chekhov. Five bucks apiece.

And then she smiled. It was the tie. She remarked on my tie. And suddenly, without asking, she reached for it, fingered it. Her fingers brushed against my chest.

She looked at its pattern: oars, many-colored oar blades, on a field of middling blue. She exclaimed at its softness and smoothness.

I don't know her name, but I know her. She's partnered with the spike-haired barmaid at the saloon down the street, a potter. In this city, we have the privilege, and the burden, of having encountered one another before, for there aren't so many of us anymore. I make an effort to patronize her haphazard store of great piles of used books. She knows me, as she knows me, as a man who is her customer, but not a poetry-slam reader nor a neighborhood hangabout, nor a graduate student, nor a professor in an open-neck shirt. I am the suit man. I am the tie man. I am the man iconic, against whom she was educated. I am, by my tie and by my starched shirt, my pressed trousers, my polished Oxfords, the enemy patriarch. Yet I am also customer, if infrequent customer. And I get a smile, and the surprising tactile intimacy of my tie being touched, my tie, its color and its pattern and its formality, my silk jewel.

It speaks like a Montreal novelist of our city's earlier era—when her father's clothing was like mine, when men like me and her father went to a place called Downtown.

Downtown is where the great men's clothing stores were, especially the one that owned all the handsome facade of the Brisbane building all around its curve on Lafayette Square. One could be fitted for a suit there, and look out the window to see the Downtown library where Mark Twain's manuscripts and the great John James Audubon portraits of birds are housed amid the big buildings, the banks and courts and offices full of men who wore ties and women who wore stockings. A suit and a tie, shoe-shines and cigar stores, barber shops with straight razors and hot lather and strops, blocked hats, and cocktails, the great library with its important books—they were all Downtown.

I carry that geography with me. For thirty years, I have been wearing suits and ties and shined shoes through airports and in offices, in committee rooms on Capitol Hill and at press conferences, at lecterns, at church. These days, I walk across campus in the crowds of students moving between classes, and they know me to be other than them, dressed, as I am, in icons of class, race, age. Among the adults there, too, I am mistaken as the other, as a member of the administrative branch, for the professoriate does not wear silk or press its trousers, nor does it shine its shoes. Downtown is far away.

It was actually destroyed here, in our city. There is no men's store downtown where one can buy a shirt, or a suit, or a tie. The center, the pinnacle, the place of fathers and of enemy patriarchs exists in every other city, and yes, it is not all destroyed, it does still cling to existence here, but not like Richler's Montreal or Bellows's Chicago, or my own 1970s Chicago, or my current Washington. My city is of middling size. It has Main Street, but Main Street has not a single store that sells a silk tie. The ties and the shoes and the stockings, too, moved away, to the suburbs. Everything moved to the suburbs when they dug up the streets. Many fathers then died, the ones who wore suits Downtown.

I'm new to the campus. My Downtown suit does not fit here. I do own a Harris tweed jacket, the kind that professors in movies wear. My tweed jacket's pockets are full of sunflower seeds. Its elbows gave out some years ago, so I had suede patches sewn on because I just like it so well, smelly old thing. I used to take my daughters to the nature preserve just over the bridge from Downtown, and walk into the snowy woods, and reach into my tweedy seedy pockets for a little bunch of sunflower seeds, and hold them in my cupped hand, arm outstretched, and wait for the chickadees to come alight on my sleeve and on my thumb, and take a seed, and flit off. My girls loved seeing that. They liked trying it. They liked the feeling of those tiny living bold birds, so near to weightless on their own hands. Then they outgrew visiting the chickadees. When the city has gotten snowy these past few years, they haven't come with me to feed those birds. Perhaps when they are older, visiting me with their friends who have never fed wild birds, who have never seen the surprising herd of white-tail deer in our feral precincts, they will indulge me, and let me convince their friends (I'm so annoying, I always speak with the friends) to come with me and feed the birds and see the deer.

I will wear boots or overshoes, old-fashioned overshoes of the kind that the men of Downtown used to wear when I got my first suit at Kleinhans, which was the week when my grandfather died. Grandmother had wanted me to wear one of his suits, because we'd loved each other so closely, but I'd grown too tall by then. I don't recall what became of his ties, but his hats—his rabbit-felt hats, with the ribands of satin, blocked, each hat in its own box—his hats were a marvel to me, the most firm statement that he had come from another era entirely, just as my tie tells store clerks how separate my native space will ever be, and how lost to all of us.

Embracing civilization, fighting savagery

The war against terror requires that we understand and accept that there is a difference between being Civilized and being Primitive. The real topic is war. Not metaphorical war, but real war. Who will kill us; who will live, who will die.

President Bush has spoken about the threat to our civilization. We are daily witnesses to the brutal, savage, primitive warfare that is waged against our soldiers and against civilians in Iraq and Afghanistan. We've heard rhetorical conflict too, between the Pope and those who accuse him of having slandered Islam. A powerful government faces threats from non-governments: our American legal system is having a very difficult time coping with Guantanamo; the international legal system embodied in the Geneva Accords is being challenged.

Our very words are culturally charged when we try to describe the conflict between us and them. And as heirs to and practitioners within the Anglo-American legal tradition, we tend to see the conflict now in law enforcement terms.

But the language of war and the language of law enforcement are uncomfortable together. The Pope asked for interfaith dialogue between Islam and Christianity; the response was murder and lawlessness. The language is important; the clash of culture became a trigger for the violence of primitive war.

Ten years ago, James Keeley wrote a revolutionary book about primitive warfare that has a peculiar relevance to current events.

First, contrast, as Keeley bravely does, civilized warfare from primitive warfare. Civilized warfare is almost like crime-fighting, for civilized warfare is about rules. Civilized war between nations means professionalized soldiers, an official or legal code of conduct binding on all parties, and very low casualty rates for the societies at war.

Primitive war is not about professionalized soldiers. Every man, *every* single male in a primitive society was a soldier. There was a code of conduct, but that code is not about law. And casualty rates in primitive war were and are staggeringly high compared to the casualty rates in civilized war.

When the French and the Germans fought in the Franco-Prussian War of 1870, for example, the casualty rate for both countries was under 1 percent. Primitive war is not like this. It is not restrained. Its warriors do not delegate. It is also not large. When fifty-two Assiniboine warriors went on a raid of the Blackfeet in the northern plains in 1852, the Blackfeet killed every single Assiniboine on that raid and tried to kill every single Assiniboine in the village from which they rode. Primitive warfare was about annihilation.

When the Senecas first came to western New York in 1658, it was to annihilate the Erie nation, to kill the Erie nation, to eat the Erie nation, and to forcibly adopt what was left of the Erie nation. Jesuit missionaries wrote accounts of this atrocity in blood-curdling detail.

The language gets inflammatory, but it must: primitive is a word that we must not shrink from. Civilized is a word that we must not shrink from.

But we do. Our language about primitive people since World War Two has constrained our ability to think clearly.

I am an object lesson in avoiding clear language about primitive people, even though I did fieldwork among, learned a language of, and even underwent arduous rituals with primitive people. The Assiniboine people of Saskatchewan and Montana taught me that primitive does not mean simple, or stupid; it is not a term of condemnation, nor is it a term of endearment. In the issue of war, the difference is fundamental.

Civilized countries have soldiers; primitive peoples have warriors. This is a critical difference. In fact, I believe that today, as we face terrorism, we are fortunate to have soldiers who can draw on a warrior tradition.

I know many soldiers, and a few warriors.

Soldiers wear the uniform. Many of you who read this have worn the uniform. You wore it during the Cold War. Notwithstanding any rhetoric, there was not much question of civilized versus primitive during the Cold War. Those who served on the front lines of the Cold War were soldiers pitted against other soldiers from other civilized countries. You were not sent out to fight a clan or a warrior society or a kin network. Your war was a conflict between great powers.

Today, the conflict is not between great powers. The conflict is between the many great powers which together constitute the civilized world, versus a dispersed, internationalized, self-refreshing conspiracy. It is a conflict between international civilization, on one side, versus a cultural movement on the other that expresses itself in acts of terror against the civilians who constitute that civilization. It is between we who are defended by our professional defenders, versus a movement of direct actors that motivates *them* through suicidal devotion to a religious doctrine.

The analytical framework of Primitive versus Civilized is, however, challenged, because never has primitivity endeavored to seek world domination. That religiously motivated actors use primitive means suggests that we should understand primitive war, as if we are fighting it.

We thought we knew what terrorism was. Think back to 1995, when a white kid from Pendleton named Timothy McVeigh murdered 168 of his fellow Americans.

Timothy McVeigh and his coconspirators thought themselves to be the vanguard of an international movement. Americans generally took them to be a terrorist underground that was going to shake civilized society to its foundation. But they weren't any such thing. Their international movement consisted of European skinheads and neo-Nazis, who were really just street thugs and soccer hooligans. Timothy McVeigh and his like never had a cohesive ideology other than anti-Semitism, misogyny, antipathy to visible minorities, and love of beer. Here in America, they organized a few so-called militias composed of working-class jobless small-town white men led by jailhouse lawyers, conspiracy theorists, and anti-tax scammers, who were egged on by radio talk show hosts.

The reason we have not heard much about the alleged terrorism of these very marginal actors is that our law enforcement personnel took them down.

Oklahoma City was indeed a blow against civilization, but it wasn't an expression of a worldwide political-religious movement using the tactics and mentality of primitive warfare.

But the first World Trade Center bombing in 1993 was exactly that—a planned expression of a worldwide political religious movement using the tactics and mentality of primitive warfare.

The tactic is the raid. The target is the civilian, to prove that the enemy cannot defend his own people, his own family. The change is that the terrorist, unlike the Assiniboine warrior of old, is not trying to bring property or booty back home, except metaphorically—bringing home the prize of the enemy's humiliation. But the new primitive warrior is just like the old primitive warrior in this respect: they both seek hero status, and renown, and glory. Their glory is the slaughter of civilians.

But we ought to ask ourselves some questions about this new type of primitive war:

First, why did it take us so long to figure out how this works?

Second, can we preserve our most precious values and achievements as a civilization—and by that I mean our laws—and still prevail against our enemy?

Third, can we accept that this enemy requires that we employ warriors like my Assiniboine friends and not just soldiers?

And last, what is it that we are asking our defenders to defend?

Answering these questions means understanding why we have had such a tough problem accepting that there is a difference between the civilized and the primitive.

In his book about primitive war, Keeley tells how he started out in the 1970s as an archaeologist excavating the fortified, palisaded villages of ancient northern Europe. In Belgium, he looked at 7,000-year-old village sites. He saw wooden posts surrounding these village sites. Aha, he says. These are Neolithic forts. These are fortified villages. On the outside of these forts were arrowheads and spear points. In a few sites he found skeletons of men, women, and children who had been killed by arrowheads or knives or spears, as evidenced by the existence of arrowheads stuck between their ribs, and by scars on their skulls—skulls that had been scalped—European skulls scalped in Europe.

Keeley confronted a scholarly consensus that had developed in the post–World War Two era. Archaeologists had decided that precivilized Europe was a peaceful place. Scholars had come to consensus that precivilized everywhere was peaceful: that there had been a golden age, and that that golden age was ruined not by primitive war, but by civilization. Not just brown people or black people were wrecked by civilization—even ancient white people started out peaceful and primitive until civilization brought them war.

In other words, scholars decided to ignore all the physical evidence of spear points and mass graves and scalped ancient Belgians and scalped ancient Assiniboines and palisaded villages from seven thousand years ago. They decided to ignore the Jesuits' accounts of the Senecas eating the Eries in western New York.

What this meant is that they decided to throw out the entire Enlightenment idea of progress. They decided to deny the great driving ideology of the nineteenth century that the British and French and Russian and American empires had had, which was that civilization was good and primitivity bad. They decided to resurrect the myth of the noble savage: Rousseau, not Hobbes, became the guiding light. Now a consensus is emerging that it is this myth, of the noble savage, that has impeded our understanding as we try to cope with the new reality of terrorism.

How curious, even to the point of insanity, this confusion is. Insanity? Consider that the people of Goethe and Beethoven and of the ancient universities of Central Europe eschewed their civilization, bulldozed the rule of law, burned their neighbors' books and then their neighbors themselves. In the years after World War Two, which is to say, in the years after the German people were forced to confront the Nuremburg Trials, and during which many thousands of German civilians were marched through the concentration camps to see what they had condoned, and what they had indeed done, what did the term "civilization" mean? What did that experience of state-sponsored savagery do to the reputation of civilization?

We know what it did. Civilized people had acted savagely as a matter of state policy. It was an inconceivable breach of every notion of law that anybody civilized had ever known. The West was utterly traumatized, especially the sensitive intellectuals of the West. So the myth of the peaceful Jean-Jacques Rousseau savage—the myth of the golden age of peace that had been ruined by civilization—became an entrenched idea because civilized people had finally seen total war close-up, in their own hometowns, conducted by their own home boys, and civilized people had recoiled in horror.

After we Americans won that war, we reasserted the idea of civilization. The way we did this was by asserting the idea of law.

In our generation, we accept that the Germans under Hitler were not civilized soldiers. When we think of Germans in World War Two, we think of them in the same terms we think of the more recent examples of Slobodan Milosevic and General Mladić of Serbia: we think of them as war criminals.

Civilized men who break the law are criminals. That's why the victors of World War Two put the Nazis on trial at Nuremburg. That's why we put Milosevic on trial in den Haag. We're still seeking General Mladić and Radovan Karadžić—to put them on trial for war crimes.

But what do you do with uncivilized men who slaughter civilians? How do you fight warriors who aren't soldiers?

There seems to be some confusion on this issue. Much confusion, actually.

The president asked the United States Senate to consider relaxing or rewriting the laws on interrogation and torture. The president's attorney general argued for a more expansive or elastic reading of the Geneva Conventions on what is and what is not permissible treatment of prisoners of war.

Two American combat veterans objected. Colin Powell and, in a more nuanced manner, John McCain, the future presidential candidate, told George Bush, in effect, that a state cannot undermine its own law as it pursues the defense of civilization. The Supreme Court said essentially the same thing in the Guantanamo detainee case, to wit: civilization is law; and the state cannot relax or evade law in its defense.

All the lawyers in the room understand this. But where does that leave civilians: does adherence to the rules of civilized war doom us in a fight with primitive warriors?

The answer that the old empires had was to conduct total war until total victory, but to stop short of annihilation, because it was imperative, under the old empires, to understand who was who. Primitive warriors kill everybody. Civilized soldiers stop short of that, except that the Ottoman Empire massacred Armenian civilians, and the British Empire burned my wife's great-grandparents' Cape Province farmsteads and put noncombatants into concentration camps, where, mostly, they died. The record of Empire is cloudier than the bright clarity of Empire's laws.

Old empires, and our empire as well, devised a solution. Empires used and continue to use proxies. And we use warriors when it is legal to do so.

Robert Kaplan's little book *Warrior Politics* is a reading of classic texts and of recent history as well in a search for a pathway to clarity on this issue. He says that we should all read Winston Churchill's own writing from his experiences, especially, in Sudan and South Africa. Kaplan's reading of Churchill and of history has yielded conclusions as clear as what the anthropologists are beginning to say. Kaplan writes about the choices that military and political leaders have to make, and his conclusion is that if we're going to fight primitive warriors, we have to know their tactics, know their methods, know their aims . . . and that we have to use their ruthless means.

Therein is the difficulty.

How does a state, which is a society organized under law, undertake its defense against the lawless and the stateless?

Robert Kaplan says that we have to act as an empire. Kaplan believes that the United States today is one of history's great empires. He approves of this. Kaplan wields wide influence. He has become a friend of, a defender of, and a strategist for the professional American military class. He warns that civilian leaders had better get a better understanding of what our civilization means, too, because our military class is getting less and less interested in defending a society overrun with casino gambling, rap videos, rampant consumerism, and slack discipline.

Robert Kaplan believes that we must know the enemy and that we must allow our military to prosecute its role by *whatever means necessary*.

So what are we up against?

Another recent book's title says it all: *Insurgents, Terrorists, and Militias*. The authors Schultz and Dew describe the street-fighters in Baghdad as tribal networks who want to annihilate our soldiers, and who do so for power, certainly, but also for honor, for personal renown and for the esteem of their extended family networks. Religion is their vocabulary and their justification, but the rules of honor and of obligation in the tribe are paramount. Every man is a potential warrior. Every person is a potential target.

Our politicians did not understand this, but our military planners did understand the difference between primitive war and civilized war. Our military professionals understood that Saddam Hussein had kept the tribal networks of the Sunnis intact inside his military, his secret police, and his political party apparatus. When Saddam's police and his Ba'ath party were gone, the tribes were still there; it's the tribes that became the sources of insurgency. For the tribes, every man is a potential warrior. Every person is a potential target. This is the Assiniboines versus the Blackfeet on the northern plains of 150 years ago, except with millions of tribesmen rather than hundreds. This is not France versus Prussia in 1870, with uniformed soldiers arrayed against uniformed soldiers and generals far in the rear. The casualty rate is not 5 percent or 7 percent in the professional armed forces; it is 5 percent or 7 percent *in the society*. Every year. Year after year.

That's primitive war. A larger share of the entire population gets killed than if uniformed, law-abiding soldiers are at work.

What is so terrible to see every day on the evening news is that the anthropologists and historians including Keeley, Schultz, and Dew had it right a very long time ago. So did our own military planners, whom the ideologues of the Bush administration ignored. Professionals predicted what would happen after the conventional structures of the deeply flawed Iraqi state were stripped away. The conventional structures were unsanitary, but the conflict between the Sunni and the Shi'a had been suppressed under Saddam. The mutual enmity of communal adversaries had been managed by a state system of centralized control—but when that control was destroyed, the communal violence, using the techniques of primitive warfare, ensued, exactly as had been predicted. And the military expression of these communities is primitive: raids, ambushes, hostage-taking, the targeting of civilians, the pursuit of individual and subgroup revenge. In what has happened in Iraq since the U.S. military toppled Saddam Hussein's regime, there is no analogy to the conduct of warfare by a nation-state.

There are other places where the tribes are in charge, and where there is no state.

Afghanistan, Yemen, Somalia, Chechnya, and Lebanon are now in the category of Failed States, defined as one where central authority, a regular army, and the normal apparatus of a civilized society is lacking, and where primitive warfare, conducted by warriors and not by soldiers, rules.

Schultz and Dew point to these places that have no regime but rather only tribes in charge—heavily armed tribes—that are as content to annihilate each other as they are any outsiders. They also describe the rule of the clan system, and of the personal vendetta, in Chechnya. The religious motivation for terror among Muslim Chechen tribesmen against the Russian state amplifies grievances that are personal, tribal, communal, as well as national; the Russian response has been to break every rule of civilized war in order to suppress the Chechen resistance, or backlash, or insurgency, or jihad. Russia is winning, but the costs have been unfathomable. Russia uses proxies—other Chechens, and people from the small, neighboring, hostile, or opportunistic ethnic groups—the Asiatic Kalmyks, the Christian Ossetians, and others—but Russian racism and their claim that the Chechen issue is a matter of internal state security mean that the destruction of Chechen terror has been horrific for every Chechen.

We could use some good news.

James Fallows, writing in the *Atlantic Monthly*, argues that we have won the fight against global terror. Fallows says that our law enforcement and military people together have won the war against al-Qaeda. America, he argues, is safe now. The ideology of terrorism persists, but now the conspiracy that flew the airplanes in the World Trade Center no longer has the means to be a threat.

Many disagree with that happy conclusion. They point out that Fallows is talking only about America's success in detecting and preventing any more bombings like Timothy McVeigh's or terrorism like Nine Eleven.

And they also point out that our civilization is not just North American but Europe's, too, and that Europe has a terrible structural problem. Muslim immigrants in North America continue to practice their religion, but are integrated, for the most part, into North American culture. In Europe, Muslims do not learn Dutch or Norwegian or German or Swedish; Muslims dwell overwhelmingly in ghettos, alienated and isolated from the host society. Welfare and unemployment rates are astronomical. Honor-killings, forcible child marriage, polygamy, and crimes on non-Muslims, especially women, are now part of life in Oslo, Copenhagen, Amsterdam, and elsewhere. This behavior is, of course, against the law in each of the countries in which it occurs. Four second-generation Pakistani men in Britain got onto the Tube in 2005 and tried to kill thousands, succeeding in killing themselves and dozens of innocent civilians. Alienation and isolation keep the European cauldron bubbling; politics keeps the cauldron bubbling and steaming; and as a result, anti-immigrant politics is no longer just the province of "Pig" le Pen, the frankly and outspokenly racist leader of the French Right.

But while Europe stews in its indecisive responses to lawless behavior by non-natives, American and Canadian law enforcement people have indeed been effective here. British law enforcement has been effective, most recently in preventing the multiple bombing of transatlantic airliners.

But the contrast between the ghettoized Muslims of Europe, and the melded-in or dispersed Muslim populations of North America, is stark. The scariest book you'll ever read about contemporary Europe lays out how a gay New Yorker went there to get away from George Bush and found Europeans still cringing at the memory of World War Two, still in the grips of the myth of the noble savage, still believing that they somehow owe the poor immigrants from western Asia and the Middle East slots on their welfare rolls, still unwilling to enforce their own laws when they are broken by people who refuse to adjust to their new Northern European homes.

Subtle gradations in theology thus have now become expressions of states-of-readiness to commit acts of terror.

And in a very insidious threat to the notion of law's universality, it has become the identity of the perpetrator that determines whether we treat these acts of terror as criminal acts or as acts of war. But the very categories into which we divide our world are themselves challenged; each of the authors who have reported on this phenomenon is trying to get his or her Western, legalistic, logical arms around the problem.

I think that we are getting there. Each of these authors has come to the conclusion that muddy or wishful thinking about a bygone era of tranquility, or a golden age of peace, has muddied up our ability to respond to threats that will tear our civilization apart.

I believe that they are correct. I also believe that the Bush administration's policies have been against our national interest. Those policies are a toxic stew of cynicism, naivete, and intellectual shallowness.

We as Americans are prone to idealizing our own democracy, and presidents from Woodrow Wilson to Jimmy Carter and now George Bush have sought to extend our notions of democracy and to institute them in places where despotism was the solution to containing primitivity. These American leaders each, in his own idiom, said that democracy would liberate people and peoples from despotism. This is not what happened. Woodrow Wilson, Jimmy Carter, and George Bush all failed our national interest because they failed miserably to appreciate the historical and anthropological realities of the lands for which they designed highly idealized policies. Woodrow Wilson's belief in self-determination for ethnic groups changed a stable, if decrepit, Austro-Hungarian empire into a bagful of small nations; Wilson thus, rather than stabilizing Central and Eastern Europe within a multi-ethnic federation with a common language, enabled local political independence to come, but only as a brief interlude before the next empire. Lithuania and Latvia and Estonia, Poland and Czechoslovakia and the rest enjoyed two decades as independent nation-states even as their immense neighbors prepared genocide, fascism, and then forcible reabsorption of these former territories into, first, the Nazi empire, then into the Soviet empire.

Jimmy Carter's campaign for human rights was more benign. Carter helped American interests by stimulating competition against established oligarchies; but Carter injured American interests to the extent that the Human Rights campaign failed to become meaningful international law; and when the Shah of Iran wavered on containing his own domestic opposition, and when his hesitation loosed the dogs of civil insurrection, Iran's fall undermined America's national interest.

The most recent collapse of idealism in the face of realpolitik is Iraq. Bush pushed America into a war that undermined a distasteful proxy that had been a useful bulwark against Shi'a expansionism in Iran and against Sunni collaboration with an international terror network. As newly available documents show, there never was a nexus or collaboration between Saddam Hussein and Osama bin Laden. Now, because primitive warriors in the failed state have been empowered, Bush's campaign for democracy in Iraq has made our country more vulnerable. Bush and his team failed to appreciate that there may be no way to manage or impose a transition from a functioning state to a democratic state without empowering primitive warriors.

I ventured into this difficult area tonight in part as an exercise in making sense of recent events in light of my own personal experience of and historical research on primitive people. I did fieldwork with these people in the early 1980s while I was in graduate school in Chicago. My dissertation was based on my work on Sioux-language texts, translating the autobiographical accounts of a notorious Sioux Holy Man who had turned on his people, joined the Americans, and then spent most of his adulthood fighting for what he and his sponsors believed was civilization. His job, between the time George Armstrong Custer's troop was massacred in 1876 and the Ghost Dance crisis in 1890, was to suppress ancient rituals and to bust up the cultural practices of his people. This individual failed in his mission. Militarily, his people were pacified by overwhelming force; they have since been among the most loyal, the most patriotic, and the most intrepid fighters in America's armed forces. Many of you in this room have ancestors among the tribal peoples of Scotland; there is a good analogy here. When the Americans finally got around to using the military to assimilate the Sioux and the Assiniboine the way the British Crown used the military to assimilate the Scots, we got it about right.

It happened that I got to know many military veterans among those people. A few of them can more accurately be called warriors, including an Assiniboine man we'll call Chetan, in English, Hawk.

Hawk is a veteran of the Special Forces. Hawk was a specialist in close combat. He's about my age or perhaps younger. He was about five-ten, one seventy. Being an Assiniboine, he was dark complected with straight dark hair and decidedly Central Asian features; you would not be surprised to see his face in a nineteenth-century photograph of Plains Indians, but he could have had a place in Genghis Khan's army, too. You see his face in Afghanistan; you see his face in Iran. Thirty-two years ago, he was one of the men whom Jimmy Carter sent in-country into Iran to rescue our hostages. He was one of the soldiers in what was called Delta Force. He'd had to live off the land and pass as a native; he'd killed with his knife and strangled with his hands. His fellow veterans of Delta Force and the Assiniboine Sacred Medicine Lodge held him in awe. Hawk, Chetan, was a warrior. Chetan was a primitive warrior who wore our uniform. When he came home, he was an honored veteran. He became a police officer on a reservation with about a hundred miles of border with Canada; he mainly chases drug smugglers, and he works with both Canadian and U.S. Customs on tracking down anybody else who needs tracking down. He is a Medicine Lodge Man, Ti Jax Wachipi Wichashta.

The logic here is straightforward.

Hawk is an American who is a leading man among his folks, and who is a member of our civilization too. To defend our country, when he was out in the field, he had to do to what he had to do. Here at home, he obeys the law; he enforces the law—American law. For fifty years, American law was wrong and unjust when it suppressed Hawk's religion, the Assiniboine Sacred Medicine Lodge; but bad old American law got changed when Congress acted in a civilized manner, and enacted the Native American Religious Freedom Act.

Imagine living in a society in which there is no constitutional guarantee of religious liberty, and no special legislation to correct a historic injustice against a minority racial group.

Imagine living in a society so traumatized by direct experience of war that it cannot take rational steps to defend its most central institution, namely, its own law.

We Americans are sloppy and clumsy; sometimes it takes us a long time to get it right. We should not, however, harbor illusions that endanger our very existence.

That is why I propose the following answers to my four questions:

First, as to why it took us so long to figure out who the enemy is, we can understand the difficulty better now that scholars have begun to rethink these issues—and that the key to their thinking is that they recognize that there never was a golden age of primitive peace. Civilization has its many discontents, but by the simplest of measures, overwhelmingly higher percentages of people get to live in civilized society, and to survive its wars, than get to live and survive wars in primitive society. Life is good, ergo so is civilization, so let us dispense with the myth of the noble peaceful savage. As Saint Paul said, when I was a child I thought and acted as a child, but now that I am a man, I have put away my childish ways . . .

Second, as to the question of whether we should compromise our critical institutions as we defend ourselves, the answer is in the preamble to our Constitution. I believe that it is absolutely imperative that we maintain our constitution against all enemies foreign and domestic, including an administration that refuses to listen, refuses to learn, and refuses to give up immature notions even after they have caused terrible consequences.

Third, I believe that we are blessed to have fellow citizens like the warrior Hawk, my brother from the Sacred Medicine Lodge. We need soldiers. In the years ahead, facing the struggle we face, we cannot hope to prevail without warriors, even if they must be proxies. That's the lesson of history.

Last, as to the question of what it is that we are asking our defenders to defend, I propose the following: for their sakes, and for the sake of our children and grandchildren if not for ourselves, let us resolve to conduct ourselves as civilized people. This means that we have to defend our law, but it should mean, too, that we defend our own culture as well. If our culture becomes a cluster of distractions for the masses while international financial speculators enrich themselves at the expense of every American who is not one of them, then our culture won't last, because law will come to mean nothing but the defense of internationalized capital. Our defenders will get wise to that fact, and turn on us all, distracted masses and elites alike. As well they should.

CONTESTS

Sculls

On an early October day, the Black Rock Canal was beset by a strange wind from the northeast, which makes no sense at all, because the geography of that canal is structured for a prevailing southwesterly.

The Black Rock Canal is the shipping channel at the very end of Lake Erie. It used to be that all the shipping from all the upper Great Lakes flowed with the water from the west, from Duluth on Superior and Chicago on Michigan through the Straits of Mackinac, south out of Lake Huron past Detroit, then east on Erie past Cleveland and on to Erie and to Buffalo. At Buffalo, since 1825, there has been a place for boats to go if they weren't going to unload in Buffalo Harbor, and shift their cargo to trucks or to trains; the place where boats go is up the Black Rock Canal past Squaw Island and through the locks to the calm, broad section of the Niagara River until junction with the old Erie Canal. The big boats from the west stopped unloading in Buffalo after 1957, which is when the Canadians finished their Welland Canal, just twenty miles west of the Black Rock. There had long been a Welland Canal, but there hadn't until 1957 been a Welland Canal big enough to allow big ore boats and big grain boats and big oceangoing freighters to cross the Niagara Peninsula to Lake Ontario, and then go on to the Saint Lawrence River past the Thousand Islands and Montreal and Quebec City and ancient Tadoussac all the way out to the Gulf of Saint Lawrence and the Atlantic Ocean beyond. Now, mostly, it's small boats on the Black Rock Canal, with a few freighters hauling coal past the sailors and fishers and rowers, through the locks, up to the coal-fired power plant on the wide swell of the Niagara River. Now, mostly, what comes out of the west, across Lake Erie and all the previous lakes, is weather.

Storms come, sometimes suddenly, following that route of ghost freighters now long departed. Storms drop down from Alberta into the

American plains and then proceed eastward like raging Hun armies. In their seasons, they stoop to fetch water from Chicago's front terraces, that they turn into snow for western Michigan. That water makes them stronger with new bows and new scimitars: with it, they blow past flat Michigan and past its thumb to Lake Erie, and over Erie's three hundred miles of open shallow water they fetch up more water until they meet this next west-facing shore. Then our orchards, our vineyards, our slickened streets are conquered, and our damp-holding hillsides wetted again, ever dotted with fat Holsteins up to their shins in every season's mud.

Wind that is the bane of rowing here comes here from the west and it comes over the lake. Wind here crosses over the indefinable borderline between the end of the lake and the start of the Niagara River. It's easy enough to say where the Black Rock Canal starts: there are breakwalls at the mouth of Buffalo Harbor, three of them. From high windows in the bank buildings and the courts and the government offices, the storms that come that way lift white churned water over those breakwalls and that's the work day's entertainment or at least distraction from the foolishness or self-importance of the proceedings behind all that glass. The west-southwest wind blows the water from the lake into the harbor and into the canal, not the other way around, and the flow and the wind send it down-river, the Niagara River. This would be the same Niagara River that ends in Niagara Falls, but here, it is a city river, which is separated from the Black Rock Canal by a breakwall two miles long and by another mile of Squaw Island. The Niagara flows one way, with the wind.

But on that October night, the wind turned. It came from the wrong direction entirely.

The next morning, a fine Indian Summer Saturday morning, the wind was still confused and various, still northeast. Eights and fours stacked on two trailers were pretty much loaded already, all stacked up and ready to be trucked out for a Sunday regatta an hour east in Rochester, on the Genesee River, which is easy water compared to the Black Rock Canal because it's so sheltered.

I walked a club single past all those naked empty racks, down the inclined concrete path to the docks. I chose River Dock, river side, to put in. The wind made it a day for the heavy hatchets, the grays, from the long row of oars that the club owns. These grays are oars whose blades are shaped to catch more water and to force more work, and they do.

A heavy rig is a good thing in a wind. A northeast wind is a good thing, rare as it is, for right out of the boathouse, it is a headwind. The resistance of more water and more wind means that the two miles of water between the boathouse and the locks is a distance for warming-up that is a harder piece of work to do, and what is rowing but work?

Rowing north out of the docks is the normal course in the Black Rock Canal. Rowing north is usually easy because of the following wind, the normal wind that geography makes so predictable. One starts out with help from Alberta, Chicago, Cleveland, and Erie, when the wind is normal.

But there are those who like a headwind. There are those who find that a headwind has a certain stimulating effect. Its smell is of land. Its breath is inconstant, even as it fades with the fading sun.

The next day was Sunday. The wind had sorted itself out by Sunday. Rowing north and downstream from the docks was easy with the south-southwest tailwind of a few knots, such that the air feels breathless and there is the illusion of smooth water, but of course this is cheating and every rower knows it and we would all be ashamed at this business of sparing ourselves the work except that all of us know what to expect. What we expect is a headwind on the way home, and that means ripples that become chop and chop that grows to waves when the Huns ride. This is why one gets up early to row, for as the sun warms the air, the winds awaken, and before the winds wake up, we are safe in Rome.

That is not, however, what happened on Sunday. Put-in came a little later in the morning than one would have preferred. This was all, all the fault of the Sunday morning news being full of big news about big changes in grand schemes that only pretend to be grander than the real plan, the same plan, the only plan for any day, and that plan is, simply, to row.

To write about rowing, as I do to tired friends over and over again, is to refocus on the moments just undertaken. No doubt they would prefer a normal diarist, one who revisits the same personhood day after day, and brings a gift of flowers or new humor or refreshed love with each visit. A diarist is something of a barnacle or a pretty coral that reaches out and traps whatever happens to be passing by, and measures it with the intense and focused application of fine prejudices, and sharing that diary is a true act of intimacy. Perhaps this is never the case with the work of a rowing diarist. A rowing diarist is one who overlooks or rather looks past this tiresome business of personhood in order to explore the power of minute variations. The rowing diarist says that those items that vary are wind, water, light, and air as they act to change the response of the same old equipment in the same old course of water with the same old person moving the process along. What does not vary is the rower's obsession with the experience of feeling wind, water, light, air, and feeling breath, sweat, aches, joints, muscles, and feeling the glide over an element and through another, through fluids, under sky, being born and reborn, borne by a boat, in a canal.

Thus to read a rowing diary is to read repetition. It could be an immersion experience, if it weren't so common: millions row, or have rowed, in the two hundred years or so that rowing has been a sport and not just transport or work or an instrumentality of the hunt. Rowing is not, however, however populated it may be, very welcoming of others' attentions. I said, to parents watching a regatta last spring, that the only people who watch rowing are those whom the rower loves. They were embarrassed by that admission, but there was no disagreement. We were watching our children race. The races were, as most rowing races are, utterly without suspense, because here's how it is in a rowing race: if one boat is clearly far ahead of the other two or three boats in the race, and the race is a normal 1,500-meter or 2,000-meter race, or a 5,000-meter "head" race, then chances are very good that the order of boats at the finish line won't have changed. There is no suspense, mostly.

And then there is sculling. I scull, solo. Sculling is a solitary activity even when there are spectators.

The next day was the Columbus Day holiday. I got up. I stretched. I made herbal tea, and while I drank it, and as the children slept late on their school holiday, I listened to a performance of Chopin's posthumous nocturne in C minor, which is so simple: a balancing of the right and the left hands along the theme that has the rhythm of a waltz and a very geometric or meditative melody. Everything in that piece is balance. Everything in that piece is symmetry. Everything is minute adjustment. Everything is minute adjustment to keep the balance and the symmetry of a long thin line, and the variation of performances of that piece is a variation of intensity.

This is sculling.

On Monday morning, dockside was at a more respectable hour, just an hour past dawn, which is still a fat time in October, being that dawn comes around seven. There was an eight putting in, boys, young ones, maybe novices. Came the hail from its coach. The coach is a typical coach. He is a man of fifty or so, who himself rowed but as a boy. He is Irish American; the rowing scene in Buffalo is an overwhelmingly Irish American scene. They are so acculturated that none of them have yet admitted or commented at the irony that we all think that the pinnacle of rowing is the annual race at Henley-on-Thames—not our lovely Royal Canadian Henley that is held twenty miles west in St. Catharines on Martindale Pond, but the *echt* Henley, on Thames. This fine man, this coach, this volunteer volunteering his coaching early on a holiday morning, is happy to talk about his son who has rowed and who has won at Henley-on-Thames. Dad wears a Henley tie with pink Henley hippos that his son acquired there.

Coach yelled to me as I put in, "They'll let anybody row here," and he got me but good, man—me quipping back to him but swallowing it, as his eight of boys was launching. And then as penance he helpfully added that there were too many boats down below the Iron Bridge downstream, so I should instead head upstream to the Gap.

So the Gap is where I headed. The normal wind was back; the heavy rig, the gray hatchets again. I hugged the breakwall past the wide gulf at Bird Island, which is that bend of the ancient breakwall in which shelter cormorants and Canada geese perching on just-submerged rocks, and this meant scudding over some Clorox-bottle buoys that the Buffalo Yacht Club sailors set for themselves, exercising, without benefit of statute, their home-water privilege. They pride their club for its age, second-oldest in North America. Nearby Niagara-on-the-Lake has the first-oldest golf course in North America. Past this place was where the first sailing ship penetrated North America, in 1688, piloted by the Sieur de La Salle and his liar of a passenger, the egregious Belgian priest Louis Hennepin. How this old town downwind of Alberta seeks its legitimacy in age, no matter who was young back then.

The breeze made all that open water all choppy. The cormorants slid their snaky heads up out of the water, and the fat, splay-foot Canada geese stood on the rocks like Christs out past those Clorox buoys, and some of them had the audacity to complain about the intrusion of a single solo sculler. Their chatter is the white noise of sculling, not even a distraction. The wind is something to be avoided even when it's light, so I slid up alongside the breakwall because then the Hun wouldn't see me. There were more Canada geese, and mallards and migratory black-bodied white-billed coots who all complained and complained, for I was taking their monopoly of calm water in the lee of that breakwall and interrupting their butts-up dabbling.

I pulled and pulled in that thwarted breeze. I pulled and pulled and left perfect swirls the way that good oarsmen do: two tiny tight whirlpools at the end of each stroke, one each for each side of each oar-blade. Pulling against that mitigated wind, pulling despite it, sliding my virgin butt back and forth with each massive push of my massive powerful pudgy thighs. This is the stuff of dreams, and voila—the dream came: what if we were to get clever and organize a party of botanists to plant a windbreak on this breakwall? A line of sturdy arborvitae cedars, native North American cedars that are thick and low, dense and bent by this wind into a sheltering hedge? That's the dream.

The reality was good enough: not glassy, not spotless, no mirror, but at least a moderated course of a thousand meters of racing water, with a fresh breeze to cool the neck, is what it was.

It was delicious. Scullers know what this is—good water with no current, and nostrils tickling in air that was moving just half-a-body above the sternum. Conditions as follows: bright, just under 60 degrees Fahrenheit, smooth water unchurned by motors or eights, with new air whistling past the ears and that sharp clarity as from new lenses that high barometric pressure in autumn gives. One thousand pure unobstructed meters, it was.

It ends. It ended at the Gap itself, where there was no more protection from the southwesterly. There was no choice but to turn.

So steadily, and strong with the lake's breeze fanning, is how the shell turned and then coursed with the unobstructed wind downstream past the mile of LaSalle Park, past the second-oldest yacht basin proper, tight in past the Navy Reserve's ramp, past the new construction for the new Frank Lloyd Wright–designed boathouse, past the West Side Rowing Club, past Cotter's Point which would have been the logical end, but the hard weather of the rest of October would come in snow-blasts only four days later, so that wasn't the end of it, no. Down-channel, past the international Peace Bridge and past all those original limestone blocks of the old Erie Canal that nobody but rowers ever looks at except for an occasional coal boat, and occasional users, like sailors, the rich ones, who motor their sailboats with sails furled to a seasonal anchorage on the wide shore of the widened, flattened Niagara down past the locks.

Along the Black Rock's city-side runs a highway. It is elevated by ten feet of stone even above the canal stones, and these are faced with concrete, and that concrete is the palette of champion rowers in this town. Each ephemeral victory of real note is emblazoned on those walls above which the unseeing drivers speed, like this: 2000 Henley women's lightweight 8 West Side Rowing Club, and all their names are there, from coxy to bow, and coaches' names too, and in West Side colors, maroon, black, white. Another, more compact painting hails the 2001 and 2002 national pairs in West Side colors, the brothers with the German names, and you see them at the boathouse, coaching, authoritative, two slight men with black short hair. A sign reads: 1996 Canadian Schoolboys four, but it's fading, for these paint jobs don't last through the ages, and they don't even call that spring race the Schoolboys anymore, due to the advent of girls. It's the Canadian Scholastic now, but the boys and girls alike still call the race Schoolboys, and what a pageant it is: a couple of thousand rowers all gathered at Martindale Pond a mile from the Ontario end of the Welland Canal, just twenty miles away from these canal stones, at the Royal Canadian Henley racecourse. A hundred crews go there, orderly strong gangs in their colors. The mighty Canadian private schools, Upper Canada College boys and Branksome Hall and Havergal girls, Ridley College and Sir Winston Churchill, and the Michiganders and Ohioans and Pennsylvanians and New Yorkers, perfect children in their unis, pronounced you-knees. Kids who win races at Schoolboys paint their names on the walls of the Black Rock Canal, and never a car driver nor a car passenger sees those trophies, and then the trophies fade, and are painted over.

Downstream, there are more paint jobs, about victories in U.S. and Canadian national races. The newest: girls' eight, Royal Canadian Henley, gold. There's only gold at Henley. You either win at Henley or you lose, it's so refreshingly simple. Nobody keeps the time and there are no other metals or medals but gold, gold. The walls are silent except gold, such as the boys of a Catholic high school, coached by a local Olympian, won in the American Nationals this year. Such wins are why the rowers of this continent hold West Side in high esteem. Everybody who rows out of this boathouse knows cold, and knows wind. Everybody knows that their job is to be imperturbable in the face of such conditions. Everybody who rows against them knows about these conditions.

Below the Iron Bridge of Ferry Street, which connects the city to Squaw Island which is where the Underground Railroad used to ferry folks to freedom just a mile across the Niagara, there's more water for rowing, a couple of thousand meters more, until the railroad bridge, and the locks beyond.

The kids' practice route is this: from the boathouse downstream to the locks, back upstream past the boathouse to the Gap, then back downstream to the boathouse. Locks Gap Back.

Locks Gap Back. That's what I'd wanted. Boathouse to Locks is about 3,300 meters. Locks to Gap is 5,000, back home to the Boathouse a last 1,700. It's a 10k circuit. I wanted it all, but the crews were headed in, so I opted to turn at the first buoy beyond the Iron Bridge.

I was warm.

I was ready.

I set the rotating dial on my watch.

The plan: a fast start, a steady pace for 1,500, then a 500-meter sprint.

Ready.

Tick.

Go.

The Chopin piece, as described before: symmetry along a long line. Everything in each piece is balance. Everything in each piece is symmetry as I struggled against the Hun wind out of Alberta which comes from a much, much more ancient place, perhaps Baikal. Everything is minute adjustment. Everything is minute adjustment to keep the balance and the symmetry of a long thin line that I created with my effort, four tiny whirlpools at the tips of my blades, and then watched disintegrate and fade.

This was my race, into the wind, without any competitors, without the urgency of a crowd watching at the finish. Two thousand meters as if it counted.

I won.

The sports

Winter

The main purposes for maintaining one's residence in the city, or for living deep in the country, is so that one can drink in peace and drink in plenty and never have to worry about the cops. Thus suburban life has never made sense to me. Suburbs consume the nation's energy, and the world's, because the people who live in suburbs spend all their time driving around buying things to span those yawning empty hours that we city and country people fill with one another's company, and with drinks.

This is especially true in this city in wintertime. Here, the bars close at 4 a.m.

This is a feature of life that has shaped this community entirely. It is a critical formative experience for a boy or a girl to close a bar, and to go from beers to breakfast at a Greek diner on Allen Street, on Elmwood Avenue, on Hertel Avenue, or on one of the great eastering boulevards of old—Genesee, Clinton, Broadway, William—but on those latter, of course, radiating as they do in Pierre L'Enfant's wheel-and-spoke design from this city's diminished downtown, there are precious few restaurants, Greek or otherwise, because of racism's tremendous success in having wiped out commerce of most any kind. If you know the West Side of Chicago, or the South Bronx before gentrification, or just about any stretch of inner Detroit, or the places in Los Angeles, Libertyville, Pigtown, or Kansas City where cops and social workers and teachers and an occasional mobile psychiatrist are the only Caucasians ever to visit, then you probably are a cop, a social worker, a teacher, or a doctor licensed to dispense psychoactive medications, and so can claim to have firsthand knowledge of this landscape.

In our town, it all looks better when it has been snowed upon.

Feta cheese, edge-burnt charcoal-broiled chunks of beef or of spiced lamb, eggs, butter-soaked toast: manna, and the ice melts into puddles under one's rubber-bottomed boots, and coffee makes one clever again, and one wonders one's just-legal head about what these immigrant boys—curly black hair, white smocks, gray checked trousers, their long knives for trimming the gyros off the spit—what could these hard-working boys think of all that deep white snow, and of all these young men and young women marching into the diner at 4:18 a.m. on a Saturday morning, still not tired of one another's company, and the shopping mall the last thing on their minds.

Summer

Mason is rarely in the city on weekends in summer. Mason on Fridays drives out Route 62 south from Hamburg village, then through Eden Township past the high school on Route 75, then left for a mile on New Oregon Road, which tracks the course of the South Branch of Eighteen-mile Creek, to his house in Clarksburg. Clarksburg is a non-village—a non-hamlet—with neither store nor post office, only an intersection of one-lane roads and a one-lane bridge not even a hundred yards down-stream of the creek's falls. This place is the home of the Clarksburg Club, which is an unheated mid-nineteenth-century flour mill that has a great stone fireplace in a great open room with a slate flagstone floor on which picnic tables are set, and among those flagstones are set two ancient round millstones.

There are tennis courts. There is a field for softball. There is a staircase down the ravine to the great shale shelf overhanging the swimming hole at the base of the falls, which are a trickle for most of the summer because the upper creek dries so thoroughly. But this summer, we've been having rain, rain like March or April, or like November, heavy gray rain from pewter skies that seldom break, so the falls are vigorous. The turbid water in the swimming hole has risen so high that it spills over the wooden dam. When the runoff calms, the swimming-hole water clears, and the sediment settles to the soft sand bottom. But any new storm roils it within an hour, and nobody wants to swim amid branches, mud, drowned opossums, disoriented garter snakes. There was so much rain last Friday that Mason broke his weekend routine and stayed in town. He took his guest to dinner, and then on a steamy moist Saturday morning at eleven he called Fish looking for a game because it was too damned hot and too damned wet to be outside.

Fish arrived first by about fifteen minutes, because Fish has been insisting to himself that this business of showing up five minutes before a match and then getting on the court cold has got to stop, because he's past fifty by some notches and it's about time, he thinks, that he got serious about warming up, running a few minutes or biking or doing a few flights of stairs and then stretching before opening the glass door and starting to swing a squash racquet.

He made it to the sauna first. It was hot. But get this: he had just escaped the midday heat, and the stuffy lobby, and the airless lounge. Dreading what he'd find, he had then proceeded to check the court to make sure that the staff had put the air conditioner on, for it is pure oppression to play squash on a hot court. Happily, they had. The court was adequately cool. He'd sighed with whole-body pleasure as he'd entered the much cooler locker room. He'd pulled off his cotton trousers and put on his white squash shorts with the club logo embroidered in gold and green thread, and his white squash shirt with that same logo, and had gone on to the cedar room and to its radical, medicinal, incongruous heat.

Fish sat on the lower bleacher. He turned and lifted his left foot onto the bench and stretched his left hand out to his left sneaker because it's his left hamstring that needs most to be stretched. That's his focus after using the rowing machine too, or after sculling on the Black Rock Canal: the left hamstring. He's not much of a stretcher. He's never again going to get his face down to his thigh or his nose to his knee as he did so easily when he was a skinny teen, but he can get his fingers to his toes, and with patience, he can get his fingers beyond his toes to the ball of his foot, and with warmth and a few more minutes, he can get his fingers beyond even there, to the arch of his foot.

This was the second time he'd stretched it in the same day. He had stretched it the evening before, after the session with the dog in the backyard, when the dog had awakened to the presence of a small young cat, entirely black, that had taken them both so utterly by surprise that the leashed dog had yanked him quite abruptly, aggravating his aggrieved lower back. Only stretching the left hamstring provides Fish with relief.

Fish could have stayed in the sauna until the sweat came, but he'd heard voices, jolly banter from the locker room. Fish was warmed but not sweating, and told himself that he should walk past the squash court, and then past the hot tennis court that gets so hot because the skylights trap the summer sun, and that he should then walk down an antique low corridor to the room with the machines, the stationary bikes and treadmills and those machines that simulate the action of running without stressing the knees. What I should do, he told himself, is warm up.

Instead, he opened the glass door to the squash court, stepped in, closed it, and started hitting the squash ball through the nicely cooled air.

Fish hit it high over the cutline so that it took an arc up along the sidewall and made it all the way back to the rear wall, the glass wall, and bounced off, and came forward toward the service box, where he hit it again, high and just slightly harder. He was taking care to hold the racquet face open, and to hit a few feet above the cutline, so that the ball would fly up, so that he could focus on his form: left foot forward, body square to the wall, racquet head whipped back, weight shifted, elbow of the racquet arm tucked tight to the body on the follow-through, keeping the body away from the wall, preventing the wrist from turning over on the grip. He wanted to hit the ball ahead of his torso. He tried to hit the ball with precision, and then with force, but it needed warming before it was going to become lively enough for that, for even on a summer court, a one-inch hollow of black rubber lacks bounce until friction warms it. So he slipped into his usual warm-up, which was to hit the ball hard, very hard, crosscourt to the center of the front wall well below the cutline, so that on its rebound it hit the side wall a few feet ahead of the service line, and thus came out to the center of the court ahead of the T, where Fish hit his backhand, this time toward the forehand side of the front wall. The ball bounced from front to the right sidewall, and Fish snapped it back to the front wall on the backhand side, and repeated the circuit.

Fish stepped lightly. After some minutes of that corner-to-corner drill, he let the ball fly past him, so that he could bounce on his toes and thus test his Achilles tendons. They appeared to be springy. So he picked up the ball, went back to the forehand, and again sent it to the front wall and then to the left wall, and he turned to the backhand position, racquet up, waiting for it. He opened the racquet face, sent the ball up high over the cutline with a smooth backhand, and it sailed crosscourt back to the right rear wall. It came off without much energy but still enough for him to pick it up and drive it hard with a strong full turn of the shoulder straight down the rail. Fish hit a few more of those and the ball started to liven up.

Mason arrived. He came into the court wearing dark shorts and a dark shirt. Fish wore white. His shirt had the same insignia as his shorts. His socks were white, his shoes as well. He was *de rigueur*. This was somewhat a comical reversal of roles, as the men laughingly noted.

It was time for the conflict. The usual run of things between Mason and Fish is that they have no contact outside of squash. They expect that Mason will hit the ball as hard as possible, except for when he slices a tiny crosscourt drop that Fish won't get to, mostly won't even try to get to, at least in the early points. They also expect that Mason will rely on his crushing forehand to take any loose ball and smash it an inch above the tin so that it flies back low, too low, despite the velocity, to make it all the way to the rear wall, and that often enough, it will nick out, which is when a round ball hits the intersection of the wall and the floor, and rolls, and ends the point. They expect that Mason will win the first game while Fish is just beginning to warm up enough to move adequately, and that Mason will win the second game by just one or two points, because Fish will have warmed enough to start asserting himself at the T and to actually start catching the low forehand smashes. They have come to expect that Fish will lose the third game too, because he really hasn't been able to command much of anything on a singles court recently, and has been hinting broadly that maybe his days as a singles player should be fading while his new career in doubles tennis, a game in which people don't have to do much moving, should soon begin.

But this is not what happened.

Fish put the first serve where Mason likes it, but Mason's smash return was tin, loud tin. They joked about the high quality of their previous evening—and that Mason tends to call Fish for a match the morning after Mason enjoys breakfasting in Greek restaurants at a very, very early hour.

Second serve was to the forehand, and somehow, nonsensically, Mason couldn't grab it off the low wall. Third serve was to the backhand again, and this time Mason hit it reasonably, down the rail with speed but not terribly tight, so Fish got to it, racquet high on the ready, and put it forward with some authority over the cutline, again down the left rail, and slid back to the T. Mason went in again for a long backhand rail and succeeded, forcing Fish's decision to go deep again. They exchanged places again, and then again, in the same sequence. Mason was being patient, retrieving off the back wall, and going for another rail exchange, but Fish perceived that this was not going to last, and indeed, Mason began telegraphing a low, rolling boast. Fish saw it. His racquet was low. Mason was going for the right front corner. Either the ball was not yet warm, or the sidewall smash too weak. The ball hit mid-tin, and Fish had a third point.

The fourth point was a more typical exchange. Fish knew that his lead was fragile or worse, undeserved, for he was not yet moving with any flow. He did hit a decent spinning high-wall serve, but Mason was ready with one of those decisive forehand smashes, millimeters above the tin, that come back as far as the service line and then either nick out or hit the back wall and immediately die. Fish's lunge for it was clumsy and stiff and heavy. He sighed. The usual pattern was about to reassert itself.

But when Mason served, he hit the ball out of court. "Come on, Jesus *Christ* that's bad," he said, humorlessly.

Fish checked Mason's readiness. Mason would never call a quick serve in those terms. He didn't call "let" but did say "sorry" whenever he was crowded. Fish always offered a stroke and expected Mason to turn it down with "just let," but left it to Mason to decide.

Fish served hard, and Mason returned hard, but crosscourt, and low, to Fish's forehand side, and so well in front of the service line that Fish's easiest choice and his best choice, too, was a forehand rail. Mason never left the back of the court. He lunged for the forehand, hit a strong low rail, but with Mason locked in the rear, Fish was poised to boast, right sidewall to front to side, and end the point cheaply and quickly. It worked. The ball nicked out in the front left corner. Four-zero.

Serving for five, Fish knew to go lighter. Hard-serving Mason was generally ineffective. Hard-serving when Mason's forehand rail was working was a waste of rubber and of sweat and of breath. Fish hit an off-speed serve designed just to get the ball into play. Mason, anxious to smash it, again tinned, and swore.

Six-zero. Mason took service with a high hard rail and went to the T just like in the manuals and coaching videos. Fish followed it in and tried a skid-boast that was reasonably tight but Mason caught it and tossed it back in a high arc back along the rail, using every inch of the wall below the red out-of-bounds tape, and waited at the T. Fish couldn't handle the reduced speed; he was into the left rear corner too deeply to put his racquet under the ball and toss it back where it came from, and he didn't have the skill to put a full swing into the ball and send in a high crosscourt and thereby lever Mason out of the T, so he hit boast, albeit a high one, which bought him an extra second. Mason saw it. Mason felt Fish behind him, reaching for the T but still trapped, so Mason hit his favorite shot, his reliable, his "patented" hard low forehand rail. Fish knew it was coming. He had had no chance to get to the T, so he waited in Mason's shadow for the inevitable and hoped he was up far enough to get it. He was, just. Fish replied to this aggression by hitting a high hard forehand rail to get Mason the hell out of the center of the court, and it worked. Mason raced to the back court. And once again in this unlikely game, Mason smashed the ball into the loudest part of the tin. Seven-zero Fish with Mason scowling, loudly, "Come on, Mase."

Fish by now had a cocked eyebrow. He hadn't taken a set from Mason in weeks. Friendly match notwithstanding, winning is the superior experience.

"Seven-zero left," Fish said, to remind himself.

"Excellent squash. Just the best," said Mason.

Fish looked at him. Mason was ready. Fish served, another hard one, immediately regretting it. Mason put it down like a bear slapping a salmon, effortlessly, decisively, and won the serve. The exchange lasted less than a second.

"Alrighty then," said Mason. "Zero-seven on the right, coming in."

Mason's serve was in, and it was good, and Fish barely scraped it off the backhand wall such that his return was a poor fat rail that was neither a drop nor any useful length at all, but rather a mid-court gift to Mason, who dropped it crosscourt while Fish stood feeling worthless somewhere west and south of the T.

"One-seven, on the left," Mason stated.

His serve to Fish's forehand was hard, but just moderately hard, so that when Fish tried to take it off the back wall, his stroke was off-balance. Mason, astride the T like its owner, had Fish behind him again, and took the occasion to hide a forehand crosscourt smash deep in the left rear court. Fish got to it but he was again off-balance, so his return was uncontrolled—aimed high on the rail so that he could get himself out of purgatory, but poorly hit, because as he happily went back toward center court, the ball sailed back high as you please, only to touch the wall high above the red out-of-bounds line.

"Two-seven right. Good ball," said Fish. This was an attempt to regain emotional control. The loser of two points who lost them more or less on serves is the loser of two points on serves not in tennis but in squash, where the serve just gets the damned ball going. Squash is not like tennis, where there are service aces expertly hit, serves that cannot be returned. A serve can be difficult in squash. It can be annoying. But one is expected to adjust. Squash is about endurance and speed and unflappability. In squash, if one is running, one is losing. If one departs the T, one gets lost. One is not to swear, or to whisper, or to talk to oneself in the far confines of the court because there are no far confines in a squash court. It is a small room, and there are no secrets, and the acoustics for secrets as for shouts alike are appalling. And so the point of Fish's utterance and congratulation was that Fish wasn't waiting for Mason's self-congratulation. Fish was taking the opportunity to praise first, which is to say, to remind Mason of his generous spirit, of his imperturbability, of his rocky poise. He was asserting self-confidence for all to hear, all two of them, in a place where there is no room for secrets.

Mason served a Mason serve, a teenage-boy serve. He served hard, very hard. The ball came off the back wall and skidded on the backhand sidewall such that it was past Fish's racquet well before Fish swung for it. It was a change-up, this harder-than-hard serve, designed to keep the momentum going, the off-balance momentum. Fish would be the one intended to be kept off-balance.

"Four-seven . . . left?" Mason asked.

Before he finished, Fish was saying, "Three-seven left. Three-seven." Firmly.

"Alrighty, here we go."

Fish knew Mason wanted the momentum, so he pushed himself up level with the service box to receive. Adjusting. This is the tiny increment of demonstrativeness which asserts that the fooling is over. True to form, Mason served it hard. Fish, ready for it, took it early, hit it hard crosscourt where Mason's racquet was drooping toward forehand in preparation for what he had obviously assumed was going to be Fish's forehand rail, but Fish hadn't done that. He hadn't passively waited for the back wall to take the starch and momentum out of the ball. He hadn't been formulaic. He'd stood forward and smashed back what had been smashed at him. Mason's racquet couldn't get set fast enough. Mason hit the ball with his rim, and sent it to the ceiling. Out of court.

"Good ball, Fish. Seven-three, your choice," said Mason.

"Seven-three right," said Fish.

The serve was normal, mid-speed, high on the backhand. Mason hit a hard backhand drop and Fish was on it, way up front, with a quick boast, obviously working a theory. Mason saw it unfolding and went on the offensive in the right forecourt, getting there and hitting a decisive low crosscourt in the classic manner that wrecks the lower backs of all middle-aged squash players and makes them leave the game for doubles tennis, because the sudden reversal of direction is a strain, a mighty strain. But Fish collected it, and sent it back along the backhand rail because that's the way to move one's man off the T. Mason ran deep but ran it down and magically tagged it high on the front wall, high enough so that he could step back to the T and get a breath while Fish tracked it. Fish tried a bold one: taking a big backhand swing, he scraped the ball off the shoulder-high post not, as expected, on a replay of the left-wall war of rails, but crosscourt, like a pro, up to the front wall five or perhaps even seven feet above the cutline, and back it sailed in a high lob toward the rear forehand corner. Mason tracked it like a duck-hunter watching a shot bird fall, waiting to loose his dog to the correct place in the marsh to retrieve. But there was no retrieving. The ball fell out of the lob to the floor, where it died. He could have shot it from the sky, but he had waited.

The last point was all running, snakes on sticks, up and down the rails, a good long point that ended in a misconceived Mason reverse-corner on the left, which came out so fat to the center that Fish, from the T, blocking out all sight, raised his racquet high on the forehand, shaking it above his shoulder like Muhammad Ali pretending to be Popeye winding up his fist for a big punch, but instead of sending a hard crosscourt back to the deep backhand, or a Mason forehand obliterating all hope with a harder-than-possible crack down the forehand rail, Fish sent a dribbling forehand to nowhere particular in the general vicinity of the right forecourt. It was a cheap lure, a dog bone for a scavenging Labrador. Mason went for it, got infected by its weakness, touched it with his slicing drop crosscourt, but Fish saw it all, and sent it to a dribbling ignominious lousy stickiness deep along the backhand wall.

First game Fish.

"Excellent squash, man. How about a beer now and we just let somebody else play?"

They exited through the glass door of the glass back court for water, and settled for water. Fish sat down to stretch the left hamstring. It was the first game, and he considers himself a peacemaker, so he gave it back. "Yes," he said, "I was particularly impressed with my hard serves. The ones that you usually put away, but I want to thank you for tinning them today. You had about eleven of those, right?"

"Twelve," said Mason, and they laughed.

When they went back on court for more, the true and normal structure of the universe was restored. Mason won three straight. Fish's right knee swelled and his left hamstring tightened and his sciatic nerve complained. Summer squash, just like winter squash.

Spring

The most pressing issue is that the hands hurt. At some point in our ongoing conversation, the correspondent asked about how a summertime rower manages during the winter. The question was about the difference between working out on land versus on water, and whether it is comparable to a runner running on treadmills versus running out of doors.

Here are the differences:

1) Rather than sitting in front of the television, and having the dog nuzzle up when he sees all the back and forth and hears the gears of the rowing machine and all the heavy breathing, being on the water involves neither dogs nor TV;

2) On the rowing machine, it is easy to ask a kid to pop a Netflix video into the DVD player, whereas on the water, one must stay away from the canal-side park because it does no good to tell the city kids who hang around there not to fling their sharp-hooked fishing lures at you, because they just do, and then they swear and grab their balls and utter incomprehensible oaths, but at least they don't shoot their guns, not yet anyway;

3) On the rowing machine, one can set one's workout to run a certain set pattern that the timer times and that the stroke meter counts, whereas on the water, one goes by landmarks (the Canadian water tower, the big green sumac bush near the 1,000-meter marker, the green buoy) and the wind changes everything, especially the consistency of one's technique, which has, so far this season, been truly embarrassing;

4) On the rowing machine, one grows nice little calluses at the bases of the fingers and at mid-finger, calluses that remind one of what a good diligent trainer one is, but on the water, after only five or six times out and long before one's technique has returned for the season, there is a big open sore on the left side of the right palm where the nice thick rowing-machine callus just tore part-way off today, and there's a mirror of that on the left palm except not so deep, and the left thumb still needs to be wrapped with white tape because its winter-callus tore away, and it all stings when the fetid Black Rock Canal water gets on it, sort of an ongoing test of immuno-sufficiency; and most importantly,

5) On the rowing machine, the only danger is around the corner in the kitchen where there is always half a bottle of eight-dollar Spanish Tempranillo, which one sometimes drinks before rehydrating with water (as a reward if one has plowed ten thousand meters or more), whereas on the water, today, not one but two barge tugs came chugging down the canal from the Iron Bridge, coming on at about ten knots, bearing down just after one had finished another 500-m sprint, and the single shell just barely got back to the dock in time for those sunzabitches to rock on by, leaving a wake that was at least two feet high, that swamped the dock, and the boat, and that drenched the sculler.

So God has smiled yet again, because, though one can't quite wash the smell off, the first plan was to head north past the Iron Bridge and all the way to the locks, but something, some bug or insect or twitchy nerve gave the instruction to stay near the boathouse, and to do sprints, between the Peace Bridge and the finish line, and good thing, for one would have been run down by those monsters, and churned into additional Black Rock Canal pollution by their sharp spinning propellers.

THE NEXT SEASON

Being cold in Buffalo

In trench coat over sweater and two scarves, with a fleece toque and with leather gloves, one awaits the furnace repairman. The temperature in the house at breakfast-time is 52 degrees Fahrenheit.

The first child to school got a cold Japanese minivan but at least a heated seat; the second and third got warmed leather and warmed air and the calm radio voices from National Public Radio explaining about the carnage among the Shi'a and Sunni of Iraq. The streets are dry: they are black but edged with gray like Stewart Granger's temples because the salt from the city trucks sits first on the crown of the blacktop then, as it is variously dissolved in snow and allowed by gravity to trickle as wet precipitate, or pulverized to dust in the absence of snow, it slides the slight inclines to the sides of the streets and whitens the pitches from mid-lane to curb. That stuff will sit there through March. Winter has all its storm weeks and lingering or persistence yet to run, unless all the cold and snow left to this season is headed south to the convenience of the ski hills, with the city left to take cold showers that will black up the blacktop again and wash the white out.

This day, precipitation is a theory. Barometric pressure is high. The sun is up early and strong, and one makes do as bravely as one can by hoisting up the quilted blinds on the east-facing windows, the better to catch that radiant heat with old Buffalo rugs brought from Persia and from Turkey back when Qajars and Osmanlis yet reigned. Those were dark oppressive times to be sure, which yielded dark red rugs that for a hundred years have been soaking up a warming winter sun on Buffalo floors that are that old themselves. Oriental potentates were caricatured in newspaper when this fine lumber was hewn out of the oak, cherry, and maple forests of Cattaraugus and Allegheny; the would-be American commercial dynasts got rich denuding the hills, and showed off what they'd cut. One buys a hundred-year-old house in Buffalo first built to celebrate the success of one such proud American, for one likes the look and the central-city siting and also the price: one gets all this wood, these floors, this wainscoting, the broad nineteenth-century slate sidewalks, the hundred-year-old shade trees—the look of old wealth more or less honestly got, or at least one does not dwell on the crimes that produced it—for the price of a three-bedroom split-level in a new far-suburban cul-de-sac. But as these places are handsome and classy, so are they needy. They must be retrofitted as sure as old men need new knees. The roof must be removed (all six roofs, actually) and replaced. The galvanized pipes must be replaced with copper. New wires must be threaded through the walls along the courses of ancient wires. And one must replace the decrepit furnace with a new high-technology, high-efficiency boiler that will make the handsome hot-water radiators warm. Only after all that purchasing and installing, that thankless plumbing and heating and roofing, does one hunt for the red rugs of Qajar times.

The furnace man arrived. He knew without one telling him the way to the basement. He spent some personal, quality time with the unit with which he and his colleagues have spent so very much time since they installed it just two seasons back. One heard him speak excitedly into his cell phone, but the voice was muffled by the exquisite old flooring that is set between this doctor below and the patient's anxious relative one floor up. The muffled chatter stopped. Various pipes were heard to ring, as if a faraway carillon was being played. A period of silence ensued. Then, unaccompanied by any jolly humming or whistling that a jolly workman would bring along, and with a set or rather a glum look about him, he ascended the basement stairs. He arrived in the dining room. The thermostat read 51 degrees Fahrenheit. Then he spoke. When he did so, he did not allay the anxiety there present in the room.

What the furnace man did was as follows.

He protested the limitations of his expertise.

He told the customer that the customer's next call should be to the manufacturer of the unit, and not to the installer or to poor servicemen such as him.

He was not an expert, he said. He would be coming here no more, he said.

He then reached into his pocket, pulled out a pen like a concealed weapon from a holster, then wrote down the phone numbers of the manufacturer's local distributors. He accompanied the act of so writing with a narrative, the gist of which was that his company never installs this particular model anymore because there have been so many problems.

Then he left.

One was speechless.

One is not about to get into a legal argument with a serviceman. He is not a serviceman because he understands the nature of the relationship between the vendor and installer, on the one hand, and the customer, on the other. He does not know the Uniform Commercial Code.

One must maintain one's calm in circumstances such as these, and calmly check the indicators of the unit in question. One must be patient.

An hour later, the temperature reported by the thermostat remained the same. But this of course is a large house from the end of the nineteenth century. Much energy would be required to raise the temperature of such a house even one degree, and wasn't it obvious, from the hum of the boiler, that energy was being used? One must have patience with these things.

After another hour, the temperature was actually down a degree. Fifty degrees flat. One despaired. Was there no radiant heat from the front window? Was the ancient nomads' woven wool of no use in trapping the gift of the sun? One had no choice. One had to get into the Japanese minivan and go for a drive, just to warm up. Heat from anger would shed no light. One had to get out and give it some time. The thing was humming, dammit. It just needed time. Time.

A cold creeps into one, and with it a negativity. One's interior monologue turned into a depressive rant that went something like so: "Rip-off bastards. No big city would ever let them keep a license with that attitude, not even filthy New York or corrupt Chicago. This is a sign—a sign of the decline of Buffalo. This is a once-great place one should never have returned to. This is an irretrievably fallen place. Everything is broken here. Nobody in their right mind would come here from a decent, thriving place. It's colder in Boulder, but their furnaces work there. The clean white snow outside this house would be a glory in any resort; here, it's just more oppression."

Snow. One sighed. One huddled in the coat and hat and scarves, waiting. One dozed . . . then woke with a start. Snow. The sight of it out the east-facing window made one immediately, abruptly angry. The monologue began again . . . "Johnny Carson was right to mock Buffalo in the 1977 blizzard. Snow. Snow on top of rusting decrepit steelworks. Snow on the losing football team. Snow swirling around a hockey team that gets to the finals but can't clinch. Snow that creeps into every crack in every old house, and here all the houses are old or they are new and they are cheap and nasty. This place is the unreconstructed Eastern Europe of America. Its unions are thugs. Whiny thugs. Its capitalists are ridiculous because their money is covered with snow. Its news media have long since frozen. Everybody without frostbite has left for a growing market. There must be a place where the sun actually shines more than twenty days a year, or where an educated person isn't a pariah." So it went.

One's mood, in short, fell with the temperature.

There was nowhere to go but into the Japanese minivan.

Most strangely and unexpectedly, there was warmth already inside: the morning sun had actually caught in that small space. Driving off down the empty salt-crusted street, the glove box and the various cubbies and hatches got searched for sunglasses, for the snow-glare was that intense. The heat came on presently, and the focus shifted from interior darkness to the winter light, of which there was actually rather a lot.

With the warming, with the scene having changed from the chill empty house to the bright crisp day, and seeing it from comfort, one turned to consider the stuff. Snow. Snow had settled pristinely on the white marble exterior of the great art gallery. Snow in good quantity had covered the sloping lawns and the wide playing fields of the parkways as well. Snow is a reputational curse here, as if every viewer is frigid in a heatless house whose new boiler, still on warranty, is on the blink with some serviceman passing the buck and raising one's blood pressure.

But why should that be?

Comfortable now, snow was no longer a threat or a rebuke or a negative at all, at all. Snow became, as one knows it is, a feature of God's nature. Snow is fit for contemplation. Reveries thrive in it. Special and specific childhood reminiscences of it are there in one's inventory of formative images: snowmen made, snowdrifts in which one tunneled, snow angels, deeply placed bunnies' turds so black against the whiteness of the snow. Puffs of snow like talcum dust in the dimmest light when a white owl smashed down into a drift and emerged with a wriggling mouse, and fanned off silently, leaving little tornadoes of snow just for the merest moment. Snow hanging on the eaves of houses so tall that only very old, very very old, and very rich unknowable people must be living there. Snow on elms as straight as soldiers in salute. Snow as high as one's head in shoveled phalanxes on either side of the sidewalk on the way to school.

Snow and Buffalo: strangely but of course not strangely at all, it is never pictured by the national media as the soft gesture of a gentle nature that saves Buffalo from Gulf hurricanes. Snow is part of the same divine design or weaving of features that spares Buffalo those California earthquakes and mudslides. Our ancient terrain was scraped and pressed by glaciers and antique mounds of snow, but is blessed by it now, not threatened like Tacoma or Seattle, seated there in the next spillway of a pyroclastic flow that will start from Mount Rainier's snows and end in magma, glacier-melt flood, and catastrophe. Here our snow frosts our ski hills and collects like dollops of whipped cream into suggestive shapes in every neighborhood grand or small. It has become a commonplace for northerners of every burg to call it magic but at least let us admit that snow makes commonplace things into shape-shifters. Forms that in the other seasons are mere bushes or houses or unlovely automobiles become with this winter-dressing these rounded, quieted, smoothed, frosted cakes just precisely in the same way that homemade warm cakes are frosted, and that is sweetly. Snow takes the edges away, until one cheerily goes out there with one's blade, and cuts it, and packs it, and achieves dry pavement like our plowmen do, and frosts our walks with salt, and puts the real frost where it belongs, there, in piles to look at and walk past.

Driving, comfortable, through the range of landscape here: lake, river, escarpment, plains, wandering like a wind-blown crystal that originated far away, in a cloud. This is the end of winter, and one must think of what is to come.

So one thought about the next season, when our snow will retreat to soak our strawberry fields and our giant peach and apple orchards and our rolling miles of juice vineyards. It shall retreat and in so doing it shall green our golf courses and refill our ponds and all those streams that tumble happily through the ancient stable geology here, our strata filled with fossils that say that life has always flourished here at least for the past four hundred million years or so, and that water has always flowed, as it flows still here, in its seasons, toward our own broad bright great lake that never even iced over this winter.

Out in the winter, safely, one drives. One warms. The sun shines. One passes stands of sugar maples whose tappers love such days as these—bright in the lengthening day, cooling deep into the freezing range again in the retreating nights. One passes Frederick Law Olmsted's arboretum and thinks of the buds on all those exotic and spring-colorful trees as being just thirty more days in this stage, this winter stage of repose or potentiality, before they get to opening again. One sees the snow clean and sharp-edged like the day itself, for this is still most definitely winter and not that indistinct state of transition from the one sure season to the next sure season called summer, with an unhappy passage through one other, the dour, damp, gray, sunless season called spring.

One is warm in the car, looking at all this. But one wants to go home to check on the progress. They say that a watched pot does not boil, so one drives around for another hour.

But enough. One breathes in the last of the small warmth of the car. One is still wearing layers and layers that swell one to twice one's normal size. One is thus ready for confrontation. There is still time to call the serviceman's boss if there's no change. There is time to call the lawyer, too, if the people who sold and installed the damned thing try any foolishness about whom one is to call. There is time enough to go to the installer's shop and personally explain one's preference for immediate satisfaction, should the need arise.

The need does not so arise. By some stroke of luck, it was all just a misunderstanding—a sensor's misunderstanding of the signal that one part of the apparatus sent to another. Resetting was all that was required. It is four hours after the serviceman's departure and the temperature reading is now above 60 degrees Fahrenheit. We are on the return path to civilization. We are in one of the typical woody domestic interiors of Buffalo, of the sort so lovingly crafted at the end of the nineteenth century, when the merchants purchased a domestic space that was ample of dimension and framed with the best of the regional forest down where the snow collects heaviest, on the ski hills. With 60 degrees and a warming trend to follow, Buffalo is a good choice again. It is handsome. It is comfortable. It is uncrowded. Its windows give on to a prettied landscape that every season pretties, even spring. All those concerns about decay, abandonment, irretrievable loss, economic decline, about sagging late-nineteenth-century wooden houses that cannot be insulated and that cost more to heat than anyone can bear, houses that continue to decline rather than appreciate in value because of the endless flight of the earning classes farther and farther away from the region's first havens for said classes, in houses such as this—all these worries fade like a February snowdrift succumbing to March. It is Buffalo. We are warm. We are back to our great interior life, and now to our west-facing windows, full of the last sun of the day, which was a good day, a cold, clear, bright winter's day like so many other winters' days in Buffalo.

Christmas morning

The children are still asleep on this calm morning. The sun has climbed behind a mountain of clouds, but this new sun is so strong that the snowy landscape has amplified its light and banished all shadow. Light though it is, something about this sky doesn't give color a chance, but I don't mind. There hasn't been a car down our wide city street since dawn. Not a sound escapes any bedroom. And beyond our window, the chickadees flitting from feeder to branch are a silent movie of the old type, black and white and gray.

Forty and a few years ago, something curious happened on a Christmas morning very much like this one. How much like this one? Well, I'll tell you. There were clouds in the sky but still a strong bright sun. There was deep and fresh new snow as smooth as whipped cream spread expertly over every lawn, topping off every shrub, frosting every tree branch, naked bark leaf-tree and conifer alike, and quieting the street, too. Christmas grownups were doing the snoozing then, I'll give you that.

My grandfather's backyard was the place for me. I was dressed already. I zipped up my overshoes, retrieved my knit gloves all warmed from the radiator, and carefully exited through the kitchen door, and here's why the care: it's because we had a practice, back then, of taking crusts of bread and crumbs from the dinner table and often as not some eggshells from breakfast, too, and setting it all on a sawhorse for the wrens. Now my grandfather's cats (they lived in the barn out back) expected something for their work. They'd come trotting up with their unmoving hunter faces to see if my grandfather was going to give out a few scraps of beef kidney which he got all wrapped up in that old kind of butcher paper, kind of brownish or rather liverish in color, just a few blocks up Main Street from where we lived. But I didn't have anything for the birds. I didn't have anything for the cats. We never took anything to the rabbits that hid under the south end of the barn, tucked away behind the raspberry brambles and on the other side of a pair of hemlocks. Rabbits are very very quiet and very self-sufficient and those rabbits somehow had arranged peace with the cats. I saw plenty of blackbirds, blue jays, mice, and shrews dead and delivered to the kitchen stoop by those killers. They made meals of the birds except for the heads, which they brought home to us, bird tongues distended, neck cords bloody, but never rabbits.

I shuffled through the unbroken snow like an arctic explorer. I shuffled past the great poplar tree whose limbs reached out across half the yard and half the neighbor's yard, too, and from which in spring dropped tons of poplar catkins. I walked past the sawhorses still set up from summertime, when my grandfather and I put them to good use for skinning catfish and largemouth and calico bass, because you need to drive a nail through those tough-skinned fishes if you're going to have a hope of getting the barbs and fins and bass-scales off. The cats loved those sawhorses Saturday and Sunday afternoons, fish-guts and fish-heads galore. On Christmas day forty-some years ago, they were just two incongruous ridges of snow set near the swing-doors of our barn.

What I was hoping for was to actually see the owls hunting in the fields behind that barn. These flat-faced white owls lived up in the peak on the north side of the barn, above the highest height of the trumpet-vines which in their season did so well with hummingbirds. White owls, white snow, suddenly a little shadow over the snow and one of them would pounce and fluff up the powder like the little cloud when you pour talc into your hand, and, from nowhere I could see, there would be a wriggling black mouse.

I stalked them soundlessly in this black-and-white world. They weren't perched up there in their peak under the eaves. So I shuffled around toward the back, past the cherry trees and the plum trees whose fruit the birds around there always made off with, but they were sour cherries anyway, and no good unless my grandmother baked them into pies, in which case they were fabulous. I can't say now that I can remember every second of my mind's journey then, but I remember the approximate geography just fine: happy at the kitchen door, excited at the poplar tree when I thought to look for the barn owls, determined under the fruit trees looking for them, disappointed at the compost heap where we dug for fishing worms three seasons, blank when I rounded the corner and saw the expanse of field where my grandfather's big vegetable garden was but a memory under all that snow.

Now there is, or should be, in every child's life, a sense of mystery connected to a place. In my small life then, just nine or ten or twelve years into the process, my grandfather's gray and white and black winter yard had a mysterious edge, a perimeter defined by trees and tangly bushes, beyond which was mystery. Now how could that be, you might ask. This was a village, after all, not a big city. In leafless winter when all the maples and lilacs and skinny walnut trees and buttress-like sumacs were denuded, the wall they were in summer was a lattice through which I could see what lay beyond. No mystery, then, that my grandfather's yard ended only half a field from the sturdy bricks of the village high school. No mystery either that the woods, winter-stripped, defined the near neighbor's yard, and that there was a house or two on the other side. What was mysterious was that sense of boundary, though, that persisted no matter how well I got to know the immediate environs. Or let me try it this way: all the magic was contained in my grandfather's yard. His barn, his trees, his bordered landscape of corn, beans, summer squash, vine after tangled vine of cucumber, muddy beets, rhubarb that nobody could ever get me to eat; wren-houses on the barn, set high up, far above cats' reach in any season; trumpet-vines on the shady side, plums worth eating and cherries worth not. And there, on Christmas Day when all but I slept, a bright world with no shadow, but no color, either, the mystery was that anybody would care about the boring and inconsequential world beyond this border.

But then, the marvel of the new was revealed. From out of that thicket, calm as you please, marched the first color of that day. I knew what it was, of course, because I was an outdoors kind of boy. But it was so bright against that snow, such a surprise, and so near, that I couldn't comprehend.

Pheasants. Ring-necked pheasants. Christmas birds. Bright as ornaments with red and blue and green and golden long feathers. Pecking at the snow, unmolested by cats, untroubled by dogs, unworried by hawks or owls. Christmas colors, like presents in bright wrapping paper from the world beyond our yard. And suddenly, I knew that I would have to leave home one day, just to know where new things come from.

Christmas night

For some years now, the Christmas Eve observance has been a pleasant party, a most diverse and polyglot party, where the celebrants are not Christians, and where the hostess forbids gift-exchange—that last vestige of my own tradition and arguably the cause of most of the trouble of Christmas. Midnight Mass had been discussed but never pursued. Where would the group go anyway? In most years, most of the adults at this party are observant Jews. One is Greek Orthodox, two or three Catholic, but lapsed. I and my children are the Episcopalians, but we, or rather I, had long since lost enthusiasm for a churchly Christmas Eve because of a new pastor with a decidedly anti-traditional demeanor. Ten years ago, he came to the big Victorian edifice we'd attended, and removed what remained of Caxton's English, and also spurned the incense and much else of the comforting continuity of old "high church" or Catholic-derived ritual. If such Episcopal practice endures, it may be found, I guess, in some other hall, perhaps at the Episcopal Cathedral, or across the nearby bridge in Canada, or in that assertive parish where the recent, sexuality-oriented innovations of Episcopalianism are eschewed.

At Christmas, one craves the familiar, not the conflicts of politics, or the bureaucratic indignities of cross-border travel. I remember with great fondness the Christmas Eve when my youngest daughter was the baby in the manger, and her two older sisters were cuddly sheep, in the Christmas pageant, and I was the happy dad up there at the pulpit, reading the Lesson in my best baritone. That sweet memory was of an eye-blink in cultural continuity.

This Christmas Eve, at my generous friend's home, this grumpiness and sense of loss, or of too much accommodation, was making me bad company. I sat around drinking whiskey and being a bit too clever. But I had announced early on that we'd be leaving for Midnight Mass and would ferry any and all churchgoers, but as in previous years, there were no takers—not even my eldest, the twenty-year-old student of anthropology, or my eighteen-year-old who attends a Catholic university and has, by her own choice, been reintroduced to a version of what she'd known as a child.

Tired of sounding ungrateful for my old and cherished friendships, I abruptly commanded my youngest that she would be driving me to attend the Polish church deep in Buffalo's East Side. Driving is new to her, and so she is ever-ready for the keys. I had described the place to all at table: as a place unknown to me, whose parish council is led by a friend, a church that is an allegedly beautiful structure, recently the destination of a group of Pauline religious from Poland, as a community treasure in a rough place—

That brought a response.

"It's not rough over there. It's damned well devastated."

"You'd better park in the parking lot because you'll get killed driving around there at midnight."

"It's in a war zone."

"You're taking Lydia? Will she be safe?"

We drove down Parker Street from the comfortable middle-class white neighborhood, through the stretch of big houses known as Central Park, and cross the border, Main Street, where Parker becomes Fillmore Avenue, and where the residents are almost all black and victimized by gangs of young men so alienated and abandoned that they lash out in every season. South a couple of miles to Broadway and what had been the very heart of a dense and populous Polonia in my youth, then east just a bit past the Broadway Market, which is still Polish except that most of its day-to-day customers are the successors to the Poles who, in the main, moved out over the last thirty years, leaving behind their churches.

I have long railed against the Catholic hierarchy of Buffalo and of the other great Catholic cities of the Great Lakes. In the 1960s, as the new Protestant migrants from the American South arrived, the Catholic hierarchy either bought into the myth of growth, or just did nothing, sat passively, as one hundred years of Central and Eastern and Southern European cultural continuity—in the physical form of great churches beautifully adorned—were abandoned. Why would American priests stand idly by and watch the neighborhoods decline, neighborhoods of the successors to those who had beaten back the Turks and survived the Mongols? A century or more of pennies scraped up to hire great Buffalo church artists like Mazur to paint and to make stained glass—abandoned, just because of cultural conflict with Protestants? Because of the blandishments of suburban developers? Dozens, hundreds, many hundreds of church buildings in our freshwater cities are abandoned, derelict, their art peeling, their altars roosts for pigeons.

Corpus Christi Church is down Clark Street a block from once-bustling Broadway. Its twin towers are not so towering, though in that neighborhood of very small one- and two-story frame houses on very small lots, it was the largest structure. Its dusky exterior was unremarkable.

When we opened the church's door, however, it was as a cinematic experience: the space we entered was overpowering. I glanced at Lydia: what was she experiencing?

Three stories up, the ribbed and vaulted ceiling is sky-blue. Far, far to the east, before a pyramid of red flowers, distant priests in gold-edged white vestments were chanting in Polish in melodies that originated long before polyphony and counterpoint. The vast space was full of light and color and sound. At that hour, there was no sun to illuminate the tall stained-glass windows that were made for mornings, but between each on the stucco walls was a large painting of a Station of the Cross. In our hands was a four-page folder of lyrics, in Polish, with unfamiliar diacritical marks and impossible clusters of consonants. And all around us in that vast space were people, people in overcoats, all of them Caucasian. Polish people. Americans perhaps, but Americans less essentially than something else.

Now and again, some English came from the altar. One priest read a lesson from old Isaiah, the prophecy of the eventual Messiah. Then there were prayers in Polish, and singing. Before the priest who read the Gospel read it in his heavily Polonized but precise English, another, with a white beard, swung the smoking censer around the lectern and over the missal; not even the most Catholic of the High Church Episcopalians ever get that Catholic. A lay reader, a woman, read something in Polish, and the head priest assisted her by adjusting the microphone so that all the vast congregation could hear her. A whimpering infant became loud, and mother walked her out of the hall. I gestured to Lydia to follow my pointing finger to the image, in an alcove, of what I think was the Black Madonna of Czestochowa.

And so we witnessed a world previously invisible to my child, and for so long unattended by me—the world of a continuity, of an unapologetic or even urgent persistence, for in this neighborhood that had been their refuge back in the years when I was a child, a neighborhood which they had since left, mainly, leaving it for the next wave of poor immigrants, these Poles had not only not abandoned their church as so many others had, but had refreshed it. Their teens were in attendance, of course in much smaller numbers than the gray- and white-hairs, but remarkably many of them. Eight ushers in tuxedos came through at the offertory, asserting that this is a special place, an extraordinary church. To us visitors, cultural tourists from across town, so much was so well elaborated, so forcefully asserted: we were guests in this particular section of America, whose music is unfamiliar, whose language is not American English. As persons from another tradition, we got distracted by things as small as the Catholic practice, as the Host was prepared, of the priest ringing a handbell. But the large, inescapable reality of the place and of the event—even as the Apostle's Creed was led in English—is that there is a dogged courage and embrace of life in evidence there, and our presence was a happy event for us, but of no relevance to them.

We left as parishioners filed forward for Communion, for this was not the time for plunging back into Christian practice. How challenging, though, is the insistence of that society to hold on to its self—as Poles did after 1796, when Russia took the east of their country, Prussia the north and west, and Austria-Hungary the south, and left the Poles no country but their church, and their language. How persistent these people, whose revolution in 1980 was led by shipyard workers asserting their Catholicism.

This Christmas, the internal conversation of Episcopalians—all about matters of gender—seems less urgent than the Polish insistence on mere survival, though their country was again and again ripped up, though their American refuge became another kind of war zone, with crack and guns and young men who are not Catholics so often, sadly, terrorizing the elderly of all races who persist on Clark Street.

The Poles of the suburbs came out at midnight this Christmas. They sang in their language, and in English. Their very formal ushers gave us pages with Polish-language lyrics on one side, and English-language lyrics on the other. The disconnect between the English and the Polish was evident, even to my ignorant eye: while most of the Polish-language verses had the terms "swiaty" and "Bog" and "Christ" and "Betlejem," the English-language songs on the flip side, which we did not hear sung there, included "Jingle Bells" and "White Christmas" and "Up on the Rooftop," and I wanted to tell those priests, those new ones over so recently from Poland, that they do not know about our fine English traditions of sacred Christmas music, in which there is dignity and spirituality, and that there is a difference. But they know enough about difference.